The Beginning of Western Philosophy

Studies in Continental Thought

Martin Heidegger

The Beginning of Western Philosophy

Interpretation of Anaximander and Parmenides

Translated by
Richard Rojcewicz

Indiana University Press
Bloomington and Indianapolis

This book is a publication of

Indiana University Press
Office of Scholarly Publishing
Herman B Wells Library 350
1320 East 10th Street
Bloomington, Indiana 47405 USA

iupress.indiana.edu

Published in German as Martin Heidegger, *Gesamtausgabe 35: Der Anfang der abendländischen Philosophie, Auslegung des Anaximander und Parmenides,* ed. Peter Trawny
© 2012 by Vittorio Klostermann GmbH, Frankfurt am Main

English translation © 2015 by Indiana University Press

Manufactured in the United States of America

Library of Congress Cataloging-in-Publication Data

Heidegger, Martin, 1889–1976.
[Anfang der abendländischen Philosophie. English]
The beginning of western philosophy : interpretation of Anaximander and Parmenides / Martin Heidegger ; translated by Richard Rojcewicz.
pages cm. — (Studies in continental thought)
"Published in German as Martin Heidegger, Gesamtausgabe 35: Der Anfang der abendländischen Philosophie, Auslegung des Anaximander und Parmenides, ed. Peter Trawny © 2012 by Vittorio Klostermann GmbH, Frankfurt am Main."
Includes bibliographical references.
ISBN 978-0-253-01553-2 (cloth : alk. paper) — ISBN 978-0-253-01561-7 (ebook)
1. Anaximander. 2. Parmenides. 3. Pre-Socratic philosophers. I. Title.
B208.Z7H4413 2015
182'.3—dc23
2014028442

1 2 3 4 5 20 19 18 17 16 15

CONTENTS

Contents

Chapter III
The other dictum

PART TWO
INTERPOSED CONSIDERATIONS

PART THREE
The "didactic poem" of Parmenides of Elea, 6th–5th century

Conclusion

Appendix

Translator's Introduction

This is a translation of a lecture course Martin Heidegger offered in the summer semester of 1932 at the University of Freiburg. The German original appeared posthumously in 2012 as volume 35 of the philosopher's *Gesamtausgabe* ("Complete Works").

The editor, in his afterword, identifies the sources he drew on to compose the text. These sources are varied, and the book at times does consequently display unevenness. Not everything is expressed in full sentences, and some few passages are quite cryptic. I did not attempt to alter the diction, for example by supplying tacitly understood verbs. The translation is meant to read to an English ear the way the original does to a German one.

This is the first of the *Gesamtausgabe* volumes to provide the pagination of Heidegger's manuscript. These numbers are placed in the outer margin, with a vertical line to mark the page break. All cross-references in the book are to the manuscript page numbers. The running heads correspond to the *Gesamtausgabe* pagination.

I used square brackets ([]) throughout the book for my insertions into the text, and the few footnotes I introduced are marked "Trans." Braces ({ }) are reserved for the editor's interpolations. German-English and English-German glossaries can be found in the back matter and invite the reader to pursue linguistic connections I was unable to capture. Heidegger himself translates here all the extant fragments of Anaximander and Parmenides, obviating the need for a Greek-English lexicon. Even someone without facility in ancient Greek should have little trouble following the thread of Heidegger's inimitable interpretation of these two so-called pre-Socratics.

Richard Rojcewicz

The Beginning of Western Philosophy

PART ONE

The dictum of Anaximander of Miletus, 6th–5th century

Introduction

§1. The mission and the dictum

a) Cessation and beginning

Our mission: the cessation of philosophizing?[1] *That is, the end of metaphysics;* by way of an originary questioning of the "meaning" (truth) of Beyng.[2]   1

We want to seek out the *beginning* of Western philosophy (cf. p. 31!).—Western philosophy takes its *start* in the 6th century BC with the Greeks, a minor, relatively isolated, and purely self-dependent(??) people. The Greeks of course knew nothing of the "Western" and the "West." These terms express a primarily geographical concept, contrasted against the East, the Oriental, the Asiatic. At the same time, however, the rubric "Western" is a historiological concept and signifies today's European history and culture, which were inaugurated by the Greeks and especially by the Romans and which were essentially determined and borne by Judeo-Christianity.

Had the Greeks known something of this Western future, a beginning of philosophy would never have come about. Rome, Judaism, and Christianity completely transformed and adulterated the inceptual— i.e., Greek—philosophy.

b) The dictum in the customary translations

We want to seek out the beginning of Western philosophy. What we find therein is little. And this little is incomplete. The tradition ordinarily calls Thales of Miletus the first philosopher. Much is reported about him and his teaching. But nothing is handed down directly.

After Thales, Anaximandros (ca. 610–545) is called the second philosopher. Preserved for us are a few of his words and statements. The one reads:

---

1. Cf. *Überlegung II,* 89. {In: *Überlegungen II–VI.* GA [Gesamtausgabe] 94.}

2. [Archaic form of "Being," to render *das Seyn,* archaic form of *das Sein.*— Trans.]

ἐξ ὧν δὲ ἡ γένεσίς ἐστί τοῖς οὖσι καὶ τὴν φθορὰν εἰς ταῦτα γίνεσθαι κατὰ τὸ χρεών· διδόναι γὰρ αὐτὰ δίκην καὶ τίσιν ἀλλήλοις τῆς ἀδικίας κατὰ τὴν τοῦ χρόνου τάξιν.

From Simplicius (Commentary on the *Physics*) based on Theophrastus (Φυσικῶν δόξαι).[3]

In translation: "But whence things take their origin, thence also proceeds their passing away, according to necessity; for they pay one another penalty and retribution for their wickedness according to established time." Diels.[4]

"Whence things have their origination, thence must they also perish, according to necessity; for they must pay retribution and be judged for their injustices, according to the order of time." Nietzsche.[5]

---

3. {*Simplicii in Aristotelis Physicorum libros quattuor priores commentaria*. Edidit H. Diels. Berlin: Reimer, 1882. *Phys.* 1:2, 24. Cf. also *Die Fragmente der Vorsakratiker. Griechisch und Deutsch von Hermann Diels.* Vol. 1, 4th. ed. Berlin: Weidmann, 1922. Heidegger underlines the words τοῖς οὖσι. Diels has a comma after οὖσι.}

4. {This translation is not in Diels. The 4th edition of *Die Fragmente der Vorsokratiker* reads: "But whence their birth is, thence also proceeds their dying, according to necessity. For they pay one another penalty and retribution for their wickedness according to the order of time." Cf. also the afterword to Heidegger's "Der Spruch des Anaximander," GA78, 339ff.}

5. {Friedrich Nietzsche, *Die Philosophie im tragischen Zeitalter der Griechen.* In *Nietzsche's Werke: Gesamtausgabe in Großoktav,* 19 vols. *Nachgelassene Werke,* vol. 10. Leipzig: Naumann, 1903, 26.}

Chapter I
The first phase of the interpretation

A. THE FIRST SECTION OF THE STATEMENT

§2. The theme of the dictum: beings as a whole

a) The meaning of τὰ ὄντα

About what is Anaximandros speaking here? About τὰ ὄντα. τὰ ὄντα—plural of the neuter τὸ ὄν—the being; plural: the beings. Yet from early on, already in Sanskrit, the neuter plural does not simply mean a multiplicity of individuals; instead, it signifies the many individuals in their unity: hence "that which is," thereby thinking of *that which is* [das *Seiende*] as particularized into many individual beings, into *the beings* [die Seienden]. We could use "the beings" as a translation of τὰ ὄντα only provided we recognize there is no question here of arbitrary, individual beings. More clearly at first: singular—that which is—and this indeed now requires some comments.

That which is—about beings pure and simple (cf. below p. 35, sec. a, *τὸ ἐόν*)—not about just any arbitrary individual extant thing in its accidental obtrusiveness, e.g., the sea; also not the being we call the land; also not what is in the sea, on land, in the air, not the plants and animals; also not humans and their work, their trouble and joy, their success, their triumph, their death—all such is *a* being, not that which is. Even all this totaled up does not constitute that which is. For as soon as we start to seize any being whatever and ascribe something further to it, we have just as immediately wrenched that individual out of that which is. We do not first of all have nothingness and then the individual beings; on the contrary, first and last we have that which is. The latter is not simply *all* individual beings thrust together; it is *more* than all these and then again at the same time *less*. That which is means that which is before and around us, below us and above us, and includes ourselves. That which is: not this being and not that one and not everything together, but more than "everything." Then what?

2   Is there | something that could be "more" than "everything"? "Everything" does not tolerate still "more" outside of itself. "Everything" includes each thing and leaves nothing out. But if, for example, we carefully take apart and lay out "everything" that pertains to a plant, viz., root, stalk, leaves, blossoms, and if we omit nothing, then does all this together give us "the plant"? No; something is still missing. The whole of the plant does not result from thrusting together all the pieces but is on the contrary *prior* to all the components, even if these are not expressly present at hand but are, e.g., still in the bud or in the seed grain. Everything that pertains to the plant is not *the* plant as a being, is not the whole being.

And so we will say: that which is—if it means more than all individuals, then it means the *whole* of beings.

We do not mean thereby that the whole of beings would be the same as, for instance, an immense plant or some other "organism." The wholeness of a whole is not simply and necessarily the wholeness of an "organism." Yet even if we take this reservation to heart, may we then equate "that which is" (τὰ ὄντα) with the whole of beings?

For could a person ever grasp all beings individually and then gather them together? Even if it were possible to grasp all particular beings individually and go through them all, would we not continually have to set aside the ones already grasped? How could a person claim to grasp all beings at one stroke? We saw, however, that that which is does not mean everything but, instead, means the whole of beings. Nevertheless, is not the whole of beings even less graspable? For that, the person would need to utterly encompass beings, stand outside of them and beyond the whole, and not belong therein himself. Outside the whole of beings is only nothingness. "That which is"—if we take this expression to mean the whole of beings, is it then not precisely vacuous? To be sure! That which is means for us therefore not the whole of beings—neither this nor "all beings."

Thus we said advisedly: "that which is" is more and at the same time less than all beings. More, insofar as it somehow proceeds to the whole; *less*—how so?

In this way: insofar as there is not at first or ever any necessity to grasp *all* beings in order to understand truly what was said. Indeed what is not decisive is the *magnitude* in number or in scope of the beings we explicitly know; and how much we scientifically know is utterly inconsequential. The farmer, whose "world" might strike the city dweller as narrow and poor, in the end possesses "that which is" much more intimately and immediately. The farmer's experience proceeds quite differently into the whole and comes quite differently out of the whole than the agitated squirming of the city dweller, who clings only to the "telephone and radio." The smallest and narrowest sphere of known beings has nevertheless its expansion into the whole; even narrowness is always still an expanse—an expansion into the whole. On the other hand, the widest variety is largely lacking in expanse, so much so that it—as mere scatterings and their running on and on—never even amounts to a narrowness.

That which is is always less than all beings and is also not the whole of beings purely and simply encompassed and intuited. It is rather, as we say, *beings as a whole*—in that way indeed more, essentially more than each and every summation, even the greatest possible.

τὰ ὄντα—that which is—means beings as a whole. From this is to be distinguished all beings as well as the whole of beings. Yet let us not fool ourselves. We do not have a fully clear understanding of what is meant here. Nevertheless, something is indicated for which we have a quite sure feeling. This "as a whole" is so ungraspable in an inceptual way precisely because it is constantly what is closest and most familiar to us: we always skip over it. Indeed, even further, for the most part we unwittingly misinterpret it and render it unrecognizable. In order to experience that which is, i.e., beings as a whole, we do not need to undertake gymnastically any sort of mysterious contortion of thought and representation. Quite to the contrary, we only need to loosen somewhat our everyday shackling to what is currently obtrusive and incidental—and already we will have explicitly experienced what is astonishing in experience. | To be sure, only quite roughly, but this "roughly," this "as a whole," is in itself something completely determinate and essential, even if we are now still far removed from comprehending it.

Let this be a provisional elucidation of what Anaximandros is speaking *about*. We will now ask: 2) *What* does he actually say about it, about "beings"? "Whence (that out of which) beings step forth—precisely into this also their receding happens according to necessity."

b) Beings in γένεσις καὶ φθορά

a) *Stepping forth and receding pertain to beings.* α) γένεσις in general β) ἡ γένεσις ἡ φθορά [*the* stepping-forth *the* receding]. γένεσις and φθορά are readily taken as "coming to be and passing away," and so in short: alteration, becoming other, or in general: *becoming.* That is very understandable and is not artificially formulated. For us, however, the question is whether the ready translation does not unwittingly introduce something un-Greek into the content of the whole statement. Here it is in fact so; stepping forth means originating arrival, arriving emergence, self-manifestation, *appearance*;[1] correspondingly, receding means disappearance, withdrawal, going away. So what is the difference between these and coming to be and passing away? We are accustomed to think of coming to be as development, as a sequence of processes in which the earlier ones are always the causes of the following ones, as concatenation, transition, progression, as *direction*, as from . . . to, out of . . . into; and correspondingly we think of passing away as downfall and annihilation. For the Greeks, what is decisive is not the causal sequence, the coming to be out of and through one another, but purely and simply the *stepping-forth*, the looming up. Our term for it in short will be *appearance*. (Cf. below p. 8; need to carefully set aside every relation to later meanings of the word as a technical term, even the relation to the Kantian concept, although Kant does, within certain limits, use "appearance" genuinely and originarily. It is only because "appearance" becomes the counter concept to "thing-in-itself" that we cannot appeal here to Kant.)

Appearance is emergence: not the becoming seen and apprehended of something, but a character of the happening of *beings* as such. Only subsequently applicable to a being in its becoming perceived and grasped. To appear: to remain in apparentness—or to withdraw from this. To appear: as we say "a new book has appeared" or "the president of the society thanked the appearing guests for making an appearance." Appearing can be understood only very broadly and originarily, and it oscillates within the meaning of γένεσις—thus not coming to be, but stepping forth. And receding, disappearance, is merely a distinctive mode of appearance and belongs completely to it; for only what has appeared or can appear can also disappear and specifically such that the appearing is retracted.

> c) ἐξ ὧν—εἰς ταῦτα—the whence-whither—our characterization of stepping forth and receding. Inadequacy of speaking about a "basic matter"

b) *The* stepping-forth and *the* receding are to beings not just any random occurrence but are instead precisely *essential* to the ὄντα. And now both are *characterized more closely* in a determinate respect. ἐξ ὧν—εἰς ταῦτα; the whence of the coming forth and the whither of the disappearing. And it is said: *the whence and the whither of appearance (disap-*

---

1. Up—forth. γένεσις qua "genesis" only later; in Aristotle only when grasping κίνησις, and even then still primarily in terms of ποίησις, i.e., production—εἶδος.

pearance) are the same. The whence is the whither, and conversely.—
This information is exceedingly meager. We would very much like to
know what is this whence and whither. And if we speak—as do all
interpreters since Aristotle—in a completely wrong-headed way, i.e.,
if we speak of coming to be and passing away, then we are thinking
of the *coming to be* of the world—"world" as nature—whereby it seems
that to ask whence beings come to be is even to engage in the most
thoughtful research. Whence something comes to be is ordinarily called
its matter, and if beings—all of them—come to be out of, and decom-
pose into, the same matter, then the whence-whither is the basic matter. And people go out of their way to praise Anaximandros for having
already advanced so far in physics and chemistry. As if sciences as such
were an advancement; as if advancement for philosophy could ever
be a mark of distinction. And, above all, as if Anaximandros had ever
asked about matter and the basic matter. This view of Anaximandros
and his physics is not even false; it is so far removed from the content of his teaching that it does not grasp the least of it and so does
not even rise to the level of the false and wrong. This way of taking
him or, rather, this mis-taking is encountered at every turn; it is mentioned here only in order to be discarded. For even to enter into dia-
logue with it is otiose. | 4

At issue here cannot be matter and the basic matter, for: 1) the
questioning in general does not aim to establish a sequence, the coming to be of things out of and through one another; thereby no occasion is given to ask about something as a matter out of which things
are formed. 2) the questioning of a basic matter must from the outset
equate "beings" with the material domain of lifeless nature. τὰ ὄντα,
however, signifies beings as a whole and precisely not any individual
delimited or distinctive sphere of beings. Therefore the whence and
whither apply to beings as a whole, just as appearance applies not
simply to the emergence of water or air or animals, but to everything
that happens.

Now, to be sure, the whence-whither is different from beings as a
whole, precisely as that out of which beings as a whole have their appearing and to which they revert. But what is different from beings
and is *not* a being nor beings as a whole must be addressed by us as
nothingness. Be that as it may: if indeed the whence-whither must
remain differentiated from beings as a whole, then we arrive at the
brink of nothingness. We must not shrink back here and must rather
consider this: if we want to grasp beings (the Greeks say delimit, place
within limits), then we must, indeed necessarily, proceed to the limit
of beings, and that is nothingness. Accordingly, what was said about

beings comes to us initially and for a long time hence as saying *nothing*. It says *nothing* to us, because we are used to apprehending only beings. And this saying nothing also implies that we can at first, as the expression is, "do nothing" with the statement that the whence and whither of appearing are the same.[2]

Before we consider more closely what lies in such a pronouncement, the task is to lay open in full what Anaximander says about beings.

d) The whence and whither of the stepping-forth and receding κατὰ τὸ χρεών—according to necessity

c) The whence and whither of the stepping-forth and receding of beings are the same κατὰ τὸ χρεών—according to necessity. What this says about beings is that their receding, disappearance, into the same as that from which comes their appearance, stepping forth, is not something that just happens to occur at one time or other. It is not left to the choice and pleasure of beings to accept or not to accept, so to speak, this sameness of their whence and whither. On the contrary, it is necessity—more precisely, τό, *the* necessity.[3] In this sameness of the whence-whither, the necessity comes to light.

Thus we have now commented in more detail on what was pronounced about beings: stepping forth and receding (appearance), the whence and whither in their sameness, the latter as necessity.

Everything said about beings tells us how beings comport themselves, what the situation is with beings. But heed well: what is not recounted and established is how this or that individual being behaves, which properties and quirks it displays. Instead, what is supposed to be addressed is how beings, precisely as the beings they are, comport themselves. The way the singing [*singend*] bird comports itself we call singing [*das Singen*]. The way the extant [*seiend*] being comports itself we call Being [*das Sein*].

Therefore, Anaximander's pronouncement about beings as a whole speaks of the Being of beings. But it does not simply enumerate all sorts of things that pertain to the Being of beings. At the same time, as the later section of the dictum shows, it says *why* the enumerated characters pertain to the Being of beings, (why they constitute Being). |

5

---

2. Completely if we heed: plural—therefore not at all a ἕν! Or indeed—something—which does not exclude multiplicity—| but *essential fullness*—plural—indication—of the *ungraspable*? Overfullness. Cf. below, p. 11, sec. b.

3. Essence—as *necessitating power*—compliance. {?}

B. THE SECOND SECTION OF THE STATEMENT

§3. Beings in the relation of compliance and noncompliance

a) Stepping forth and receding as giving
way before, and against, each other

διδόναι γὰρ αὐτὰ δίκην καὶ τίσιν ἀλλήλοις τῆς ἀκικίας—they (viz., the beings as such) reciprocally bestow compliance and correspondence in consideration of the noncompliance. Reciprocally—the one to the other and the other to the one.

This is supposed to supply the *grounds* explaining why what was said earlier constitutes the Being of beings. With that intention, beings are characterized anew—indeed while the previous declarations are still held fast. Stepping forth and receding are not arbitrarily now this, now that; instead, in stepping forth and receding, beings are *interrelated*.

Where is the evidence for such a reciprocal relation in arrival and departure? We do not need to lose ourselves in roundabout ways of artificial investigations; it is excessively extravagant to contrive anything like that. What is required is this: we should merely hold clear and open the broadest and simplest life view in order to experience that night gives way to day, and day to night: σκότωι φάος ἀντίμοιρον (Aeschylus, *Choephoren,* 320).[4] To darkness, light is the counter-destiny, a rising (of the day) and a disappearing (of the night), and conversely. This is *an appearance,* which for the Greeks (above all others!) stood in an inconceivably clear importance in the broadest expanse of their experience. And no less: winter and summer, tempest and calm, sleep and waking, youth and age, birth and death, fame and disgrace, shine and pallor, curse and blessing (cf. Sophocles, *Ajax,* 670f.).[5] The one gives way reciprocally to the other, and this giving way is at once arrival and departure, i.e., appearance. *Appearance oscillates in such giving way before, and against, each other of the stepping-forth and receding.*—We want to cast this simple and yet great and free glance at beings, for thereby appears what is properly closest and constant. From this, Anaximander can say what beings are. We of today must first be educated to this glancing. Instead of: subject-object and the like. Only insofar as the "things" are appearance *in* all this are they present at hand. Not by any

---

4. {*Aeschyli Tragoediae.* Recensuit G. Hermannus. Editio altera. Tomus primus. Berlin: Weidmann, 1859.}

5. {*Sophoclis Fabulae.* Recognovit brevique adnotatione critica instruxit A. C. Pearson. Impressio altera. Oxford 1924.}

chance presence at hand merely the "presence" of a thing and from there alone the domain expands. Not to be sought in the abstract, arid, and sparse field of a so-called chemistry and physics!

b) The inadequacy of the juridical-moral
meanings of δίκη, τίσις, and ἀδικία

To the way beings are extant, i.e., to Being, Anaximander now provides the already cited grounding. He says: beings bestow on one another compliance and correspondence in consideration of the non-compliance.

This translation already shows that I reject the long-customary and facile interpretation of the statement. The terms justice (δίκη), retribution (τίσις), and injustice (ἀδικία) refer to juridical-moral, human relations. As a rule, the words of the text are taken in an even more emphatic sense by speaking of penalty, recompense, atonement, wickedness, guilt. And it will have to be admitted that, with this statement, according to which "beings pay penalty and retribution for their guilt," Anaximander is giving things a juridical-moral construction and evaluation.

If, in addition, we note what was said earlier, namely, that Anaximander's is taken as a doctrine about the basic matter of nature, then it is very easy to see here an intertwining of primitive natural science with the projection of human experiences into things—as indeed is usual among primitives. This interpretation is as old as the sources handing down the statement to us; it goes back to Theophrastus, the student of Aristotle, and indeed it can be traced to the latter himself—4th century BC. To be sure, Theophrastus directly says of the statement: ποιητικωτέροις ὀνόμασιν αὐτὰ λέγων—Anaximander is speaking here in poetical words. But these words are "poetical" only if one gives them an emphatically juridical-moral meaning and in addition holds fast to the unfounded presupposition that at issue here is the knowledge of nature. Actually, the words are poetical in the genuine sense of the poetry of Being—a poetizing of Being; but that is precisely the abandonment of "anthropomorphism" and therefore shows the impossibility of such a way of thinking!

If, however, right from the start we do not accept this presupposition, since at issue here are beings as a whole, then at least initially it is impossible to insert a wedge between the knowledge of nature and the moral evaluation of things. Certainly—yet then it precisely still remains: the whole of beings is interpreted in a juridical-moral sense. But only as long as we uncritically impute to these words concepts of justice and morality deriving from a subsequent ethics or even from that of late antiquity and ultimately from Christian ethics. Not only do we have no right to do this, but we also know positively that in ancient times these words had a broader and deeper meaning.

c) ἀδικία as noncompliance, δίκη as compliance

Because we may not attribute to these words—or indeed to any of the basic words, above all to "beings" and "Being"—the conventional meaning which is therefore determinate and apparently full, the semblance then arises that in antiquity these words were still indeterminate and empty. But this indeterminateness is hardly that of something superficial and idle; instead, it is the not unfolded element of an earlier originality and power.—Proceeding now to the individual words, we find ἀδικία translated as guilt, wickedness, and we read elsewhere of an ἄδικος ἵππος,[6] a guilty horse, or a profligate one, or even a sinful one. That is of course not the meaning; it is a matter instead of a horse that is not broken in, a horse that will not I run in harness,   6
does not fit in, is not pliant, is *without* compliance—here a noncompliance reigns. Compliance—that is harmonization, the dovetailing of the totality of something coordinated in itself. Compliance therefore characterizes something *inter*-related; we see this in phenomena such as day-night, birth-death, etc. Its opposite is noncompliance, where the being is somehow out of order; ἀδικία is noncompliance, in this original sense. Certainly at times ἀδικία means injustice or something similar, and later it takes on this sense exclusively. In our context, however, the word has no moral-juridical meaning, but just as little does it mean "structure" in a neutral sense or the like.

How we need to take the counter-concept, δίκη, is thereby already expressed: compliance (cf. also "with full compliance" [*mit "Fug und Recht"*], as we say). Compliance: that which incorporates something, which provides the cadre for something and which has to accommodate this something. None of the usual notions of justice, judgment, penalty, and recompense may be admitted here; and so also the third concept, τίσις, cannot immediately be translated as "retribution" or "atonement." Instead, τίω originally means "appreciate," take the measure of something in its relation to something else, determine whether and how it *corresponds* to something else. Therefore we will translate not with "retribution" ("atonement"), but with "correspondence." Whereas δίκη—compliance—emphasizes the *belonging together* as such, τίσις brings out the *respective measuring off of the correspondence*. It is clear that *this* meaning of τίσις supersedes its meaning as retribution and atonement, and it is just as clear that there is no necessity or

---

6.[Heidegger is perhaps referring to Xenophon, Κύρου Παιδείας, B, 2, 26.—Trans.]

even possibility to speak automatically of retribution upon encountering the word τίσις.

Hence we must not maintain that in antiquity these words had *at first* an individualized-practical-moral meaning which was then subsequently altered and transferred to nonmoral relations of beings from other regions. It is the reverse, and we must think that in antiquity *individual regions of beings were not at all separated out yet.* The delimitations arose for the most part only in connection with the rise of the sciences and had the effect of diverting and making murky the original comprehensive view of beings as a whole.

d) Translation of the second section of the statement

All these discussions of the basic meanings and of the origin of the cited words can and must serve in the first place only to make palpable the difference between the following two juxtaposed translations of the Greek passage: διδόναι γὰρ αὐτὰ δίκην καὶ τίσιν ἀλλήλοις τῆς ἀδικίας.

1) "for things pay one another penalty and retribution for their wickedness." (the usual translation)

2) "they (beings) bestow compliance and correspondence on one another in consideration of the noncompliance."

A translation is always the result and final gathering together of an interpretation. Translation is never the mere exchange of a foreign language for the mother tongue; rather, it amounts to being *trans*-lated with the original power of one's own language into the reality of the world manifest in the other language.

Our translation will receive its properly cogent confirmation only from the completed interpretation of the whole statement and of what has come down to us immediately from Anaximander. This requires first of all, however, an examination of the full statement.

We maintained that the just-discussed section of the statement is supposed to supply the grounding, as the word γάρ clearly indicates, for what was previously laid down as belonging to Being. If so, then Anaximander is trying to say that the whence and whither of appearance are the same *because appearance is itself nothing other than the bestowal of compliance and correspondence in consideration of the noncompliance.* Is this a grounding? What we demand of one is that it provide *insight* into what is to be grounded. And the presupposition for this is that the grounding itself be accompanied with insight, such that we are "content" with it. Yet is this grounding insightful? I would think it is anything but, for it notes and appeals to the fact that the bestowal happens in consideration of a noncompliance. Which noncompliance? Not just any, but *the* noncompliance, the one which obviously concerns beings as a whole, for only that is at issue here. Beings as a whole—noncompliance? *And we experience anew:* an attempt to delimit beings in what they are, in their Being, leads us to the brink of nothingness and to the abyss. For does not an abyss exist and yawn open if we think deeply into Anaximander's pronouncement: beings as a whole, more precisely, their Being—noncompliance?

With this outlook on nothingness and darkness, we come now to the last section of the full statement. | 7

C. THE THIRD SECTION OF THE STATEMENT

§4. Being and time

a) Beings κατὰ τὴν τοῦ χρόνου τάξιν. Time as measure

κατὰ τὴν τοῦ χρόνου τάξιν, "according to the measure of time." This final section of the full statement still belongs to the grounding; it says that the reciprocal bestowal of compliance and correspondence, which indeed characterizes appearance, happens according to the measure of *time.* The overall task is to state *how* beings as a whole *are* as beings, what the Being of beings is. Thereby time now finally turns up, and the issue is the τάξις τοῦ χρόνου.

Beings—(Being) appearance → noncompliance—time.

It is superfluous to remark again that with regard also to the basic words now under discussion, χρόνος—τάξις, what was said earlier still holds. It seems there is no danger of misinterpretation here. For it is clear that things and all processes elapse in time and that time is therefore the universal order (τάξις) of the sequence of positions which pertain respectively to every event. Certainly—to us today this is commonplace, and we of today are quite capable of invoking the testimony of philosophy, namely, the fact that Kant indeed apprehends time as a form in which the manifold of the sequence of appearances is ordered, and so time is a universal form of the order of succession of things as appearances. This characterization of the essence of time is hardly self-evident. It views time purely and simply as time presents itself in the calculative investigation of nature, especially in physics. I.e., time is understood here purely and simply with respect to the sequence of natural processes in the sense of their succession according to antecedent and consequent, cause and effect.

We see, however, that Anaximander: 1) asks not at all about a determinate region of beings as nature but, instead, about beings as a whole and 2) understands beings not at all primarily as development, as causal generation and degeneration, but as stepping forth and receding, as we said: appearance. If Anaximander speaks of time, then he certainly does so with regard to its connection with this appearance. But then what is meant here by time and by the τάξις of time? This question has never been posed, because precisely this statement by Anaximander sounds so obvious—i.e., for thoughtlessness. It will be brought up that at issue here are indeed γένεσις and φθορά, coming to be and passing away, and precisely in their relation to time; for things come and go in time. Time is indeed precisely the transitory, the temporal in distinction to the eternal. Nothing could be more a matter of course than that Anaximander, when he speaks of γένεσις and φθορά, coming to be and passing away, must then also think of time. On the other hand, γένεσις does not mean "coming to be," but arrival, appearance, and φθορά does not mean "passing away," but disappearance, withdrawal from appearance. And time is perhaps then also not an unwinding cable on which each thing has a fixed position such that time would supply precisely the framework of the order of succession.

Indeed, the pronouncement is about nothing like that at all, but is instead concerned with beings as a whole and with the fact that beings bestow on one another compliance and correspondence in consideration of the noncompliance. It is with this that time is brought into connection—time and the noncompliance. Yet indeed we still do not know what that means at all: the noncompliance of beings as a whole. And so it will be difficult to make out what time means here and how its relation to beings as a whole should be grasped. Only one thing might have become clear: the facile bandying about of the contemporary notion of time, a notion that is in addition highly confused and, above all, ungrounded—this procedure leads nowhere and leaves us standing quite outside the content of the pronouncement.

b) Insight into χρόνος by appealing to Sophocles

How should we grasp χρόνος? A simple expedient offers itself. We will ask not Kant but the Greek philosophers themselves what they think about the essence of time. Aristotle has written a great treatise on time. But it will not be of use here, for this treatise articulates precisely that conception of time in which Western thinking about time in philosophy, in the sciences, and in everyday occupations has moved ever since. And Plato also tells us very little, even if it might seem to be much, for between Plato and Anaximander lie two centuries, and not just indifferent ones but ones in which Greek philosophy changed essentially. We will proceed much more surely if we go outside of philosophy to inquire whether and how Greek Dasein expressed itself about time. That cannot be presented here in full; we will offer only one instance, but, to be sure, one chosen on good grounds and not at random. The passage is from Sophocles, *Ajax* 646–47. The passage itself will immediately tell us why it in particular is introduced here. ἄπανθ᾽ ὁ μακρὸς κἀναρίθμητος χρόνος φύει τ᾽ ἄδηλα καὶ φανέντα κρύπτεται.[7] Powerful, incalculable time lets emerge *everything* not manifest and conceals everything standing in appearance. Time has all things in its power, (namely) it lets emerge the concealed and conceals (lets disappear) what has appeared.

Accordingly, time stands in the closest connection to everything that appears, everything that has stepped forth as appearance and is present at hand. But, as was established, the very operation of appearance includes disappearance; what disappears *withdraws*, | becomes   8
non-manifest. That is, everything non-manifest either still remains in a state of disappearance or has reverted to disappearance. In this very broad sense, however, appearance is the character Anaximander attributes to beings as beings; it designates their Being. Sophocles now speaks of a connection between *this* Being of beings and time. Indeed it is an essential connection, inasmuch as appearance and disappearance happen precisely *through* time. Heed well: it is not simply that appearances lapse "in time." That is not the point. Instead, time *lets* disappearance happen. It is of time that Sophocles says κρύπτεται: *it* conceals that which was previously manifest in apparentness. Likewise, time is what brings to appearance the non-manifest, the concealed. Sophocles uses for this a most notable expression: χρόνος— φύει. φύειν means to let grow—φύσις is growth—the grown and the growing—"nature."

c) Being and time as φύσις

The word possesses today, as it has since long ago, two senses: 1) Nature in distinction to history or art; nature as a determinate domain of beings, one which the natural sciences make the object of their research. 2) Nature in an essentially broader sense: we speak of and interrogate the nature of a historical process, the nature of the work of art, in general the nature of something; nature as equivalent to the essence of something, that which a being is, its whatness, how it is. In early Greek philosophy, φύσις has neither of today's senses but, instead, means in a very general way that by which beings live and thrive—their Being. The philosophers at the beginning of Greek phi-

---

7. {*Sophoclis Fabulae*, op. cit.}

losophy ask about physis, but they are not interrogating "nature," as if they were natural scientists. Instead, they are asking about beings, whose Being is φύσις—φύειν.

Have we not stressed throughout that for the Greeks the Being of beings means the same as appearance, remaining in apparentness or withdrawing from it, disappearing? Certainly; but that is not in the least contradicted by the characterization of this Being through φύειν and φύσις. On the contrary, here lies merely a quite decisive confirmation of our earlier interpretation of γένεσις and φθορά, provided we understand φύσις in the actual Greek way and do not read into it modern notions according to which what essentially counts in a natural process, thus even in growth, is the causal succession of states and properties. We would thereby miss the essential moment implicit in the Greek use of φύσις and φύειν: growth, coming forth—precisely out of the earth and thus *emergence,* self-unfolding, self-presentation in the open, self-showing—appearance.

χρόνος φύει—time lets the concealed emerge. It allows appearance. *φύειν is the counter concept to κρύπτεσθαι,* conceal. (On this basis we understand the pronouncement of Heraclitus (D 123): ἡ φύσις κρύπτεσθαι φιλεῖ—beings contain an intrinsic striving to self-concealment. That is possible only if beings as beings are at once *appearance;* only what appears and can appear, i.e., can show itself, can also conceal itself.)

What do we draw from the passage in Sophocles for the characterization of time? Time stands in relation to all beings and specifically to their Being; the *office and essence* of time is to *let beings appear and disappear.* (Cf. the connection between time and sun, light and darkness.) Time ever measures out to beings their Being, their appearing and disappearing. Time places before (present), takes back (past), and holds back (future); cf. in contrast the emptying and disempowering of the essence of time to a form of numerability. *Time—here what measures out Being,* time ever provides the "syntax"—τάσσω, "to allocate place"—time is the *allocative* in general, τάξις Being which a being possesses. Time: the giving of measure to Being; thus our translation: "according to the measure of time." It is not a question of the order and sequence of succession and of its numerical calculation and stipulation.

Sophocles therefore also calls time ἀναρίθμητος; in the full context, that does not simply mean "innumerable," as if to say that there is no end to counting and numbering time. Counting and numbering are not at issue here at all; instead, the meaning is: time is outside the realm of calculation. With regard to time, precisely as what brings and takes away beings, *all human calculation and planning fail.* Time is μακρός, not long in the sense of mere endless duration, but broad, broadly encompassing, powerful, inasmuch as time, in its en-compassing power, possesses all beings in their Being.

Let this suffice as an initial clarification of the words χρόνος—τάξις χρόνου.

We have now worked through Anaximander's pronouncement in all its sections and have commented on the individual words and phrases. To recapitulate: "But whence beings take their stepping-forth, thence also their receding ensues (happens) according to necessitation (compulsion); for they (the beings) give compliance—maintaining correspondence with one another, *acquiescing* to a correspondence with one another—(in consideration of) in return for the noncom-pliance according to the allocation of time." *Will we dare to say we have understood this pronouncement?* On the contrary, what initially looked like a exceedingly naive poetic-moral observation on the usual course of things besets us now as a thoroughly obscure pronouncement on the *Being of beings as a whole* (Being and time). Can the obscurity be cleared up? | 9

Chapter II
The second phase of the interpretation

§5. The unitary content of the pronouncement
on the basis of its central core

a) The essential power of Being as noncompliance

We must at least *attempt* such a clarification before we dismiss the statement as unintelligible. That would be as arbitrary as the surely still more fatal approach which degrades it to a primitive poetic-moral outburst. We will therefore now proceed beyond commenting on the individual elements and grasp the *unitary content* of the pronouncement on the basis of its *central core*. For that, we must once again gather up what was said hitherto.

The pronouncement speaks about beings as a whole, how they are, how that which is is (Being), what the situation is with Being (*how Being essentially occurs*)—thus it speaks of the Being of beings. Specifically, in the first section: initial indication of the characters of Being—appearance, whose whence and whither are the same. In the second: why Being has this character, why the whither of disappearing is the same as the whence of stepping forth—because beings must bestow compliance and correspondence on one another and must do so in consideration of the noncompliance. In the third: for this bestowal, i.e., for this consideration of the noncompliance, time provides the allocation; time in each case measures out to beings their Being. Consideration of the noncompliance according to the power of time—the *essential power of Being.*

Such a clear structure to the statement—and yet it is basically inaccessible to us, alien. If pressed, we can clarify it this way: an alternating of coming and going can be found in beings. But that this reciprocal giving-way should have the character of a bestowal of compliance and correspondence, that precisely therein should lie the consideration of the noncompliance—there we take exception. Thus what we really find shocking is that *beings persist in a noncompliance*, that beings in their Being are noncompliant. Yet precisely this is the *core* of the whole, for indeed on this basis the entire character of the Being of beings is determined. In this noncompliance is grounded the way beings are. If we desire to penetrate the content, that is what we must clarify.

b) The noncompliance. Day and night as the basic appearance

In what does the noncompliance persist? How does it persist? These two questions are one. The core allegation of the pronouncement is that the Being of beings consists in noncompliance. We will have to ask: how did the previous interpretation grasp the Being of beings? Will a further elucidation permit us finally to gather how the non-compliance persists and why it persists?

The only basic character of beings that was mentioned up to now is appearance, along with its most properly concomitant disappearance (γένεσις—φθορά). Reference was made to day and night, birth and death, etc. This reference initially served as an illustration. But it would be a fatal misunderstanding to take day and night, birth and death, merely as examples and particular cases of appearance. Such a conception already distances us from appearance in the Greek sense, provided we were ever in its vicinity; we remain victims of modern thinking. For, day and night are not to the Greeks just any random appearances among others; on the contrary, in day and night the *originary* appearance reveals itself. And that is not simply because day and night encompass everything; day and night are the *basic appearance* in the genuine sense because they constitute the ground of all other appearance. They permit all appearances to arise. For while the day shows itself, the light—brightness—appears; and precisely this appearing light first lets appear all other beings: sea and land, forest and mountain, human being and animal, house and homestead. As the day recedes, giving way to the night, it in a certain way takes the appearing things along with it and cedes sovereignty to the night which conceals everything. In the luster of the day and of the light, beings appear. The light, the sun, what allows appearance—allows beings presence in Being—that is time. Today we are not one step further along; on the contrary, our artificial light essentially does not exceed the power of light. At most, we thereby completely mistake the light—and forget our original bond to it.

c) Noncompliance: persistence in contours over and against contourlessness; compliance: return to contourlessness

What does that mean? Every being sets itself out in relief, every being raises itself up over and against others. Appearance is not merely a stepping-forth; the stepping-forth is an *entering into a contour* and into the limits of the contour. Set out in its contours, standing out in them, the being "is," i.e., *comes into the light of day.* Contour—not an indifferent framework, but the *integrating-gathering power* and inner substantiality of things. Thus through the clarification of an appearing thing in its appearing a new essential character of the Being of beings has obtruded. More precisely, appearance as emergence has been better determined as an entering into contours. Appearing—*emergent entrance into contours.* The experience of beings as what appears in possessing such Being—that is the primal experience of the Greeks.

Yet what is this to us, this sharper and fuller formulation of the essence of appearance? It should bring us closer to an understanding of the Being of beings. But that in turn is for the sake of understanding, on the basis of such a grasp of Being, how Being persists in the noncompliance which constitutes the noncompliance of beings. If the noncompliance is not something tacked on to beings, in the guise of a defective property or a belated epiphenomenon, but if it belongs, as Anaximander basically says, to the essence of beings as beings, then a sufficiently broad and penetrating elucidation of the essence of Being must I clarify how the noncompliance predominates here in beings as such.

10

That which appears, that which stands in apparentness, is *as such noncompliant, out of order.* What can this now mean, in terms of the expanded clarification of appearance? We will try to clarify it in the context of the pronouncement, by way of a free construction, so to speak.

Appearance means emerging entrance into contours; this entrance-into is supposed to be out of order. Whence steps that which enters into contours? Out of a lack of contours. What holds itself in apparentness persists in contours over and against contourlessness. The noncompliance would then consist in the possession of contours.

Seen this way, what then is disappearance? Let us remain within the basic experience of the Greeks! When day gives way to night and darkness falls over things, then contours and delineated colors disappear, the limits of things become indistinct and fade away, things lose their substantiality and individuality—everything is concealed in the gaping void (χάος) of darkness. Disappearance is accordingly a stepping-back out of the possession of contours into contourlessness. Returning to appearance is then a giving-way to a persistence in contours. In giving way to it, the appearance takes into consideration the noncompliance occurring through an abandonment of contourlessness.[1]

The receding acquiesces to the contourlessness and in this acquiescence testifies to it (discerns the compliance). Thus the noncompli-

---

1. [Reading *Umrißlosigkeit* for *Umrissenheit,* "possession of contours."—Trans.]

ance would then be: *persistence in contours over and against contourless-*
ness; and compliance: *return to contourlessness.*

In both, noncompliance as well as compliance, a contourlessness
shows itself. It ordains that what appears as such is noncompliant, and
it has at its disposal what compliance is and the fact that compliance is:
abandonment of contours. The contourlessness, thus the *limitlessness,*
would then be what by ordaining disposes of the noncompliance and
the compliance, i.e., their opposition. To give way reciprocally, however, is appearance, i.e., Being. The contourlessness and limitlessness
show themselves first and last in all appearance (stepping forth and
receding)—they have priority and preeminence. The limitless is what
disposes of compliance and noncompliance, i.e., *disposes of the Being of
beings.*[2]

On the basis of the essence of appearance as emerging entrance
into contours, we have clarified what the noncompliance can consist
in and what compliance can mean.

---

2. What lets Being essentially occur. Being and only Being essentially occurs.

Chapter III
The other dictum

§6. *The sovereign source of beings as the empowering power of appearance*

a) The ἀρχὴ τῶν ὄντων

It is not the case, however, that the noncompliance merely *can* mean this (persistence in contours over and against contourlessness), and likewise for compliance; on the contrary, ἀδικία and δίκη *must* have this meaning in the pronouncement of Anaximander, if indeed, as was shown, they are disposed by contourlessness and limitlessness. And it is in fact so; for Anaximander says, in the second statement that has come down to us, ἀρχὴ τῶν ὄντων τὸ ἄπειρον. The source of beings, and precisely of beings as such, i.e., with respect to their Being, is the limitless.

Before we offer a comprehensive presentation bringing out the intrinsic unity between this second pronouncement and the first, let us briefly explicate it, as was our earlier procedure.

1. τὰ ὄντα; at once we see that here, too, Anaximander is speaking about beings as a whole. Not about this or that being, not about any particular sphere set out above others, but about beings as such, for the issue is the

2. ἀρχή; ἄρχειν—"to precede." ἀρχή—what precedes everything, from which everything else proceeds. The issue is the *beginning of Being*, of appearance, of the entrance into contours, of what precedes in appearance, *comes into view in advance*. And that is precisely the contourless, that which in appearing enters into contours, maintains itself there, though under constraint, and compels a return to contourlessness, the abandonment[1] of the possession of contours.

ἀρχή—initially not a being, therefore not source in the sense of that by which something begins and is afterward left behind as in-

---

1. [Reading *Aufgeben* for *Aufgehen*, "emergence."—Trans.]

consequential and discardable. On the contrary, in the philosophical employment of the word ἀρχή we must hear its other meaning—precedence as *sovereignty* ("mon-archy"): source and sovereign for beings as such, i.e., for their Being. Here ἀρχή is precisely not *terminus* [boundary]. Even in Aristotle, who fixed the lexical meaning of the word, | the basic sense of sovereignty recurs: cf. *Met.* Λ, XII, at the end.[2] His whole treatise on the ἀρχὴ τῆς οὐσίας concludes with a verse from Homer's *Iliad,* B, 204: οὐκ ἀγαθὸν πολυκοιρανίη· εἷς κοίρανος ἔστω—shared sovereignty is not good; let one be sovereign, lord.[3] After all this, it is hardly necessary to stress that the later meaning of cause must be kept at arm's length—not merely because this meaning developed only subsequently, but because in the context of questioning Anaximander it would make no sense at all.

ἀρχή as the *sovereign source* remains present precisely in everything, shows itself first and last in all appearance and disappearance.

b) τὸ ἄπειρον as the empowering power of appearance

This ἀρχὴ τῶν ὄντων—indeed τῶν ὄντων and precisely as such, i.e., with respect to their Being (specifically including their whatness and thatness)—is τὸ ἄπειρον. πέρας—limit, but not so much in the merely negative sense as that by which and at which something stops and can go no further but, on the contrary, that which outlines something, its contours and inner delineation, that which in each case gives to all that appears, all beings, their closed peculiarity and security, their composure and their stance.

περαίνω—bring something into its limits, i.e., into its contours, produce, bring forth: let appear.

On the basis of πέρας arose the concept and meaning of τέλος, the determinate end in the foregoing sense. Later this basic notion of Greek philosophy was, for various reasons, misinterpreted and falsely transformed to mean purpose and goal. Teleology, purposiveness, that every Being has its τέλος—this means in the *Greek* understanding: *every being as a being stands in contours.* Later, it means: every thing has its purpose and goal and hidden, deeper function. That sense might be applicable in the biblical account of creation and in Christian dogmatics, but not in the basic propositions of ancient philosophy about beings.

Yet what is the meaning of τὸ ἄ-πειρον—the limitless, contourlessness? Grammatically, it is a privative expression: α- means "without,"

---

2. {*Aristotelis Metaphysica.* Recognovit W. Christ. Leipzig: Teubner, 1886.}

3. {*Homeri Ilias.* Edidit G. Dindorf. Editio quinta correctior quam curavit C. Hentze. Pars I. Leipzig: Teubner, 1896.}

thus something that does *not* have limit. Not to have is usually to lack, but here in no way is the meaning a not-having in the sense of doing without something on account of a defect. Here the not-having has the sense of disdaining and dismissing on account of superabundance, superiority over everything formed, everything enclosed in contours. τὸ ἄπειρον is *what disposes of beings as such* and, as this kind of disposing that ordains, constitutes Being. It is what allows all appearance, as entrance into contours, to come into noncompliance without letting it loose but, instead, so as to fetch it back into disappearance and compliance.

That beings are and insofar as they are—that is what the noncompliance consists in, *because what appears must forsake limitlessness and persist in contours.* The expression noncompliance does not merely signify disavowal of compliance, without compliance, for at the same time "compliance" remains in the sense that it signifies the ineluctable cadre of Being.[4] (Abruptly back to the first pronouncement!)

Beings, inasmuch as they are, stand under the constraint of Being. τὸ χρεών—the noncompliance disposes of them out of the ἀρχή, the cadre that disposes. And now we understand better what it means that the whence and whither[5] are the same origin of what appears, which is out of the limitless and returns to it in receding. In appearance as such, there happens a constant confirmation of the limitless. This latter, in all appearance and disappearance, has a privileged self-showing—the disposing—the *empowering power.*

As what appears disappears, it gives compliance back to the noncompliant. This giving-back happens in such a way that the individual beings correspond to one another—in the sense that they dovetail seamlessly into one another in the correspondence which is co-posited through the possession of contours, the delineation of the relations in which one appearance stands to another. The ἀλλήλοις is to be referred emphatically to τίσις, and that means: what appears does not disappear just in any way and at any time, as long as in general compliance is given back to the noncompliant; on the contrary, καὶ τίσιν ἀλλήλοις—and specifically in such a way that the enduring correspondence of day and night, birth and death, fame and disgrace is *maintained:* "acquiescing to a correspondence with one another."

---

4. inadequate—not *contour* as such, but that the contour *endures* without *escape*, departure, insists on tarrying. {Trscpt[1]}

5. ἐξ ὧν—εἰς ταῦτα [plural]—I but then why not ἐξ οὗ—εἰς τοῦτο [singular]? Because τὸ ἄπειρον, *as the superiority of the superabundance* of appearance and disappearance, is what *releases them and takes them back* (cf. above, p. 4), *not* as some sort of present at hand void of what is completely indeterminate.

It is not the case, as is falsely translated, i.e., falsely understood, that the things pay retribution to one another (no individual being has to exact compliance from another). Instead, if there is indeed to be payment, then the compliance is attested with reference to the superior power of the ἄπειρον—yet such that *this giving way to one another acquiesces to the correspondence* in which beings stand to one another according to their respective kind.

With this, the first pronouncement has once again been carefully discussed in its context, up to the last topic—the τάξις τοῦ χρόνου. The first task is now silence, but not without keeping in sight the inescapable, namely, the fact that what empowers beings in their Being is connected to the *essential occurrence and power* of *time* and thus precisely not to the *eternity* which is usually brought together with *infinity*. For ἄπειρον does not mean infinity, at least provided we do not let slip into this work some sort of later, Christian notion.

We have now brought the two pronouncements into their *intrinsic unity*. They throw light on each other. The second elucidates noncompliance and compliance; the first provides insight into the ἀρχή-character of the ἄπειρον. Both in their unity testify that the concern here is to say what beings as beings are. Being is no longer merely "appearance." The essence of Being is τὸ ἄπειρον as the empowering power of appearance and of disappearance, i.e., as the ordaining of the noncompliance which recedes into compliance. | 12

c) τὸ ἄπειρον, or, the difference between Being and beings

The two pronouncements have now been brought into their intrinsic unity. They throw light on each other. From the second, briefer one, we first understand the core of the first, namely, the meaning of noncompliance and compliance. And we now see how indeed the word γάρ does usher in a grounding of the fact that Being is not merely in general appearance and disappearance, but that the whence and whither must be the same.

Conversely, from the first-discussed statement we now understand in what sense the ἄπειρον is ἀρχὴ τῶν ὄντων, namely with respect to the way they are, i.e., with respect to their Being, and thereby at the same time we understand how the ἄπειρον holds sway as this sovereign source: disposing of the noncompliance and ordaining the compliance.

From the intrinsic unity of the two pronouncements, we first see what is said here about the Being of beings. We must now no longer be content with the introductory characterization according to which Being is appearance. That is not wrong but is insufficient; the essence of Being is to be understood on the basis of the ἄπειρον. Being is the cadre for and disposing of what is noncompliant—*there is manifest in Being as such the empowering power of appearance and disappearance.*

It would be otiose to engage ourselves in the controversy that has long occupied scholars, the question of whether the ἄπειρον of Anaximander is to represented quantitatively or qualitatively.

The question presupposes that the ἄπειρον and what Anaximander calls the ἄπειρον is a being, something present at hand, of which one could demand that it be intuitively representable in some way.

It is said, presupposing the issue here is chemistry, that the ἄπειρον is a basic matter extended in infinite space or is this limitless space itself. The retort will be that precisely then the ἄπειρον is delimited against the immaterial and the unextended, is not such, and is instead restricted to a determinate region of beings and consequently is incapable of furnishing the *most universal principle* of beings. It is then postulated that the ἄπειρον should be represented as the qualitatively limitless. These answers are all equally nonsensical, because they are responses to a question that itself is intrinsically impossible and thus they radically mistake the genuine intent of the pronouncements. The intent is to speak about *Being*—and *not about beings;* the question of what sort of a being Being is is accordingly, in this form, preposterous.

And if we ask, no doubt also unsuitably, for the genuine result held out by these pronouncements, then it is this: *beings are indeed on the basis of Being, but Being itself is not a being. Being and beings are different—* this *difference* is the *most originary* one that could ever open up.[6] Therefore the result: Being is not the beings. A comfortless message, perhaps comfortless indeed; the only question is whether such pronouncements about Being are called on to bring us comfort. Or if not comfort, then at least some clear and grounded insight. Where is that to be found?

---

6. Cf. manuscript on the essence of *this* distinction as the *originarily and essentially occurring* one—| this distinction and the bifurcation. {In *Zum Ereignis-Denken,* GA73.}

PART TWO

Interposed considerations

§7. Four objections to the interpretation

a) The dictum is too far removed and is antiquated, crude and meager, unreal

Appearance—noncompliance—time—limitlessness: are we not floundering here very unsteadily amid empty words? With what *right* do the pronouncements at issue present themselves? How do they intend to demonstrate their *truth*? On what path are they acquired? Are they not all mere decrees, conceits of a flighty arbitrariness, and not "strict science"? Yet it makes no difference whatever they may be, whether science or philosophy or poetry or something else for which we have no name, since these pronouncements are inaccessible to us, we feel no nearness to them, they are no longer of any concern.

Moreover, if we accept what we had to concede right at the start, namely, that little has been handed down and that this little is even incomplete (cf. below, p. 31), then does not the entire project of seeking out the beginning of Western philosophy become problematic in the highest degree? To be sure. It is accordingly time to pose relentlessly the objections to which our project is exposed. We will reduce them to four: | 12a

1) Between us and that beginning of Western philosophy lies a temporal span of two and a half millennia. The world and mankind have radically altered in the interim. That early time is so far removed it must remain inaccessible. Arranging a lecture course such as this will not simply leap over the two thousand five hundred years.

2) Yet even if it were possible, on the basis of other sources, to bridge this gap to some extent, what would the effort avail us? Only to establish finally that in the meantime philosophy has advanced very far? What then are we supposed to do with these long-surpassed issues and dicta? We of today especially, for whom the newest can never be "new" enough—how could we more sharply reproach and spurn something than by pointing out it is antiquated?

3) It might be conceded that this antiquated thought did continue on in what followed and did determine later developments and can therefore claim significance for itself. Even so, | this significance will 12b vanish as soon as we note how crude and much too meager these propositions and doctrines look in comparison, for instance, to the inner vitality of the Platonic dialogues or the compactness and full-

ness of the Aristotelian treatises or especially in comparison to the breadth and complex stratification of the works of Kant or Hegel. We who "know" all this resist such (all too) "primitive," simple, and insipid truths. And we feel it is almost an affront to be required to take seriously these ever-so-crude attempts made at the beginning—we to whom truth cannot be sufficiently intricate and provocative in order to count as truth at all.

4) Let even this be conceded: the simplicity and crude character of these propositions should not prevent us from pondering their content. In the end, however, does that not signify a mere scholarly occupation which entices us into all possible artifices of interpretation and perhaps momentarily enchants us with previously unfamiliar ideas? Yet it all remains a world of shadows and semblances, so that we do not come upon anything which could affect us of "today," let alone conclusively and lastingly change us. Instead, it is all unreal, a literary-philological invention, and therefore without any compelling power over us.

That is a compact series of weighty objections: unbridgeable span of time / antiquated / crude and meager / unreal (shadowy). Our project is exposed to such objections provided it intends to be something other than a far-fetched, obsolete, and altogether irrelevant report on a long-vanished age of human history. Can these objections be disabled, perhaps by refuting them with counterarguments?

Yet can this vanished time indeed be expected to return by way of a refutation of objections and become new and fertile and real? In fact, a reality never arises out of the mere refutation of false views. Cf. below.

b) Presuppositions of the objections in a self-delusion

To charge headlong at those objections would be useless without wondering at all about the content and essence of the *presuppositions* from which the objections arise and draw sustenance. What is speaking out in those objections? It is we ourselves, which is why they seem judicious and pressing. *We* therefore—we, the way we behave when we say: unbridgeable span of time / antiquated / crude and meager / unreal (shadowy)—we act in the reeling off of these objections as if we were undoubtedly ready to lend an ear to the beginning of Western philosophy. We act as if we were not only ready but naturally also predisposed to let it say something to us. We act as if we were even capable of deciding whether this beginning has something to say to us or not. We even think that such would be an honorable endeavor, and we flatter ourselves on the critical prudence with which we look upon the project of seeking out the beginning. We do all this, but what if we are thereby deluding ourselves? And what if this self-delusion was one that found it fitting to take shelter behind those objections? Perhaps well-intentioned, but nonetheless a great self-delusion that shelters behind the objections; shelters behind, precisely in order to shelter itself from ever becoming actually exposed to those early times? It is of course a self-delusion.

c) What the self-delusion consists in

What does that self-delusion consist in, one with which we have long been stricken? In the fact that humans have convinced themselves that the old is the antiquated, the antiquated the past, the past what no longer is, and what no longer is, as nonbeing, sheer nullity. What could be more obvious than this conviction that the old is the antiquated, and what is easier to cast off than the antiquated, since indeed, as past, it passes away of itself?

Is this self-delusion accidental? If it is, then how does it come to be so widespread? It derives from a firmly seated *prejudice* about humans and about their relation to history; the prejudice is that this relation consists in and is based on historiological cognitions. We take ourselves to be disposed and authorized, without further ado, to judge what history, and especially the past, can mean to us and is allowed to mean to us.

The four objections stem from a single prejudice, one so well-guarded today that it faces not even the least danger; on the contrary, at most it is increasingly advancing. For what age has ever acquired so many and such varied historiological cognitions as has ours? When were past "cultures" and human types ever rummaged through and psychologically-analytically probed to such an extent? When were these constantly accumulating cognitions ever served up with such a shameful top-dressing than in today's journalism, a journalism whose very successes do not allow this science to sleep? Must not finally such an excess of historiological cognitions show us the full totality of history and prompt us to believe we had a relation to history! Or is this monstrous amount of historiology precisely what rivets us to the prejudice about our supposedly genuine and authoritative relation to history? Can historiological cognition create at all originarily a relation to history? No; on the contrary, historiological cognition is itself possible only on the basis of an originary relation to history. Historiology can explain and expand this relation but can just as much also undermine and slacken it and, above all, can delude us precisely about the endangering, destruction, and thus the complete lack of any basic relation to history.

That is how matters stand today. Therefore, we can without scruples believe ourselves justified in bringing forward objections against the possibility and intrinsic value of the project of seeking out the begin-

ning of Western philosophy and also justified in finding these objections self-evident. Indeed, we even believe we are attempting to be especially critical and serious when we strive to make such objections
13   heard.[1] |

   d) The distance from the beginning of Western philosophy

Assuming, however, it could actually and convincingly be declared that our purported relation to history is merely a prejudice and that consequently we lack any *intrinsic* claim to be competent to put forth these objections, indeed, that they have been put forth only from not understanding history and from a negative relation [*ein Un-verhältnis*] to it—assuming all this, then would the objections not have to collapse, whereby refutation of them becomes superfluous? Certainly; but what would then be gained? We would not have eliminated the objections by way of a refutation but, instead, would have disabled them in advance through a withdrawal of their ground.

   Yet will the temporal distance of two and a half millennia that separates us from the beginning become less thereby? Will the beginning become less antiquated thereby? Through the dismissal of the objections do we attain the positive result that the beginning is of some immediate concern to us? Can such reflections, no matter how subtle, simply conjure up an actual relation to history and to the beginning? Two and a half millennia—the myriad changes in the world and in humanity indeed cannot be undone by such reflections, quite apart from the circumstance that we still do not see to what end that should happen. Are not beginnings rather in each case there precisely so that after them everything moves away from them?

   We remain shut off from the "beginning," whether or not we refute the cited objections, whether or not we wonder about the presuppositions on which they are based, whether or not we simply disregard them. No artifices of interpretation can transport us over this gap of millennia, no so-called empathy can magically replace something bygone with something real.—*That is how matters stand,* if we stay sober and do not fool ourselves. We must face the fact of our continuous movement away from the beginning. More precisely, we must face the fact of our *detachment* from the beginning. And is it not a splendid thing to bow soberly to the facts, especially when they are as indis-

---

1. *But what if the converse?*—Historiology *in* history and historiology allowing us in, but just as much slackening, undermining, destroying, and thereby still deluding. If then this prejudice nevertheless holds sway, the consequence is a *disempowering and a negative relation* to history. *Out of this,* the objections against a relation to history!!

putable as the constantly increasing distance of the present from the past, our movement away from it?

Yet the facts are also peculiar in not being exhausted by what we casually and obviously ascertain about them. To be sure, we usually believe that in this way we possess what the fact is. We do not take into account, and have no eye for, what in the end could be the case with the so-called fact.

§8. The negative relation to the beginning

a) The wanderer and the spring

Yet what then could this indubitable temporal gap between us of to-day and the beginning of philosophy still further be? What concealed possibility could still lurk in this naked fact? Let us indicate this possibility first by way of an image.

A wanderer in an arid region must distance himself more and more from the spring at which he first and last drew water. Viewed soberly, his distance from this spring is thereby increasing. He leaves the spring behind, and with the increasing distance he loses his orientation; the spring in the end lies inaccessibly far behind. Assume the wanderer then dies of thirst. Why did he die? Presumably because at too great a distance from the spring he no longer had a relation to it. Yet how is the too great distance from the spring no longer a relation to it? At a sufficiently great distance, does this relation cease to be a relation, or is the excessively great distance from the spring *always still a relation* to it, a *negative relation* but still precisely a relation and even one that is hardly inconsequential? Does the wanderer somehow get loose of the spring in the increasing distance? Does he step away from a relation to it? The opposite is the case. Does not the spring pursue him more importunately the closer he comes to dying of thirst? Indeed, soberly calculated, is it not precisely the very far distant spring that lets him perish? Therefore does not the wanderer in his roaming and advancing come to perish because of nothing other than this spring? An image.

What if now in our relation to the beginning of Western philosophy we were such advancing wanderers! What if not just today but since long ago the advancement of Western philosophy were a constant, ever-greater perishing because of its beginning! And what if in this history of perishing—precisely in it—the beginning pursued and importuned the one advancing! And what if in this pursuing and importuning the beginning were constantly there in the closest proximity, a quite different proximity than could be pointed to by the image of the spring and the wanderer! And what if this closest proximity of the beginning had to remain *concealed* precisely on account of the advancement!

b) The closest proximity of the concealed beginning

How do matters now stand with the naked fact that in advancing we distance ourselves from the beginning more and more? This fact has changed; it has become richer, even if merely with regard to possibility.

The fact of distance includes the possibility that the relation between us and the beginning is a negative relation, a negative relation thanks to which the beginning stands concealed in our closest proximity.

This fact not only stands before us, we also stand in it—thus in the possibility that the beginning has the closest proximity to us. But then the question of whether we can or cannot leap over these two and a half millennia is a "bagatelle" compared to the question of whether we experience and see that the beginning pursues us, and importunes us, out of the closest proximity. The temporal distance of more than two thousand years, this gigantic span of time, would in its significance be nothing compared to this negative relation of nearness. |

14 The invoking of the mere fact of this temporal distance would then at most be a deception which we only strengthen with the alleged sobriety. In the end, we must decide at least to look into the face of the possibility of the dangerous closest proximity of the concealed beginning. We must learn that here and in general in the naked fact of history the essential is hidden, that only apparently does the naked fact constitute the actual happening of history, and that the representation of history becomes even more destitute when so-called ideas are tacked on to so-called facts and ideology is used to help explain history. It has not yet been seen that this "ideologism" is the worst positivism and that the latter is even still dominant.

c) The inability to do anything with the beginning

We must therefore face the possibility that our relation, or negative relation, to the beginning of Western philosophy does not primarily depend on the extent of the intervening temporal span (cf. the objections!). In other words, it could be that we would remain as far removed from the beginning as we are today even if the beginning happened only a decade or a year ago; it could be that in our negative relation to the beginning we are so very *obdurate* that not only are we simply unable to experience and grasp its proximity but do not *want* to.

We must face the possibility that the beginning is not the old in the sense of the antiquated but that *we* are so very antiquated that we can no longer understand a beginning—and especially cannot understand when we invoke the advanced and the contemporary.

We must then also face the possibility that this inceptuality of the beginning is not the elementary and primitive, that what we call primitiveness is nothing other than the *simplicity* proper to everything great, and that we do not grasp this simplicity because we do not see greatness on account of our having long ago become too small. For only what is itself great, or at least in an essential sense knows about greatness, can in turn encounter the great.

In the end, we must face the possibility that the beginning, which no longer seems to be of concern to us, importunes us to the highest degree out of the closest proximity, that it constantly does everything with us, and that without it we cannot do the least thing. That we are no longer able to confront this importuning of the beginning is our unsurpassable cluelessness and harmlessness with which we are washed away in history (whereby the age of historiology still means such an age would stand in a living relation to history).

To put it succinctly, we, the obdurate, antiquated, small, and harmless, must face the possibility that it is not the beginning in its peculiarity which prevents us from coming close to it, but that we ourselves —indeed unwittingly—prevent ourselves from seeking out the beginning. This obstacle consists then in nothing less than our inability to do anything with the beginning.

Only one who *can* do something with the beginning[2] disposes of the inner preparation for the project to seek out the beginning.

Therefore when we said at the start of the lecture course, "We want to seek out the beginning of Western philosophy," that was not an innocuous remark and an incitement to a more or less amusing or boring engagement with a few scraps of old texts but instead, rightly understood, is the will to gain mastery in some way over our inability to do anything with the beginning.

Where do we now stand—and how do matters therefore stand with our project? | 15

§9. Meditation on the "current situation"

a) Who is asking about the beginning?
Toward determining the "we"

"We" are supposed to be the ones who prevent ourselves from doing anything with the beginning? *Who* is actually meant by this "we"? Not us as the ones here and now. Nor those many who according to their

---

2. i.e., has something done *to* him. {Trscpt[1]}

personal aims and occupations consider a knowledge of ancient philosophy superfluous. Nor those who indeed have the desire but lack
the required tools. It is we, not those accidentally here and now, but
we as the successors of a long history of the human impotence to actually do something with that beginning. We—these successors, but
these at the same time as *prior,* as the predecessors of the future ones.

We, the succeeding predecessors of that history which has done
something with the beginning of Western philosophy, of that history
which constantly happens in concealment *while* "we" perish on that
beginning. If we no longer succeed in coming into the proximity of
the greatness of the beginning, then everything is denied to us—even
this, to perish with greatness and composure.

Whether we will do something with the beginning or will perish
on it, in any case what is first is to experience the proximity of the beginning in our Dasein. That includes a previous effort to indicate the
beginning in our proximity. And that requires us to *involve ourselves in
ourselves.* Such a task is nevertheless exposed to tempting misunderstandings which could severely hinder the correct grasp of the following considerations. The misunderstandings concern the question:
who are the "we," the ones we are supposed to let "ourselves" be involved in?

It was already intimated that in the following when we speak of
us and our Dasein, we are speaking and questioning out of a long
and continuous backward glance and out of a broad forward glance.
Thus—glancing forward and back—we overlook the present. The latter shrinks into nothingness. As long as something of the present mixes
itself in, that is insignificant.

b) The concept of generation as off the path

We speak of us and do not mean individuals, or the individual, and
even less the so-called generation. It has lately become usual to speak
of "oneself" no longer as an individual but as belonging to a generation. Self-staring now happens generation-wise. One thinks in terms
of "generations," one makes comparison according to generations. And
it seems one has thereby arrived, beyond individuals, at a denser historical reality.

In truth, an unhistorical, frivolous conflation of individuals and
types of groups, the "calculation" with typologies and ideologies, has
thereby merely been expanded to massive proportions. The impotence
for historical Dasein has increased. The self-delusion about the relation
to history has hardened even further. The fact that today everyone
speaks of historicality is not evidence against this. For of what does
one not speak today?

This unbridled, apish rummaging around in one's own generation and in further expanses, in the so-called current situation, is becoming downright revolting. From this, however, one can if necessary maintain a safe distance.

What is fatal is that the excited fussing over the current situation is becoming the innermost corruption, since it exacerbates a basic delusion, namely, the opinion that I meditation on the current situation is the beginning of serious questioning and that here would lie the much-named but never carried out "decision." This procedure of considering the situation, including the evaluation of the procedure, constitutes merely an arbitrary and also perverse transfer of the attitude of moral self-reflection onto the relation to history and onto history itself. But history in its essence is all the more denigrated and corrupted when morals are mixed in. This running after the situation feigns proximity to the reality of history but is indeed the most unhistorical behavior imaginable.

15a

c) The determination of the current situation by Friedrich Nietzsche

The portrayal of the current situation, undertaken these days again and again and in the most varied forms, is not only intrinsically perverse but is also superfluous and has long been so. Already two lifetimes ago the current situation was determined—by Nietzsche. Moreover, it could indeed have been determined only then and only by him. The respective current situation cannot at all be discovered through the amusing portrayal of contemporary trends, fashions, and opinions; it is visible only to a creative view in advance, i.e., to a view that clearly sees the essential task and that is preserved and nourished by a long view out of the past.

Such a determination of the historical circumstances, with the depth and breadth of Nietzsche, is something that occurs only once and is based on a unique necessity; it is unrepeatable. The accomplishment of that work was paid for by the prodigious fate of a great man. Such a task cannot be carried out incidentally, as a parergon; it demands the entire inner and outer history of a man of Nietzsche's rank.

The complete self-delusion in which contemporary humanity, as contemporary, gaily splashes about is perhaps testified most clearly in the fact that Nietzsche, despite—indeed because of—the endless literature about him, is still not understood. Only a few are starting today to surmise something of the task and duty to grasp, i.e., to make effective, Nietzsche's fate as the basic happening of our most inward history. To be sure, that signifies something completely other than becoming "representatives" of Nietzsche's philosophy. No real philosophy can have representatives, provided such philosophy is truly understood. The "representatives" are always the ones who understand nothing.

Until we place ourselves in position, out of the power of a future, i.e., in the power of the past, to let the present disappear, or, in brief, as long as we are not successful in this essential transformation of the essence of time, we will not come to know authentically what we mean in saying "we."

It can now only be anticipated: we—not as persons of today but, instead, as succeeding predecessors of a concealed history.

We want to seek out the beginning of Western philosophy. A condition is our being able in general to do something with the beginning. That requires experiencing the proximity of the beginning. That in turn requires a reference to the possible proximity of the beginning *in our Dasein*. And for that, we must involve ourselves in ourselves, which means neither dissecting ourselves psychologically-analytically nor telling amusing tales about the current situation. |

16

§10. The grounding utterance of Being

a) The characterization of the beginning

How are we to *indicate* the proximity of the beginning in our Dasein? By what can the beginning become *recognizable* to us? Without a sufficiently sure and clear characterization, we might easily lose our way here. What have we learned up to now from our previous considerations of the beginning? We "know" the pronouncement of Anaximander, whereby we are now taking no. 1 and 2 together. "Know"? How so? Have we not ourselves subsequently placed in doubt our understanding of the content of this pronouncement, inasmuch as we even lack the conditions for such an understanding? Thereby the pronouncement indeed becomes a most problematic characterization of the beginning.

Should the entire interpretation therefore be retracted? No; but we must confess that its previous confirmation is insufficient, and its further justification is reserved for a later occasion. This does not exclude our taking from the pronouncement something that can characterize the beginning. And for that we do not now need to appeal to its most proper, innermost content, which might indeed be controversial. We will not take anything from the pronouncement, but we will take it more completely. We will now take only that in the pronouncement which "lies forth" uncontroversially and is, as it were, within easy reach. And what is that? The following: the pronouncement speaks *about* τὰ ὄντα, beings, by way of saying something *of* the Being of beings, and what is said about beings seeks in some way to ground why beings must be as they are (cf. the words γάρ and ἀρχή). In short:

The pronouncement is a grounding utterance of Being, about beings. That characterizes uncontroversially the oldest testimony to Western philosophy, consequently to the *beginning,* so far as we know. This latter reservation is imperative, in view of the provisionally still possible objection that the oldest preserved testimony does not necessarily concern the *first* beginning. The oldest testimony may very well be younger than the actual beginning; indeed this latter is perhaps not testified at all. A question which to be sure is only apparently of great bearing.

b) The pronouncement as an answer to a question

Therefore as far back as we can go, this is what is peculiar to the beginning: the grounding utterance of Being, about beings. We may take this as a provisional characterization of the beginning. What is dealt with there in particular is the "limitless," compliance and noncompliance, time, and appearance—we do not want to forget all this hereafter, but at first we will place no further demands on it.

Yet is this utterance which is of Being and about beings merely a *characterization* of the beginning? Is not this utterance the beginning *itself*? Even if it can be said with some justification that the pronouncement is not only the oldest testimony from the sphere of the beginning but is the actual first beginning itself, we still must not see in this pronouncement the authentic beginning. Why not? We take from the pronouncement: it is a *grounding* utterance. The grounding utters the ground in saying: "therefore" and "for this reason" Being has the mentioned characters. But to announce the "therefore" and the "for this reason" means to speak by referring back to a "wherefore?" and a "why?" and so is to be related to a question. Such an utterance is called an *answer.*

The pronouncement is not simply an assertion; it is an answer. The content of the pronouncement may be ever so controversial in itself and also in its interpretation, but what is beyond controversy is that, as an answer, it is essentially rooted in a questioning. The beginning therefore resides not in the pronouncement as such, but in the questioning to which the pronouncement is a response. The grounding utterance, as answering with the ground, already contains the questioning. The full content of the pronouncement is not at all grasped if this questioning is left unheeded. For this questioning is not merely the way it comes to be answered, the mere mode of origination of the pronouncement, which could be left out once the pronouncement had originated. On the contrary, the dictum does not in the least speak as itself unless it speaks as an answer, i.e., unless it is uttered at the same time and above all as a question.

Consequently, if the pronouncement is communicated merely as an assertion and is transmitted in such communication, then the communication remains essentially incomplete. Even if the pronouncement is discussed ever so extensively and is compared to other pronouncements, it is still not actually communicated, for in this way it is still impossible to take part in its full content, i.e., to take part in its questioning. As long and as often as the pronouncement is proposed and repeated merely as an assertion, the communication remains essentially incomplete, and furthermore this incompleteness produces an outright perversion of the character of the pronouncement. In that case, the questioning expressed here, provided it is remarked in the least, remains something contingent and all too obvious, in which one need not further involve oneself.

c) Questioning as a questioning that discloses Being

Only if we partake in the questioning expressed in the pronouncement do we grasp the latter's inceptuality, its beginning-character. As a mere assertion, the pronouncement is not at all a beginning, but is at most the end of a train of thoughts that is as negligible, once the result is given, as the scaffolding once the house is standing. Accordingly, when we speak of the "beginning of Western philosophy," we do not mean the dicta and pronouncements that lie there "at the beginning," i.e., | in those early times; instead, we mean the act of beginning itself, that which possibly expresses itself in such dicta. We mean the beginning as an *occurrence,* not the first, detached, deposited result, behind which we can go no further back. *The beginning is thus an act of beginning in the mode of a questioning.* In our search for a characterization of the beginning, the essence of the beginning has become more precisely determined. The beginning as act of beginning; the act of beginning as a questioning; the questioning as a questioning that discloses Being; the questioning as the *question of Being* [*die* Seinsfrage]. Can this questioning be characterized more precisely? Initially, only to the extent that we know the appertaining answer— the pronouncement. This was ultimately grasped as: the grounding utterance of Being, about beings.

The questioning maintains itself in the domain of that *about* which the answer is given. It is to beings that we turn, asking what they are. Beings are the interrogated [*das Be*fragte]. In what regard are they interrogated? In regard to that which determines beings as beings, in regard to their Being. We ask after that. Being is that which we ask after [*das Ge-fragte*]. We see, however: the saying is a grounding ut-

17

terance of Being. What is announced is not simply that Being is such and such, but *why* it has this character. The questioning of the "what" unfolds into a questioning of the ground of the "what." The questioning is a seeking out of the essence-ground, a grounding of Being. This grounding question of the Being of beings we call the questioning that discloses Being [*das Erfragen des Seins*].

d) The essence of questioning; various modes of questioning

The act of beginning: the questioning that discloses the Being of beings or, as we say in brief: the question of Being. We have thereby acquired a characterization of the beginning. Where we encounter this, namely, the question of Being and related matters, there we are in the proximity of the beginning. Yet what is this itself, the question of Being? It is now to us merely a name. What a question is, in general, is usually accepted by us as a matter of course, at least inasmuch as we can always easily pose questions, i.e., carry out a questioning, and can lay claim to questioning as such. E.g., these everyday questions: What is occurring there? Who won? When is the exam? Where will the seminar be held? Has the book appeared? Why was the lecture canceled? (Cf. below, *p. 25 middle*.) Modes of questioning that can be formally called who-what-when-where-questions; whether-questions; why-questions. In the forms of these questions, we can endlessly interrogate things of all sorts.

Not only can we do so, we do do so constantly, and not merely or even primarily when we express questions explicitly in interrogative sentences and use interrogative words such as "where" and "why." We often question implicitly, especially when we inquire[3] alone and in questioning seek and secure directions for our behavior at the time. Often, however, the question is an inquiry [*Anfragen*] in the presence of others and becomes a co-questioning with them. In those cases, we can also express our questioning through a mere way of looking or manifest our questioning whether such and such is the case through a shrug of the shoulders. (Doubt-question!)

In a quite different respect, there are questions that arise fleetingly and are no sooner answered; and also questions that persist: the social question, the Eastern Front question, the military question, the "Homeric question" of classical philology, and, especially in Bavaria, the question of the price of beer.

In another respect again, we can distinguish investigative questions, suitability questions, and figurative questions. To the first class belong all those questions that interrogate the interrogated matter itself. The case of the suitability question is different; here it is asked

---

3. [Reading *anfragen* for *anfangen,* "begin."—Trans.]

only whether the "interrogated" person understands the question and can answer. And figurative (rhetorical) questions are questions only in their linguistic formulation; in their sense, they are declarations, attempts to persuade, requests, and the like.

In still another respect, there are these widely divergent forms: semblant questions and fateful ones. What is interrogated and asked after in a semblant question is not originarily and immediately appropriated; it is not opened and illuminated by this questioning but is instead obscured and disguised. The makeup of such questions simulates participation in the matter but produces only groundlessness. Such semblant questions (example: idealism or realism?) can generate an entire literature, and there are scholars and scholarly trends and schools whose sole activity consists in propagating semblant questions and thereby complicating things to the point of unrecognizability and assuring the continuation of the groundlessness of their scholarship. There are other—rare—scholars who with a single question simplify the matter to its essentials and thereby bring about an essential advance. As to what a fateful question is, let us for now not speak about it further.

This rough survey is only meant to provide some indication of the phenomenon of the question and questioning. In the background, of course, lies the task of clarifying what sort of comportment questioning is in general and whether indeed it can be called an autonomous comportment. Furthermore, the task is to ground how something like questioning is possible; what sort of being is the only one that can question and even *must* question? Is it the case that gods cannot question, not because for some reason they would be incapable of it, but because they ought not at all to be capable of it if they are indeed gods? Is it that animals cannot question, because they do not at all need to question, to be sure for different reasons than gods? Is it that human beings can question, indeed must question, and consequently only humans can leave something unquestioned, specifically such that by this non-questioning they at the same time decide what they make of themselves and how they are to be taken? These are various questions about questioning that have for the most part never been properly posed, let alone resolved. Here belongs also the question of how and within what limits questioning can itself be questioned.

With this prospect, let us return to *our* question or, more prudently expressed, to the question occasioning these comments, namely, the question of Being. What sort of question is that? We already said: beings are to be interrogated with respect to their Being, and Being, so questioned, is to be grounded in the ground of its possibility. We said:

18   Being is to be disclosed in questioning. |

e) The question of Being as the most
originary, first, and last question

Under which of the above-designated forms of questioning does the question of Being fall? We ask: what are beings? A what-question. And we are also asking: why does Being have this whatness? A why-question. Consequently, the combination of a what-question and a why-question. Let us wait and see!

Consider this example: we suddenly hear a rustling in the hedges and ask: what is moving there, what is that? A what-question! Whereto is our questioning directed? Perhaps to the individual animal presumably moving about. Yet perhaps it is only a gust of wind, blowing in the leaves. What is it? A blackbird or a finch, a squirrel or a lizard? Consider another example of a what-question: what is a book? Each time, we are asking "what is it?" yet are doing so in very different respects. In the first case, we want to know not what a blackbird or a squirrel is but, rather, whether an individual of this species is moving about here. What is it, such that this noise is occurring? We are seeking, guided by possible species of things that could be moving here, what individual, actually what species, is involved. In the second case, on the contrary, we are asking not whether the present individual thing is a book but, instead, what a book is. In the former case, we seek what the X is to be determined as; in the latter, the present thing is determined as a book, and our questioning is directed to the determinate thing itself, to its "what," its whatness.

The question of Being is manifestly an essence-question. What are beings, in what does their essence consist?[4] In their Being! Is that an answer? We will then ask at once: what is the essence of Being? This essence-question has various levels. But that peculiarity holds for every essence-question. What is a book? Answer: a use-object. Apart from the fact that this is not a sufficient determination of the essence of a book, though perhaps a necessary one, we can immediately proceed to ask: what is the essence of a use-object, and so on. Yet how far does this "and so on" go? Especially with regard to the question of what is Being. Beyond Being, "is" there at all something still possible to which our questioning could be directed and which could be set forth and secured as the ground of the essence of Being? Something which could be fixed as something that *is*? Or, if we go beyond Being, do we not immediately and inevitably come to nothingness, with which at once every possibility of a ground is lost and there is

---

4. "Essence," essence-question—not every what-question an essence-question: what is the price of the trip?

no longer ground but only abyss? (Difference between groundless and abyssal questioning.)

The question of Being would then be an essence-question, but a preeminent one: a grounding question which, in going back to the ground, necessarily and not accidentally reaches the abyss. Even more: the question of Being is not merely *one* essence-question among others, not merely a preeminent one, but is *the* essence-question in the sense that it secures the general possibility of any essence-question, for essence means the whatness of a being: whatness a mode of Being. If Being as such is not disclosed in questioning and is not grounded, then every essence-question remains ungrounded and obscure, no matter how copiously and unrestrainedly we direct our questioning to the essence of some thing.

Finally, the question of Being is not only *the* essence-question pure and simple but is altogether the most originary, first, and last question, the question directed simultaneously to that in which the possibility of each and every question is rooted.[5] The first and last, deepest and broadest, thus not at all a semblant question but, to the extreme contrary, a—indeed *the*—fateful question "of humanity." Indeed not of humanity as such and in general, which is never and nowhere, but of the humanity whose history was co-begun, in its beginning, by way of the asking of the question of Being. Yet precisely because this question is the question of this humanity, it is also the most forgotten question. And because the question of Being is the most originary one, it also remains commonly disguised and suppressed by semblant questions. These latter are especially widespread today in everything that goes by the name of "ontology."

§11. *The actual asking of the question of Being*

a) The question of Being becoming problematic

Fine—this then is the question of Being! We have gained all sorts of information *about* it but have not experienced it itself. Despite all our discussions about questioning in general and about the various interrogative forms and the place of the question of Being amid them, despite the preeminence of the question of Being over and against all other questions, despite all this the question of Being remains nebulous to us and ultimately no more than a word. And it will remain so until we set out and ask this question; only in that way, as an asked

---

5. Thus wrongly asked if seek to encase it in fixed forms—the very form of questioning—to be grounded only on the basis of the question of Being.

question, does it become for us more actual as a question and thereby become a possible characterization of the beginning and of its possible proximity—of the beginning in the mode of a questioning. (Here work up the remaining connections! Cf. p. 17, top.)

The task is now to ask—*actually* ask—the question of Being. Thus let us ask it without circumlocution or sideward glances: what are beings, namely, with respect to their Being? Answer—we have no answer. Even if we had one, no person would want to maintain that in asking the question we already have the answer. Yet with this questioning do we not also at least have the question? Then does the questioning consist only in this, namely, that the interrogative sentence and its formulation are recited and repeated? What are beings? If we actually want to ask, must not something have become *problematic* to us here? And how else do we encounter the problematic than by its placing us into the uncertain, the indeterminate, the ungrounded, the open? The problematic brings us the unrest of indecision as to whether something is so or is otherwise or even is at all. The disquiet from the problematic can increase to the point of torment—a tormenting question. Are we tormented or even disquieted by the question: what are beings? Not at all, for if indeed this is a question it is an insignificant and "unprofitable" one with which we can neither bring order to the finances of the empire nor create work for the six million unemployed. |

19

b) The question of Being as unproblematic

The question of Being contains nothing disquieting for us; perhaps we are hearing it now for the first time, and it leaves us cold. The question is unproblematic to us. That is why we cannot actually ask it.

Yet why is the question of Being unproblematic? Perhaps because we find nothing like the problematic in it? Why so? Because the question of Being bears nothing problematic. That would be a hasty contention. For have we at all seriously sought what might be problematic in the question of Being? Manifestly not. How then can we say we find nothing there? Initially, the question of Being is exhausted for us in the recited formula: what are beings as such? The recitation does not at all need to be carried out from an actually interrogative stance. We properly ask only when we *pose* the question. Repeating the interrogative sentence is not a posing of the question.

What then pertains to the posing of a question? First of all, this: we must bring ourselves and pose ourselves *before* [in the presence of] that with which the question is meant to deal. We called that the interrogated. Prior to and so that this is taken up by a questioning, it must be familiar to us and therefore must at first stand outside of questioning. The interrogated is the initially known and unproblematic. But precisely this that is familiar must at the same time be unfamiliar in some way, or able to become unfamiliar, if it is to be interrogated. The unproblematic must become problematic with respect to that in regard to which it is interrogated, i.e., with respect to what is asked after.

The posing of the question does not simply in general pose us before the interrogated but, in addition, separates out in it the unproblematic from the problematic, in such a way, to be sure, that precisely what was unproblematic steps forth in its problematic character.

The posing of a question thus consists in a pre-questioning and a pervasive questioning aimed at the interrogated as something unproblematic that is in some way problematic. Every question has its own proper pre-questions that elaborate the state of the question and so pose the questioner before the interrogated, the asked-after, and that which is to be disclosed by the questioning. The only posed question is the one elaborated in this way, and only such a posed question bears in itself that which is problematic and can therefore actually be asked. This pre-questioning, as an elaboration of the posing of the question, is in each case different according to the type of question. If the question of Being is the preeminent question in every respect, then that also holds for the elaboration of the appurtenant posing of this question.

c) Familiar beings and unfamiliar Being

Let us therefore now attempt to pose the question of Being. What are beings? In this question, beings are the interrogated. How do matters stand with them? We already said something about that in the first lecture. We find ourselves at any time in the midst of beings, posed before beings, ourselves as beings. And specifically such that these beings display a certain affiliation, without any one of them transparent to us and without our knowing how transparency can be attained. Beings as a whole are in advance, within certain limits, familiar to us and so are known.

Within certain limits, we know what beings are in each case, whether animal or human person, stone or plant, number or tool; still more particularly: whether cane or umbrella, book or pen, dog or bird. We know beings in what they are in each case. Why then do we still ask the question: what are beings? We know these beings as blackboard, book, staircase, door—what each respectively is, its whatness, its essence. And yet we immediately find ourselves in a predicament if we try to say univocally and definitively what the essence of a book, the essence of a staircase, consist in. So the result is that we have indeed a certain acquaintance with the whatness (essence) of beings but not a genuine knowledge of it. In contrast to the latter we call the former the pre-acquaintance with beings in their respective whatness and suchness. This pre-acquaintance with the essence is part of that familiarity with beings which we grow up into and which we claim for ourselves unreflectively, without further ado.

Beings as the interrogated of the question of Being are in their essential constitution familiar to us in a certain way and are unproblematic. What then is the unfamiliar and problematic? Certainly unfamiliar to us are many regions of beings and the individuals belonging therein. Yet even within familiar regions, much is unfamiliar to us. (History . . . , nature . . .) Now, if we, in accord with the sense of the question of Being, direct our questioning to the unfamiliar in the familiar, in beings, we are not seeking out some previously uninvestigated regions of beings, the provinces of the sciences, and we are not at all asking what this or that being is, or whether this or that is a being; instead, we are asking: what are beings *as such,* just insofar as they are beings?[6] No matter of what kind or of what region, what makes beings beings at all? We answer: Being. But with this response we are not answering the question of Being; instead, we are giving the question for the first time what is problematic in it: beings are the familiar, their Being is the unfamiliar. Beings are the unproblematic, Being is the problematic. In the question, what are beings, we are directing our questioning to Being. We are bringing ourselves before what is problematic in the unproblematic. | 20

d) The familiarity with Being in saying "is"

Yet how so? How are we supposed to know "beings" and at the same time not know Being? "Beings": we can indicate them and bring them forward even if all we do is not confuse them with nonbeings, with nothingness. Yet we are protected from the danger of this confusion and mistake only if we have available some mark by which we distinguish beings from nonbeings. By what do we distinguish a being from what is not a being? By Being, for this indeed is lacking to nonbeings. Thus, as we indicate beings, bring beings forward, and indeed are familiar with beings at all, we know beings as such. We know what the word "Being" is saying. Being is known to us. Yet we did maintain that "Being" is that to which our questioning is directed in the question of Being. We said beings are the unproblematic and Being is the problematic.

---

6. In this preeminent and originary essence-question also correspondingly the *whether-question*!

Yet now we see that the problematic, Being, is also familiar to us; indeed it even *must* be familiar, for otherwise the unproblematic, beings, could not ever be unproblematic to us. Indeed, even more, Being must be familiar to us just so that it can become problematic, for how could Being be placed in question if we had no previous knowledge of it at all? In short: beings are familiar to us, *and so is Being.* And yet we have never up to now in all our lives taken the least notice of this, our familiarity with Being. Beings, indeed: they face us, besiege us, dispose us, captivate us. Beings, indeed: we are driven to them or we withdraw from them, we busy ourselves with them or we are engulfed by them. But Being and especially our familiarity with Being— that has previously never occurred to us, and indeed we might now even believe that here a mere verbal distinction is up to its old tricks: beings and Being—a *splitting of hairs* behind which there is nothing, and which in any case is of no concern to *us*!

How do matters stand with our familiarly with Being? We comport ourselves to Being when we experience some being in the way that it *is,* thus in explicitly saying "is." And how often does it not happen that we say "is" or one of its variants? How often during the day we say: "that is so and so"; how often we use the word "is"; how often we have already used it and will still use it! With the word "is," we indeed mean the Being of beings. We say, for example: "the door is closed." We see the door over there, we also see the "closed" or can sense it by touch. But the "is"—where in all the word resides the "is" that we mean when we say "the door is closed"?

Or can we dispense with the "is" as a linguistico-grammatical form to which we have long been accustomed but are not necessarily bound? For example: "Door—closed," as a child might say, or as an adult, a soldier, might say in a dispatch: "Order carried out." The "is" (or a variant) in both cases omitted. And nothing at all has changed. To be sure, nothing. Does that prove the "is" can be dispensed with? Quite the contrary, here is the strongest proof of its *in*dispensability, i.e., of the indispensability of that which we understand by it but which the objection (that the "is" is a mere verbal form) does not wish to admit. For even in saying "Door—closed," we mean precisely the door as a being that is closed, i.e., in its *being-closed.* The word "is" can be absent; but what the word "is" signifies will still be apparent and will even be expressed with more force precisely as the being-closed of the door— and will thereby not at all remain absent!—or as an order: "Door— closed!—the door should be closed.

Here even in the absence of the word, we understand Being and the "is"—indeed we must understand them. For what else is the "Door— closed" supposed to mean? The representation of a door along with the representation of closedness, even if these representations are contemporaneous, do not signify the being-closed of the door—quite apart from the fact that we cannot understand closedness, i.e., being-closed, without Being and cannot even represent it for itself without Being.

The example shows further that we understand the "is" and Being even when it is not expressed in its own word: e.g., "it keeps raining" [*es regnet*]. Here is the linguistic expression in the corresponding verbal form: rain is now occurring and is precisely present at hand. The "is" and "Being" therefore cannot count as mere word-sounds that signify nothing further; it is quite the reverse: "is" and "to be" can be used and spoken only because in them something is expressed. And this can be *ex*-pressed only because it is already present prior to the expression and independently of it. Whether and to what extent we "think" about it in an individual case is a question of lower rank. For we possess the dubious privilege of thoughtless speaking and writing. If the "is" had no meaning at all, then we could not even utter that word thoughtlessly. Thoughtlessness indeed consists only in making no use of the appurtenant meaning and of its understanding.

Still more: we understand the "is" and Being even when we do not speak at all and experience some being only in silence, perhaps perceiving some occurrence without speaking out loud and only saying to ourselves: "unprecedented"—namely, the occurrence *is* such. In fact, that word "unprecedented" does not even need to sound within us. Would we now still want to deny our familiarity with Being and throw suspicion on the "is" as a mere manner of speech and make it inconsequential as a mere grammatical form? Or will we consent at least to take seriously this casual and much-used "is" (naturally including all its variants)?

e) The familiar diversification of Being into thatness, whatness, suchness, and trueness

We say "The earth is," and we mean this actual thing in its actuality; we mean exactly that in fact the earth is—*thatness*. We say "The earth is a planet," and we mean what the earth is as earth—*whatness*. We say "The earth is round," and we mean that what is here as earth has this quality, is such and such—*suchness*. We say "The earth is a planet," and we mean that it is so (it is true) that the earth revolves around the sun with a definite periodicity, it is true—*trueness*. | 21

In all four cases, we use the same casual word "is" and mean Being; yet we understand in each case something different: thatness, whatness, suchness, trueness.

Moreover, we understand this distributive Being without making any further provisions; it simply leaps to us in this way in the "is." Clearly, therefore, we are not merely familiar with Being on the surface and in general; we know Being in its diversification.

And how surely we know Being! Much more surely than we know beings. We say "The door is closed." It is beyond delusion! But it can indeed be subject to doubt; the door might only be ajar. Whether this being in each case is such and such can be doubted, but what we understand by the "is"—Being and suchness in general—does not at all become doubtful. Indeed it even must stand beyond doubt just so that we can doubt whether the door is closed or ajar! We can be deluded about whether here or there something is present at hand, but presence at hand as such is beyond delusion.

Even further: I understand the "is" and Being not only by myself, the way I might indeed alone actually know some particular being while other people do not and thus I need to forge an agreement with them. Concerning "is" and "to be," we find ourselves always already in agreement, in harmony. One person maintains the door is closed, another the door is not closed. But with regard to the meaning of "is" and "is not," no conflict occurs.

In this way, our familiarity with the "is" and with Being becomes visibly more insistent. And yet we can elude it by considering that we "represent" nothing corresponding to this "is" and "Being." "Door," "closed," "earth," "planet," "round," "good"—but "is"? We do not understand what "is" properly means; granted, but we cannot thereby retract everything indicated previously, namely, that we understand the "is" and Being, whether explicitly expressed or not, in the diversification of their meaning, without doubt or delusion, in agreement with others—and yet we do not understand what Being properly means. Admittedly, we do not understand what it properly means, we do not understand it in its essence, and hence we have no *concept* of it. But much is familiar to us of which we have no concept and in relation to which we have still not advanced to the concept. That applies precisely to the type and mode of our familiarity with Being: we understand it and yet have no concept of it. We understand it prior to any concept.

This also is part of our familiarity with Being, namely, that we do not at all take heed of our familiarity. It remains inconsequential to us; indeed still more: it is not even inconsequential to us, for that would require our having once paid attention to it so as to thrust it aside immediately and for ever. Not simply inconsequential, but altogether *forgotten;* Being is not there at all—only beings are.

How then is Being ever to become problematic to us, if it is beyond all doubt and yet, as this, is also altogether forgotten?

f) The fact of the understanding of Being (Summary)

It *is the most unproblematic*! With regard to the "is" and "Being," matters are therefore peculiarly arranged. Since there occur in the world so many inconsequential things to which we direct our gaze, we should cease doing so for a moment in order to establish somewhat more securely the fact we have just come from pursuing. The issue is the familiarity with "Being." We elucidated this familiarity in terms of the understanding of the "is" and in accord with all the variants of this "auxiliary verb." Such understanding applies not to the word and the word-meaning but to the Being signified in the word-meaning. We will call this fact *the understanding of Being.* We are speaking here of a *fact* simply with respect to what we have now initially exhibited about that which is to be called such. In what way and in what sense this fact exists, whether in general this term offers a more than provisional characterization of the understanding of Being—all this now remains open. We will here attempt to see merely the already exhibited moments together in their unity and as ordered in a certain way.

1. The understanding of Being extends over the entire breadth of beings as a whole in the intricate and scattered multiplicity of their individual domains and strata—nature, history, work of art, number, space, the divine, and so on.

2. Being and the "is" articulate themselves, as if on their own, over these individual domains and regions into whatness, thatness, such-and-suchness, and trueness, without this articulation coming expressly into relief.

3. The understanding of Being can indeed be enunciated in the "is" but cannot be bound to this linguistic expression and instead manifests itself in all speech and all forms of speech; it even prevails in the silent experience of beings.

4. The understanding of Being is free of delusion and is untouched by doubt.

5. An agreement among all people prevails over the way Being is understood in the understanding of Being.

6. That with which we are familiar in the understanding of Being is indeed understood with certainty but is not conceptualized. The understanding of Being is preconceptual.

7. That which is understood in the understanding of Being is as such inconsequential to us; it is unheeded.

8. Not only unheeded, but simply forgotten. Yet, despite its constant use, it is never used up.

9. Being, as familiar in this way, as well as the understanding of Being are in every respect unquestioned—the unproblematic pure and simple.

This characterization of the understanding of Being is neither exhaustive nor even undertaken from the most originary and most proper point of view. But it tells us enough with respect to that which we are now trying to accomplish. |

22

g) The question-worthiness of that which is most unproblematic

We want to ask—actually ask—the question of Being and not merely recite the interrogative sentence "What are beings?" For that, as was shown, the question as such must be posed. This posing occurs in the elaboration of the question by way of asking the "pre-questions." These seek to delimit what is *interrogated* and what is *asked after*. Beings are interrogated; Being is asked after. Beings are the unproblematic and Being is the problematic. But is Being the problematic? The characterization of the understanding of Being shows us that Being is altogether the most unproblematic. If so, then it stands the farthest outside of every question. As such, it is obviously the most seldom questioned and the most difficult to place in question. And now we also note why the recital (according to its sense, a mere parroting) of the question "What are beings?" for us contains nothing at all of a questioning. It is because everything questionable is so completely missing here. At the same time, we see: the questionable is not missing inasmuch as Being is not there at all; on the contrary, Being is too fully there and too near, as what is most unproblematic.

Thus the task is to make *questionable* for the first time this that is most unproblematic. But how is such a change to happen? In the way, e.g., that we close the open door and change its state by bringing the door to? Should we in some way change unproblematic Being so that it becomes questionable, or should we on the contrary leave it just as we possess it in the understanding of Being and then look to see how and to what extent there is in it something to be disclosed by questioning? Can what is questionable be established so simply? No. In what we do not at all deem worthy of questioning we will never find anything questionable. Only that can become questionable to us which we *in advance deem worthy of questioning*—worthy to be interrogated and asked after. Only where in general something is worthy of questioning is there a possible field for the problematic and unproblematic.

Accordingly, as long as Being does not at all become question-*worthy*, we cannot exhibit anything problematic about it and so cannot direct questioning toward it, pose a question concerning it.

Yet how could Being become question-worthy to us as long as we do not know it well enough to decide whether it possesses or deserves such dignity? But we do know Being. It is only too familiar. This all-too-close familiarity is invoked when asserting that in regard to "Being" and the "is" we do think, and can think, nothing more. Perhaps, however, such assertion and belief amount to sheer thoughtlessness, one that would be no better and surer if it concluded: because we generally think nothing more in regard to "Being" and the "is," *there-*

fore these are also "nothing more" than mere words and grammatical forms making fools of us. As if something were actually decided by deporting "Being" and the "is" to the realm of "mere" linguistic usage; as if we actually did know what a word is, what language is, what linguistic usage is. How little do we know of the essence of language?—As little as we know of the essence of Being.

Yet is it actually settled that we think nothing more in regard to the word "Being"? We must pursue all this the whole way and attempt to bring ourselves closer to what we mean by understanding Being. *Perhaps* we will then come across something that *could* become *worthy* of questioning and that consequently *would* have to be made problematic in some respect and so *should* demonstrate the necessity of the question of Being.

Ever since the first session of this course, we have been speaking of the Being of beings—Being, although not a mere word-sound, still a very indeterminate signification. And this latter seems empty, the emptiest and least graspable, and yet again is what "determines" every single being and beings as a whole and as such.

We are gradually becoming unsure and impatient as to whether we will ever find ourselves on a secure path in this domain and come closer to what Being signifies.

§12. Review of the linguistic usage

a) Becoming, the "ought," thinking, semblance

This irksome question can be dispatched, however, simply by our establishing the word-meaning on the basis of the history and root of the word. We could then invoke what has been established.[7] But this procedure is as dangerous as it is simple, for it could be that the root meaning died out long ago, such that what we perhaps now believe we have established about it was actually never in use. Above all, however, we are trying to learn not merely the meaning of a word but, rather, what is signified in the meaning and is given us to understand.

On the other hand, we cannot make do without a glance at language and linguistic expression, especially since we are not taking language itself as something incidental, a mere tool for expressing and communicating already constituted thoughts. Indeed, we are now following a linguistic idiom, one in which we have been moving since long ago. Specifically, we are following it not as regards its etymology but, instead, as regards its conventional meaning-content, i.e., as re-

---

7. Cf. manuscript: Being. {Presumably in *Zum Ereignis-Denken*, GA73.}

gards that in which our understanding of Being is immediately ex-
pressed. |

We recall once again that we use "Being" for "beings as a whole."
Being—the broadest, whose limits, bounds, restrictions are found only
in nothingness, assuming we may at all say something like that of
nothingness.

Now, however, a review of the most conventional linguistic usage
shows something quite different. We distinguish Being from *becoming;*
we contrast Being with what *ought* to be; we oppose Being to *thinking*
in the broad sense; we differentiate Being from *semblance.*

We easily gather from this: 1) Such oppositions obviously *delimit* the
meaning of Being. 2) This delimitation occurs in *various* respects. 3)
On the basis of these variously directed delimitations, "Being" receives
its many-sided *determinateness.* 4) Insofar as we move unexplicitly in
this linguistic idiom, our acquaintance with the multifariously determinate meaning of "Being" must precisely be one of a *peculiar* un-
mistakability and certainty. 5) This delimited and determinate meaning of Being runs side by side with the broadest and indeterminate
meaning.

We will initially attempt to come somewhat closer to these ways of
setting Being in relief over and against becoming, the "ought," thinking, and semblance. We will be guided by the intention of establishing
what those delimitations yield for the more determinate delimitation
of "Being."

Being and becoming.[8] This distinction is common and is so not only
within the philosophical idiom. The distinction plainly means: what
becomes is not yet; what is does not first need to become. What is, a
being, has left becoming behind and in the future will resist the pres-
sure of becoming.[9] In becoming, on the contrary, we find in each case
the likes of *change,* transition from-to, unrest. Insofar as Being is opposed to becoming, Being has the sense of abiding, *persevering.* Beings are perseverant, finished, definitively resting; what becomes is
the restless, fluid.

Being and the "ought." In this particular formulation, the distinction
is usual since Kant and Fichte; as regards the matter itself, much older.
What we ought to bring about is understood by us as a demand, claim,
task, duty. We ought to accomplish or retain that which ought to be,
that which presents itself as such in the "ought." The "ought" is there-

---

8. See below, p. 41. Parmenides.

9. Cf. the new treatment, s.s. 1935, 38ff. {Martin Heidegger, *Einführung in die
Metaphysik,* GA40, 103ff.}

fore properly understood as *what ought to be as such*. In this sense, it is opposed to beings and to their Being. What ought to be, what is still outstanding or impending, is not yet. Beings thereby count as that of which it cannot be said that they first ought to be, since they are already carried out, settled, and retained: the accomplished, settled, and as such available. Or beings are distinguished from what ought to be in the sense that beings mean that of which it cannot at all be said that they ought to be accomplished since they cannot become the task of an accomplishing and producing but instead of themselves, without any assistance, make themselves and offer themselves and thus always already stand in availability (in presence at hand).

Being and thinking. For this distinction, "thinking" is taken in a *very broad* sense as representing or even having consciousness or experiencing, so that the opposition could also be expressed in the formula: *Being and consciousness,* Being and lived experience (life). If the basic character of consciousness is taken to be the Ego, the subject, then Being and thinking means *object and subject.* Even if these three formulas do not simply coincide, we nevertheless see at once the meaning now assumed by the word "Being." Meant are beings in the sense of what stands over and against, ob-ject, what is in itself present at hand and as such able to be thought, represented, grasped in consciousness. Being—presence at hand in distinction to what is present only in thought, in consciousness, in lived experience. (Being and life).

Being and semblance. Semblance is what only looks like a being but is not a being. I.e., Being now means the same as *actuality,* genuineness, truth. Beings—the actual, genuine, true over and against the merely feigned, the play-acted as phantasized illusion. The actual, graspable, present at hand, what stands firm and does not scatter into the capriciously fabricated.

b) The question of Being as provisional and narrow

If we now gather together the four oppositions in which "Being" stands, then it is indeed difficult initially to ascertain a unitary relation among becoming, the "ought," thinking, and semblance—almost capricious. But all the more clear and graspable is the meaning of Being, a meaning that comes to light in each of the oppositions. Being means: perseverance, abiding, rest, standing in availability, presence at hand, palpability, and actuality. Indeed, these are sundry rubrics which do not simply mean the same, and yet these meanings reside unitarily together in one true content which for the moment we will not pursue.

Let us merely say provisionally that this content has to do with presence—though not as something formally universal (or as still emptier dross!) but as gathering! In line with this meaning of Being, we understand beings as the persistent, constant, available, at hand, actual. Accordingly, we understand by Being something quite *determinate*. The determinateness of the understanding of Being gives us the immediate certainty and commonness of the above-mentioned delineations.

What have we gained? Being—beings—indeed not mere word-sounds in which an indeterminate meaning resounds. Instead, the question of Being—assuming we are indeed questioning—has a quite definite directionality. Being—and *not* this or that. Certainly! Yet we thereby concede something running counter to all we said before. We surely said the question of Being is the deepest and broadest. Being is so encompassing that it finds its limits only in nothingness. Yet now we see that becoming, the "ought," thinking, and semblance fall outside of Being. The realm of becoming includes nature with its processes and developments as well as history and its events and formations; the "ought" includes all human moral action and indeed all activity related to claims and tasks; thinking (consciousness, lived experience) encompasses the entire domain of the subject and subjectivity; semblance is everything opposed to truth. |

24   In this way, very broad and most essential realms fall outside the field of beings and Being. It can hardly be imagined what then could remain left over as the domain of beings. The question of Being may still be justified, but it is on no account the *broadest, deepest,* and most decisive question. And if indeed the question of Being is supposed to constitute the beginning of philosophy, then it is obvious that in the beginning only a determinately delimited realm of what can be interrogated came into question and that the long subsequent history of philosophy was required in order to conquer the other realms, beyond the question of Being, and thereby to grasp this question in its provisional character and necessary narrowness. And so it might be fully justified that the question of Being altogether disappeared from the ruling center of philosophical questioning. The same holds for the usual concept of ontology and the ontological. On this basis, it is clear that the orientation toward the basic question of ancient philosophy presents an arbitrary and dogmatic contraction. Being—versus and without consciousness (Descartes—Kant?). Consequently, intrinsic resistance today—the question of Being is not understood. Likewise, our attempt to endow the question of Being with such a high rank turns out to be arbitrary partiality. It could hold only as long as we took the word "Being" and the meaning of Being in a universality that now precisely proves to be the mere universality of the indeterminate.

The same instant we gained clarity about the determinateness of the meaning of Being, the question of Being also lost every claim to its alleged position.

Furthermore, if we note that the cited multifarious delimitation of Being over and against becoming, the "ought," thinking, and semblance is not something of today but can even be encountered, as we must show, already at the beginning of Western philosophy, then we will completely abandon representing, and a fortiori insisting on, the question of Being as the first and last, deepest and broadest. And so in the end they are correct, namely the ones (amounting to the entire previous tradition of the history of philosophy) who maintain that Western philosophy begins with the philosophy of nature, i.e., with the questioning of nature as a determinate region of what can be interrogated, a region which precisely at the beginning coincides with beings.

c) Being in becoming, in the "ought," in thinking, and in semblance

There can be no disputing that the word "Being" and the meaning of Being were used in the delineations above. Does it follow, however, that we must carry out the elaboration of the question of Being in the direction of this delimited meaning? What dictates and decides here? Mere linguistic usage or the matter at issue? I think: only the matter itself. To the delimited meaning of Being and to the usage of that meaning, we must at once reply: every something that is not nothing has some sort of Being. This usage of "Being" is just as common and justified, and indeed perhaps as necessary, as the delimited usage is a fact. What then results with regard to everything from which Being was delimited in the cited delimitations, i.e., with regard to becoming, the "ought," thinking, and semblance?

Is becoming really nothing? If something becomes, then not only does this something which enters into becoming have a Being, but this becoming itself *happens.* This happening has a Being, only precisely not Being in the sense of abiding and persevering! How much of that which, in the broadest sense, we call beings does abide and persevere? Is not, generally speaking, most everything involved in change and alteration? Will we therefore maintain it has no Being, "is" nothing?

Is the "ought" and what ought to be really nothing, or are they something? What ought to be has "oughtness," the "ought-Being" of what ought to be. Does not "ought" precisely mean "ought to be," and is not that in each case an ought-Being? This latter is certainly not Being in the sense of the presence at hand of a thing. Yet is not "ought to be" just as much a mode of Being as "must be," i.e., necessity, and "can be," i.e., possibility? Why should only necessity, possibility, and actuality make up the so-called modalities of Being?

Is thinking, representation, lived experience really nothing (*esse* is not *percipi*)? That we could so readily oppose thinking to Being—do we not betray ourselves when we say: Being and *consciousness*? Is not the presentation, thought, or consciousness of something precisely also a mode of Being, specifically the Being of the so-called subject, Ego, self? Or are we unjustified in saying "I am," "we are"? Why should we call only the possible *object* of thinking and representing a being, as if thinking itself were nothing?

Is semblance, which we oppose to Being and beings, really nothing? Should we deny Being to illusion, lying, falsehood, and error, or must we not daily admit that these are and are exercising power over us? Or, in other terms, if physics and astronomy teach us that the setting of what we call the sun and see as the sun is an illusion, should we admit it without further ado? In any case, it is still not nothing; who then says the astronomical and astrophysical sun is the actual, extant sun? On what table of laws is that inscribed? Ultimately, is not the astrophysical sun also merely an image, a semblance, although a less essential semblance than the sun and sunset of the poet or painter?

d) The question of Being as definitively lacking question-worthiness

We see that the situation regarding the delimited meaning of the word "Being" is peculiar. This meaning certainly displays determinateness. But is it not equally narrow? Why then should only that which abides, perseveres, and is on hand be a being and have Being, while everything differentiated from this does not? Especially since we have resolved not to say that becoming, the "ought," thinking, and semblance deserve to be addressed as nothingness!

(Behind this, the question: why must the beginning grasp Being as presence, why was the beginning intercepted! and thereby only the λόγος of οὐσία came to sovereignty?)

Yet we see even this nothingness not as nothing but, rather, as being in some way. At the same time, however, we oppose it to Being. What is happening here? Difficult to say, but we do see this: our understanding of Being is most remarkable. How we spontaneously understand Being in such a way that it is limited only by nothingness while at the same time we employ the word with a multifarious narrowness which lends to Being a certain usual determinateness. Is that accidental, a mere whim of linguistic usage not open to further investigation?

Is this *merely* remarkable? Only worthy to be noted once? Or is there more afoot? Being, in the just-characterized discrepant way we understand and regard it and in the way we understand it both as of the greatest possible breadth and simultaneously as of a quite determinate narrowness—is this Being not worthy to be made into a question? Are not Being and the understanding of Being *question-worthy?*[10] | 25

It will be said: questioning can certainly be directed to the multifariously characterized understanding of Being and to Being as understood therein, just as to everything that strikes us as remarkable and attracts our attention. In that regard, the situation now under discussion is nothing special versus any other remarkable thing we might easily encounter, perhaps within the sciences. The only difference is that our case is totally pointless and its investigation without any apparent practical aim or application, at most the occupation of an extravagant and abstract rumination. But all of this merely serves to reduce its "question-worthiness" even more.

Accordingly, despite all the summoned-up characterizations of Being and of the understanding of Being, we find nothing here of a question-worthiness that would justify attributing to the question of Being the unconditional priority of which we once spoke.

§13. The basic question of existence

a) Unrest as the experience of questioning

We cannot promulgate by decree that Being is the most question-worthy for all questioning. That would be not only alienating and arbitrary but also, and above all, useless. For if questioning is actually to be carried out, its essence does not allow it to be compelled or argumentatively induced. Questioning is a comportment whereby, in each case, even if in various ways and to various degrees, we rely *on ourselves* and abide *within ourselves* and *therefore* oppose ourselves to the indeterminate, open, ungrounded, and undecided (cf. above, p. 17). This holds also of the questioning which is "merely" a co-questioning with others. Co-questioning does indeed not allow the question to arise properly for the first time. Yet it does have the character of self-determination, insofar as it merges into and vibrates sympathetically within an already oscillating question. Such a merger is possible only if the person merging contributes, from his own resources, the vibration thanks to which he participates in the movement of the questioning.

---

10. The flight in the face of Beyng into *graspable* beings! Cf. Nietzsche!

This vibration must arise out of the *unrest* into which the question-worthy as such is displaced.

If it is supposed to be for us a matter of co-asking the question of Being, then we ourselves—each on his own—must merge into this questioning on the basis of an experience of the question-worthiness of Being and of the understanding of Being.

Yet how is Being to become question-worthy for us and not something merely remarkable? That could transpire of course only if we have thoroughly conceptualized Being in its essence; but that means we must have already fathomed its meaning. Here is the "circle"! We move now, however, precisely in a *preconceptual* understanding of Being. As long as Being is not sufficiently conceptualized, it is also not appraised with certainty and penetration as worthy or unworthy or neutral. And on the other hand, we conceptualize Being only if we go beyond and through the preconceptual understanding of Being and transform this understanding into a conceptualization. Again the circle! Or can Being become question-worthy to us even before we have conceptualized it? *Within* the preconceptual understanding of Being? Yes; if this understanding as such becomes question-worthy in advance. Assuming, however, that the preconceptual understanding of Being already manifests itself to us as something question-worthy, indeed even as the most question-worthy, must then Being not become a fortiori and in advance the most question-worthy? For the understanding of Being is indeed such, and takes on such and such a character, only for the sake of Being.

Therefore we can experience the question-worthiness of Being already within the sphere of the preconceptual understanding of Being, i.e., precisely where we now constantly abide, provided the understanding of Being becomes for us what is most question-worthy. But the understanding of Being is indeed what is most unproblematic. How are question-worthiness and worthiness in general to be *experienced*? It is now supposed to become the most question-worthy. And indeed not by decree.

b) The origin of existence in the esteeming of Being

Who then imparts to this that is most unproblematic the highest worthiness to be interrogated? That is the basic question of the origin of existence. Initially: whence the understanding of Being receives this highest question-worthiness need not at first trouble us; it is enough that it has this question-worthiness at all. But how are we to establish a question-worthiness in that which is unproblematic? In general, can a worthiness or a dignity, no matter of what sort or degree, simply be found lying there, the way we establish the properties of any arbitrary thing? Can we detect "worthiness" in just any thing, any person, or any "creature" whatsoever? Certainly; provided only that we see in the right way, i.e., *inhabit* the required way of "seeing" in the sense of experiencing.

We experience something like worthiness only if our comportment as such is a seeing in advance which is attuned toward and as an *esteeming*. Where we do not at all esteem, we remain blind to worthiness—and also to unworthiness. If our comportment is not an esteeming, do we then experience only the neutral? No; not even that and, strictly taken, never that, for just in order for something to be neutral to us it must be of concern to us. Even the neutral as such is not nothing but, instead, is precisely the flowing lack of distinction and of decision situated between worthiness and unworthiness; it is not totally outside of them. Non-esteeming comportment therefore does not mean degrading, denying worthiness, subtracting it, or even entirely taking it away. Likewise, esteeming does not consist in attributing worthiness but, rather, is *prior* to that as an originary *allowing of worthiness to light up before us*. This requires the esteeming comportment itself to assume the correct basic attitude, one appropriate to the thing whose worthiness is supposed to show itself explicitly and properly to this comportment. Esteeming is not valuing! Worthiness can subsequently be externalized into a value by way of calculation!

c) The insistence on beings as a whole

What is now our basic position with regard to the understanding of Being, an understanding whose question-worthiness is currently at issue? We saw that this understanding is inconsequential to us, indeed even totally forgotten. The understanding of Being and Being as understood therein do not at all worry us. We are constantly and only concerned with beings: we find our way about amid beings, we master beings, we comply with beings, we take care of them, and beings bear us, quicken us, excite us, without, on the other hand, overpowering and oppressing us; we co-fashion beings and give way to them. All our comportment relates always to beings alone; even further, our comportment has in advance entirely entrusted itself to beings. More precisely: first and foremost our comportment is such that it persists in devotion to fundamentally accessible beings, indeed even to the point of entirely losing itself in these ordinary things. | This character of human comportment, namely, its not only always relating in general to something, to beings, but first and foremost persisting in—insisting on—beings, will be termed by us *insistence*. And "comportment" will

26

always mean human comportment. Animals, stones, gods do not comport themselves; their way to be does not count for us as comportment in the sense we—admittedly with some arbitrariness—use this word.

Insistence includes a peculiar lack of worry over the understanding of Being and the Being understood therein. But this rigidity of the insistence of comportment can be slackened. Indeed, we have already carried out such a slackening, namely, insofar as we have managed to break the usual devotion to beings in their hegemony. Initially, only such that we have *in general* learned to see there is such a thing as the understanding of Being and the Being understood therein. What is is not exhausted by beings, to which we usually adhere to the exclusion of all else. Beyond and before beings, Being is given, and it is given to us precisely in the understanding of Being.

d) The slackening of insistence

Our previous characterization of the understanding of Being and of Being as understood therein was therefore nothing other than a slackening of the insistence of our comportment. Comportment is always a relation to beings. This slackening of insistence does not at all have a deleterious effect on the relation to beings, in the sense that the relation would become uncertain, wavering, discontinued, or even interrupted. Our relation to the door and to its closedness or openness remains the same afterward as before. The relation to beings is not slackened; instead, the relation in itself is loosened up inasmuch as now something steps forth within this comportment which is also over and above it. Within our comportment to beings there also always occurs the understanding of Being, precisely in the manner portrayed earlier. We speak therefore of a fact whose exhibition manifests the content of the relation as *richer* compared to what we are accustomed to knowing and heeding about it. (Once again, brief concrete reference to the understanding of Being; what—how it "is" and the like.)

This slackening is the first step toward an esteeming of Being and of the understanding of Being. We now for the first time, over and against beings, let Being and the understanding of Being come into words. This esteeming is admittedly a very minor one—we grant that Being and the understanding of Being are precisely also there. But we do not see any special rank that would deserve and require a special esteeming. The rank decides about the magnitude of the dignity that may be claimed. For its part, the rank in turn is measured according to the standard of what is sovereign and its sovereignty. We will therefore esteem Being and the understanding of Being more highly if we have to concede to them a rank over and beyond the mere fact that they also occur, even if this is not the highest rank. And we must do so if we encounter and see Being and the understanding of Being in the highest sovereignty. But we see nothing of that, nor of a special rank and special dignity. Yet our not seeing this is also no proof that sovereignty, rank, and dignity are not there. So let us attempt an investigation into this, indeed even the most pointed investigation that could be carried out in regard to an alleged rank and dignity.

e) The complete dis-esteeming of Being

We will look to see whether the understanding of Being can bear a complete *dis-esteeming;* i.e., we will attempt to deprive it of any special dignity. But then must we not first explicitly carry out this dis-esteeming? Does that not happen constantly in our *forgetting* Being and the understanding of Being? To be sure. Yet we esteem even when we forget, indeed, we often precisely then and in that way concede that what has been forgotten *is* such and such. By means of the forgetting, we precisely want—whether we know it or not—to get out of the way of the forgotten, have nothing more to do with it. Even forgetting cannot deprive Being and the understanding of Being of all dignity. It is still there. Accordingly, this dignity as such must count for us, no matter what happens.

We can attempt a complete dis-esteeming only if we purely and simply take away all sovereignty. That will happen most effectively if we assume that something like Being and the understanding of Being plays no role whatsoever in our comportment. What would then result? We would then have to arrange our comportment so that we could make do without Being and the understanding of Being. Here lies the root of the peculiar questioning of the "conditions of the possibility of something" as a stage and formula of the *essence*-question! Cf. s.s. 35 [summer semester 1935], p. 34f.[11]

Let us try it. Assume, therefore, we do not understand what "Being" or "is" means; assume we do not understand whatness in distinction to thatness and do not understand suchness and trueness; assume we do not understand Being in its particular meaning in distinction to becoming, the "ought," thinking, and semblance; assume we do not understand those linguistic expressions and, even more and above all, what they mean—what then? Then we could not at all encounter any being; beings as such could not beset us or make us happy, could not engage us, sustain us, or occupy us in any way. We could not at

---

11. {Cf. Heidegger, *Einführung in die Metaphysik,* op. cit., 80ff.}

all comport ourselves to beings, not even to ourselves as beings; we could not conduct ourselves as beings in the midst of beings. We could never wish that some being should rather not be than be, for even that requires at least some understanding of what it means to be and not to be! We could never ask whether beings are and what they are; for that, we must have already understood Being. We could never be able to experience the void of nothingness unless we understood Being.

§14. Commentary on our concept of existence

a) The impossibility of a complete dis-esteeming of Being; the understanding of Being as the possibility of our existence

The instant we actually try to take their sovereignty completely away from Being and the understanding of Being, what comes to light for us *in the most striking way* is the unconditional sovereignty of the understanding of Being *prior* to all comportment, *in* all comportment, and *on behalf of* all comportment. For what is irresistibly clear is that the understanding of Being first makes it possible for any comportment toward beings to be a comportment at all. How an *irresistible* clarity? An overcoming and an invasion—an overwhelming. The understanding of Being is not such a fact that we could, on occasion, when we please, establish and recognize. If the understanding of Being did not occur, if it did not have sovereignty and priority in all comportment, then we humans could not at all exist. Our existence would be radically impossible. *The understanding of Being is the ground of the possibility of our existence.* But what is the meaning of "existence" and "to exist"? It needs to be made more precise! Especially since the term "existence" is used in various senses and has now come into vogue.

b) On the meaning of "existing" and "existence" as delimited in relation to Kierkegaard and Jaspers

"Existing" and "existence" come from *existentia,* a word long used in opposition to *essentia.* We already know what these terms mean. *Essentia* is whatness, that Being of a being intended in asking about its essence, its whatness. *Existentia* is that Being of a being intended in asking whether a being of some determinate essence is or is not: thatness, presence at hand in the widest sense. According to this hackneyed meaning, *existentia* simply means the actuality of some actual thing of whatever sort. Even Kant still uses the word "existence" [*Existenz*] in this sense, since for him it is completely equivalent to "actuality" [*Wirklichkeit*] and "thereness" [*Dasein*]; there-ness, i.e., found here or there, present at hand.

Existence of the sea lion, of the earth, of the sun, of the rose, of humans, existence of God. It is to be noted here that the tradition, medieval scholasticism and modern philosophy (e.g., Leibniz), does not hold that a lion would exist in the same sense as God. *Existentia* not *univoce*, but *analogice*. Being grasped as the most universal determination of beings, but this not the universality of the highest genus. Aristotle already saw that. To be sure, even today we have not gone beyond this; i.e., it has not properly been grasped as an Aristotelian problem.

We will not use the expression in this broad sense for the thatness of any being whatever, but also not in the narrow sense, deriving from Kierkegaard, which Jaspers above all has recently taken up as a philosophical term. Jaspers says: "Existence is what comports itself to itself and thereby to its transcendence."[12] We will comment on this statement only to the extent of noting that here existence actually means not *a mode of Being* (namely, existing) but *a being:* existence is, i.e., *an existing being* is, what comports itself to itself and thereby to its transcendence. Thus Jaspers, as is still usual everywhere in philosophy today, employs the term "Being" at the same time for "beings"; and in the above statement, as ever in Jaspers, "transcendence" is the transcendent being, and the latter is the absolute—God. To be sure, this is not simply a matter of terminological precision; it is the place where everything is decided. Confusion in the most elementary concepts! | 27

At the center of Jaspers's philosophizing stands only existence, the existing being, i.e., the human being comporting himself to himself and thereby to the ground of the world. Accordingly, the designation of this philosophy, which Jaspers himself uses, "philosophy of existence," is entirely apt. But it is rash and absurd to name—i.e., apprehend—my works in this way. Not to mention the fact that I do not at all use "existence" in the sense of Kierkegaard and Jaspers; i.e., as regards the matter at issue, I determine the human essence differently.

Expressed in passing: 1) I hold no brief for my philosophy, precisely because I do not have a philosophy of my own; indeed, I have no philosophy at all. My efforts are aimed only at conquering and preparing the way so that those who will come in the future might perhaps again be able to begin with the correct beginning of philosophy.

2) According to the sound of the words, Jaspers and I have precisely the same central terms: Dasein, existence, transcendence, world. Jaspers uses all these in a totally different sense and in a completely different range of problems, despite the commonality in our attitude.

---

12. {Karl Jaspers, *Philosophie I. Philosophische Weltorientierung.* Berlin: Springer, 1932, 15.}

The confusion enormous and helpless. But terminology cannot be prescribed; on the contrary, if genuine it is determined based on the matters at issue themselves and on the mode of their interrogation and interpretation.

Existence is thereby always *possible* existence, i.e., never *actual*, as long as "actual" is understood only in the traditional way as "present at hand." Possible existence misleading! To come to existence by philosophizing—the essence of philosophy consists in that. For us, what counts is the question of Being—"existence" only a mode of Being, and this only on the basis of Being and the understanding of Being.

Only this in common with Kierkegaard's use of the concept of existence: we relate it exclusively to humans. That gives the meaning of existence a determinate narrowness in contrast to the traditional use of the word. At the same time, however, despite the indication of the specific direction of meaning, very little is said thereby, considering how ambiguous and question-worthy the human essence is. Existence signifies the mode of Being of humans. But not of humans in general and as such. Not all humans who are actual, were actual, or will be actual do "exist," have existed, or will exist—*in the sense* we understand existence. We use this word specifically with the signification that comes to the fore in the root meaning: *ex-sistere*—no matter whether it was used earlier in this sense, which is in fact not the case. *Ex-sistere* means: step out, pose oneself out of oneself to. This *ex-sistere* is employed to grasp linguistically the mode of Being of that humanity in whose history we ourselves stand and are. What this means should be clear at once.

c) The comportment toward beings

Existence is the mode of Being of the human beings we ourselves are. I call the characters of this mode of Being "existentials," and the questioning, investigating, and analyzing of humans with respect to their Being, as well the analysis and articulation of this Being, "existential analysis" ("analytics"). So it is in *Being and Time I*.[13] Nevertheless, in that treatise, the concept of existence is not employed with the necessary univocity and determinateness, and it falls short of the clarity of the guiding problem. A great defect. Soon after the appearance of the treatise, I attained the only version of the concept of existence that is appropriate to the guiding problem, and I have since been expounding this concept in my lecture courses and seminars.

---

13. {First edition: Martin Heidegger, *Sein und Zeit. Erste Hälfte*. Halle: Niemeyer, 1927. Now: Martin Heidegger, *Sein und Zeit*, GA2.}

Existence—the Being of the beings we ourselves are. And what is now the basic character of this Being? With respect to what can this mode of Being be seen most readily and most purely?

I am attempting to show this first of all by critically setting our concept of existence in relief against the one used by Jaspers. He says: "Existence is that which comports itself *to itself and thereby to its transcendence*" {Heidegger's italics}. If we take this determination more rigorously, so that it provides a characterization of Being, then it is trying to say: existence qua existing means primarily comportment to oneself and thereby to the absolute (the ground of the world). I ask: what does comportment mean here? Can one leave it undetermined in such a central determination of the central concept? Kierkegaard leaves it undetermined, and likewise Jaspers. Self-comportment! What does it mean? Self-comportment is always some sort of self-comportment to something; formally, it is to stand in relation to something, specifically such that that to which the comportment stands is encountered *as a being*. But what is encountered need not be an object! It is not even said that the encountered as object would be an unconditionally preeminent character of encountering. Accordingly, our manipulative dealing with things, e.g., our production or use of vehicles or footwear, constitutes the whatness of existing. Jaspers would not count such comportment existence, which includes for him only comportment to oneself as comportment of the acting self, i.e., in a broad sense, the *moral self* (the *existentiell* self). Not even psychology and a psychological consideration, which perhaps investigates one's own bodily states and the like, and thus not just any comportment to oneself, is what Jaspers means by existing.

For us, what characterizes existence is not the self-comportment, neither taking the self as a person nor otherwise as one's own body and one's own soul; instead, it is the comportment as such, i.e., the standing in relation to beings, whereby beings as such manifest themselves in one way or another. Existence is self-comportment in this determinate sense. Accordingly, we cannot say that an animal comports itself, although it does stand in relation, e.g., to the stone, and is locked in relations. Yet every comportment is indeed a *self*-comportment. That means such standing in relation to beings always sees itself as referred to beings. This does not at all require, however, express consciousness of the self such that the self becomes the explicit goal and object of another comportment. We spoke already of the fact that our comportment to beings and also to ourselves happens firstly and mostly such that we abandon ourselves in the beings we comport ourselves to, losing ourselves in them, so to speak, and adhering obstinately to the respective beings, insisting on them. Our existence is first and foremost insistent. That says: insistence is a mode—indeed, an essentially necessary mode—of existence.

d) Restraint

What then does existence mean? The determination of its essence cannot be exhausted by saying it is comportment in the aforesaid sense. Or can it? Only if we forget precisely the fact polarizing our entire consideration: the understanding of Being. If comportment is a standing in relation to beings, then the investigation we have undertaken shows exactly that comportment as such can be what it is only *on the basis of the appurtenant understanding of Being* and its priority. We now understand the pronouncement better: if the understanding of Being did not occur, if it did not have sovereignty and priority in all comportment, then we could not at all exist, could not direct ourselves to beings, neither to the beings we ourselves are not nor to the beings we ourselves are. In short, the understanding of Being is the ground of the possibility of our existence, i.e., the ground of the possibility of the mode of Being according to which, as we have already said many times, we find ourselves in the midst of beings, standing before beings, standing as beings ourselves.

The being whose mode of Being is determined by comportment has stepped out of itself, as self-comporting, without thereby losing itself; on the contrary, this being-outside-of-itself in the mode of self-relating to beings is altogether the condition of the possibility that a comporting being can comport itself to itself, can come back to itself and can be itself as a self. The essence of the self includes a stepping out of oneself, the out-of-oneself, the *ex-sistere. Only what comports itself, i.e., is existent, can be a self.* Only that which comports itself in general can comport itself to itself. Existence therefore cannot be determined by comportment to oneself, especially if it is not at all asked what comportment means here. |

28 The essence of comportment, however, includes not only the relation to beings as such but also the essential possibility of what we call the *restraint of comportment* [*die* Verhaltenheit des Verhaltens]. What we mean is this: comportment, as comportment to something, does not have to be completely absorbed in that to which it comports itself, does not have to lose itself completely therein; on the contrary, as comportment it can restrain itself, in comporting itself as *free* for that to which it comports itself, in *restraining itself over and against* that, it can maintain a *stance* [*die* Haltung] in the self (stance and to stand on native soil). All comportment belongs within a stance, one also able to assume the guise of a lack of stance or a neutrality between the total oscillation within oneself and the scatteredness of someone who is

always drawn this way or that and randomly bustles about. Here we see again how insistence constitutes only one mode of existence.

The ground of the possibility of existence lies in the understanding of Being. Existence essentially occurs therein. *The essence of existence is the understanding of Being.*

Self-comportment to oneself does *not* constitute the essence of existence but, instead, *presupposes* existence; only what exists—i.e., understands Being—can comport itself to itself. This is admittedly not a sufficient confrontation [with Jaspers's philosophy] as a whole, but it does touch upon an essential sphere of questioning. In this regard, my position toward philosophy and metaphysics is related, by way of a philosophical stance which is very different [from that of Jaspers], to Being as such, not to existence. Yet what matters here is neither Jaspers nor Heidegger.

§15. The full rendering of the understanding of Being

a) The priority of the understanding of Being as preconceptual understanding

Let that now suffice as a commentary on our concept of existence. It was clearly not an explanation of some arbitrarily assumed word-meaning but instead was *above all* a substantive characterization of the essence of humans as those beings whose Being is determined by comportment and stance. This characterization of the essence of humans, however, supplies us at the same time with the substantive context into which we now insert the fact we have come to know as the understanding of Being. What we called this fact became clear to us, on account of the investigation we carried out, as that understanding in which and from which are first made possible the comportment to beings and the composed stance in the midst of beings, i.e., existence as such. The understanding of Being possesses sovereignty over every comportment, wherein it is only a previous understanding of Being that makes something accessible as a being for a comportment. The fact—now the essential ground of existence, i.e., in each case, of ourselves.

The understanding of Being possesses this priority in and for comportment even if it remains what we called pre-acquaintance with the whatness and suchness of beings. This pre-acquaintance with the whatness of beings is not conceptual and is certainly not the result of an "abstraction" from individual cases and examples. It is a mistake to maintain that the individual givens, thus these individual trees and these individual birds would be given more originally, earlier, than the so-called "universal": bird, tree, which we would "first" acquire through abstraction. Rather, *equi-originally* given with the individual "those things there" is birdness, treeness, houseness. Reflection and abstraction do subsequently, in comparison with and in relation to the individuals, grasp the so-and-so-ness as a universal that applies to many. The applicability to many is not at all a necessary character of the whatness and the essence but, instead, is only a possible result of a determinate, grasped concept of the essence.

What is originally understood is the whatness in the sense of birdness, animalness, etc. The question of what is more original, the individuals, the ἕκαστα, or the essential *concepts*, the ἰδέαι, is a pseudo-question, because *both* of these are subsequent to the Being grasped in the understanding of Being. Therefore, the old Platonic problem of bridging the gap between the individual and the universal—the χωρισμός—is an impossible question, for if what is on either side of the gap is not, then neither is the gap. All this by the way. Decisive for us is the insight that the understanding of Being, even as preconceptual, has priority in and for all comportment.

b) The understanding of Being as the
transcendence that constitutes existence

In line with the priority of the understanding of Being, we see that this understanding does not arise from our relating to beings in order then to *abstract* Being and the relation to Being. On the contrary, it is the reverse: we can comport ourselves at all, i.e., relate to beings, only inasmuch as the understanding of Being has already happened. To say, as does generally repeated doctrine, that the concept of Being is the most abstract amounts to nonsense, for the simple reason that Being is not at all abstracted. It is not abstracted because it cannot at all be abstracted. The concept of Being, and accordingly *every philosophical concept*, is thus quite different.

We do not first need to await beings and their encounter in order to understand Being on that basis; on the contrary, we are always already over and above beings, beyond beings. We have always already leapt into an understanding, in advance of beings, in order then for the first time to let the encountered be as beings and as the beings they are and such as they are. We will give the name *transcendence* to this character of the understanding of Being, namely, its ascending beyond beings in advance. I am using the word in the genuine sense, as naming the *transcendere*, the transcending, and not as nonsensically signifying that toward which the transcending proceeds, which is falsely called the transcendent. For this falsely named transcendent, Jaspers again falsely uses the term "transcendence," transcendence as God, the absolute.

Transcendence is ascent, but *not* one beyond beings as ordinarily given precisely in sensible experience to the highest supersensible being. On the contrary, the essential ascent is beyond every being as such to Being. This ascent does not take place outside of the understanding of Being, as if it were still something different. Instead, the *understanding of Being is in itself this transcendence toward Being.* Being is given only in and through this understanding. Every comportment is a comportment only on the basis of the transcendence that constitutes the understanding of Being. *Existence is in its essential ground transcendence.*

To state, "Humans exist," does not mean, in accord with the concept of existence we have proposed, that humans are actually on hand, are not mere phantoms. The statement does not assert *that* humans are; it asserts *what* they are. Existence expresses the whatness, the essence of the human beings we ourselves are. The essence [*die Essenz*] of humans consists in their existence. And this their essence is possible on the basis of transcendence. Transcendence occurs as the understanding of Being.

c) The dignity of the understanding of Being only in relation to existence

Initially we encountered the understanding of Being simply as a remarkable and forgotten fact. We then sought to clarify its worthiness. We attempted a complete dis-esteeming by assuming the understanding of Being did not occur. The unconditional sovereignty and priority of the understanding of Being were thereby illuminated, and so was the essential dignity of this understanding.

The understanding of Being presented itself as the most unproblematic. Has it now been exposed as the most question-worthy? It would be rash to say so. For, just because we now see that the understanding of Being is not insignificant but is something which in the essence of human existence has the highest sovereignty and the highest rank and therefore deserves to be esteemed, this still does not mean we should deem it worthy to be questioned. On the basis of its demonstrated sovereignty and rank, the understanding of Being deserves a dignity and thus rightly demands to be heeded—when it is a matter of the existence of humans. But that does not mean without further ado that the understanding of Being would then precisely deserve to be placed in question. Quite apart from the fact that one can *doubt whether the questioning of something, the "interpellating" of it, ever actually amounts to an esteeming.* |

29

Should we not rather honor that which possesses rank and dignity by leaving it *unquestioned* and allowing it to hold sway? Questioning is here only a meddling, an encroaching curiosity, a disrespecting of the proper distance. Questioning takes that which is interrogated and drags it down to us and into our sphere. The result is:

1) Questioning and interrogating do not as such and without further ado constitute an esteeming. 2) It is not decided whether and how the understanding of Being, despite its intrinsic rank and dignity, does now demand to be questioned precisely as a way of showing the appropriate esteem for its worthiness.

Yet does the understanding of Being, as we stated above and believed we had established, possess rank and dignity *intrinsically* and unconditionally? Indeed not, but only *relative* to comportment, i.e., only within human existence. Only under the presupposition that human existence as such should prevail and assert itself does the understanding of Being possess rank and dignity—but not in itself and unconditionally.

§16. The liberation toward freedom

a) The coming into sovereignty of existence as a transformation of the essence of humanity

Yet *why* should human beings be as *existing*? The necessity of it is not obvious. Humans and human lineages are and have been and will be, without their Being having been determined as existence, without humans occupying themselves with their stance, i.e., without humans taking themselves as beings in the midst of beings who comport themselves to beings as such. There is a Being of humans, since they move in the highest simplicity and in the harmony of their needs and abilities with the powers that shelter humans and re-attune them. By way of such harmony and such shelter, nothing breaks open as regards beings as such. Humans *are,* and yet they do not *exist* in the stipulated sense of existence.

Assuming, however, that the Being of humans did come to existence, i.e., took to comportment and maintained itself in its stance, i.e., above all, assuming the understanding of Being *received sovereignty,* assuming all this, could it happen incidentally, such that it merely "came to pass" with humans and befell them? Or with such a transition to existence must not something radical happen thereby, something required by existence as a new mode of Being?

Assuming that the Being of humans came to existence, then a transformation of them has occurred. In the transition to existence, they are determined on the basis of existence. And existence as understanding of Being is letting-be: freedom. The transition to freedom leads to lack of shelter, thus to a liberation from something to something. But what does liberation from shelter mean? Into what are humans placed? Liberation to existence, understanding of Being, *Being*. That occurs only in a stance and in self-comportment to oneself. Stance and *selfhood*! The latter to be understood not in a moral or religious sense but, instead, on the basis of Being and the un-concealedness of beings as a whole.

The letting-be in comportment toward beings in the midst of beings is freedom (not ethically!—letting-be). There is freedom only out of and as liberation. According to its essence, the liberation to freedom can be guided only by that toward which it properly liberates, thus by existence and by what has the priority therein—the understanding of Being and what manifests itself in this understanding. The matter at issue here is the Being of beings. Only if the issue is Being in the understanding of Being and in its sovereignty can this liberation to the freedom of existence occur.

b) The asking of the question of Being as the closest proximity of existence

But why and for what end should Being and the understanding of Being be at issue? What happens when they are at issue? Nothing less than this: beings as a whole, previously concealed from self-manifestation, find *for the first time* and henceforth, in one way or another, the site and the amplitude in which they can step forth out of their concealedness in order to be at all as the beings they are. In this way, for the first time *concealment* is also provided them. Prior to that, they lacked it.

Thereby beings come by their Being.[14] They do so only if and insofar as the understanding of Being occurs. And the condition of possibility for it, namely, that this occurrence becomes history, is the transition to the existence of humans. But, again, that beings as such come to themselves is not intrinsically necessary, even if there are already humans.

Beings can remain sunk in the full night of self-shrouded nothingness, such that they are never granted the possibility of being concealed. For there is concealment only if the site of disconcealment holds good. | 29a

If, however, beings as such are to come to the light of day, if this day is to dawn for beings, then, as was shown by our attempt at a complete dis-esteeming of the understanding of Being, Being must come to be understood in advance. Yet Being can never simply be found amid beings as one being among others. Nor can it first be drawn out of "beings" by way of abstraction. Being can therefore nowhere and never

---

14. This coming together as "provenance" (appearance).

simply be encountered. Accordingly, it must be sought originally and entirely for itself; i.e., it must be disclosed through questioning.[15] Humans must undertake this questioning. And the most proximate form in which this questioning starts at all is the question: "What are beings?" This question already includes the other one: "How do matters stand with Being?" Being is thereby placed into question in advance, what is sought is *as such configured* and specifically as what is at issue when the issue is supposed to be beings as such. Through this original questioning and only through it, Being becomes what is at issue primarily and for all beings. As Being comes to be understood in this way, beings as such are empowered to themselves. Henceforth they can come to light as the beings they are. Yet now they can first also thrust themselves forward as what they are not and can thereby be disguised and covered over.[16]

Heed well: it is enough that questioning merely be directed to Being in order for Being to be found. *This disclosure through questioning brings about, as such, the essential finding;* and Being remains a finding only inasmuch as and as long as questioning is directed to it. (Being becomes devised [*er-funden*]—poetized—configured.) Only for so long is there Being! [*Nur solange gibt "es" (das Sein) Sein!* Lit., "only for so long does 'it' (Being) give Being!"] Whereby precisely this question can also "stand" as *unasked* (no longer explicitly posed).

To disclose Being through questioning means first of all to ask: "What are beings as such?" By this questioning, humans hold to themselves for the first time, and in this holding to themselves they explicitly hold themselves over and against that which is encountered in such a questioning stance, and thereby they comport themselves to what (namely, beings) is encountered through this questioning. Humans now become that which, as ex-sistent, stands out of itself toward beings as such. The questioning directed to Being is the *basic act of existence;* this questioning inaugurates the history of humans as existing humans.

In this questioning, humans take from Being (and essence) their ground and their courage and power and also the measure of things.[17] *This questioning, as questioning, is the original esteeming of Being.*

Questioning is thus the mode of esteeming that pertains essentially and originally to Being. Assuming that humans exist, then Being possesses sovereignty and worthiness not only in general; also,

---

15. More to be clarified—essence of seeking—*original seeking | seeking again*—in *this seeking it arises*—is configured.

16. Whence the "not"? The "not" and questioning! Seeking—

17. Origin of alone-ness [*Allein-heit*] and all-oneness [*All-einheit*].

this worthiness is in itself the dignity esteemed only in questioning: question-worthiness. With the existence of humans, the essential question-worthiness of Being comes into its own.

c) The unasked question of Being as the closest proximity of existence

Yet it must never be forgotten: question-worthiness (and sovereignty) are proper to Being and to the understanding of Being not intrinsically and in general but only insofar as humans claim and adhere to the liberation toward existence. Admittedly, that occurs also when and where the stance and comportment of humans have the character of insistence. For even then, comportment is the sovereign standing in relation to beings, except now the sovereign and guiding understanding of Being is forgotten and the disclosure of Being by way of questioning is abandoned.

Accordingly, if the understanding of Being is unfamiliar to us and the question of Being forgotten, it in no way follows that we do not still claim it, i.e., do not exist. Insistent existence does not abolish the understanding of Being; on the contrary, it merely entrenches a conventional mode of this understanding without giving it another thought. The understanding of Being does not disappear; it merely hides behind a mask, the mask of what is most unproblematic. As long as we exist insistently, we do not see through to what is behind the mask. On the other hand, as soon as we acquire a regard for the essence of existence, we see that this unproblematic, harmless, insignificant Being and understanding of Being can be nothing less than what, although dis-esteemed, is the most question-worthy for existence. This dis-esteeming of what is most question-worthy, however, does indeed mean leaving the question of Being unasked. Leaving it unasked does not eliminate it but, instead, suppresses it as held fast yet unasked. Suppressed in this way, the question of Being is still there. Then where? In our insistent existence. Our paying no heed to the suppressed question of Being is not a proof against its "being-there" but merely demonstrates that I in suppressing it we mean that   30
we could withdraw from it at any time. We can withdraw from it only in the way the wanderer, distancing himself more and more from the spring, semblantly dissolves every relation to it and yet perishes precisely through and on this relation of distancing himself.

The question of Being, as unasked, is in the closest proximity of our Dasein as existent. For what can be more essential to our existence, thus closer and more intimate to it, than the ground of its inner possibility? But that is precisely the question of Being—and the disclosive asking of it.

Yet the question of Being, as we heard earlier, begins philosophy. If the question of Being, although unasked, is so essentially close to our existence, then the beginning is in our closest proximity. We stand, insofar as we exist, even if insistently, in this beginning—but in the beginning as one that is no longer begun and has perhaps come to a premature end. The question of Being is indeed unasked but is not therefore nothing. This dis-esteemed question demands, in a quite different sense and measure, the esteeming that pertains to it precisely as the still never posed question. In view of the unasked question of Being, Being and the understanding of Being merely become more question-worthy, if indeed insistence intrinsically claims existence.

The results, taking all in all, are the following:

To be actually existent means for us: to become the ones we *are*.

The basic happening of this becoming, however, is: to grasp the ground of the possibility of our existence by fathoming this ground.

That means: to ask again the unasked question of Being.

And that implies: to begin again the unbegun beginning.

The moment we grasp our humanity as existent, the act of beginning the beginning becomes the first and last necessity. Then, however, the beginning no longer lies in back of us as something disposed of, left behind, past. Nor is it simply in the closest proximity as something hidden by the mask of the most unproblematic. On the contrary, it stands *before* us as the essential task of our most proper essence.

d) The historical re-asking of the question of Being as a re-beginning of the initial beginning

The question-worthiness of Being and of the understanding of Being and thus the question-worthiness of the question of Being may have become clear and pressing to us, yet it can never be deduced from this that we must consequently go back to the first beginning of Western philosophy. On the contrary, is not the beginning all the more immediately asked, the more exclusively we—today—ask it completely from our own present resources? We from our own resources—but who then are we, if we understand our Being from the ground of its possibility? We exist, in our Being we are constructed on the understanding of Being—even more, on the already-asked question of Being and on what it discloses of Being in questioning. Insofar as we exist, that beginning *still ever happens*. It *has been*, but it is not past—as having been, it prevails and keeps us of today in its essence.

Ever since, our humanity as existent has been grounded on the occurrence of the beginning; ever since, any asking of the question of Being, provided it is an actual, self-aware questioning, has become a *re-asking*, one intrinsically historical and thus properly historiological.

Historiological cognition is not merely aimed at retaining what has been and delivering back up to us what was retained; instead, its basic task above all is to take what has been and cast it up into the heights of its respective greatness.

Historiology that is not given to preserving the greatness of what has been, historiology that does not succeed in assuring that this greatness remains great, is an otiose pastime in no way justified by being carried out as an exact science. On the contrary, the unrelenting rigor of this scientific work first receives its sense and justification from such preserving and assuring. (Cf. above, p. 12, sec. b ff.)

The asking of the question of Being is intrinsically historical and historiological, as is all philosophizing. But not primarily and only because the first beginning, on account of its essentially unattainable greatness, can be and must be the paradigm and guide for our questioning and therefore the place we must begin, but because *our* asking of the question of Being, precisely if it arises entirely out of our own resources and out of our clarified essence, is of itself sent back into a confrontation with the beginning.

It would amount to pondering a pseudo-problem if we were to ask whether and how "systematic philosophy and the history of philosophy" are supposed to go together, for the separation of them is already mistaken about the essence of philosophy.[18] One of the most fatal delusions to which modern and contemporary efforts in philosophy have fallen victim is the view that the history of philosophy can be appended arbitrarily, occasionally, and subsequently, according to taste and preference, simply in order to "illustrate" the "real" thoughts. | 31

To co-ask the question of Being—a *re-beginning* of the *initial* beginning—is not an arbitrary occupation, not something that runs its course apart from beings, certainly not an indifferent consideration that would be crammed onto beings and could just as easily be left off.

On the contrary, in deciding whether and how the question of Being is asked, and whether and how it remains unasked, it is thereby decided in general *how matters stand concerning the Being of beings* and what possibility and amplitude are provided and prepared for Being in order that beings be the beings they are. It is thus decided how matters stand concerning the manifestness of beings, concerning truth as such; what is primarily decisive is not which truths we discover and which ones we adhere to but, instead, what truth in essence is for us at all—(question of Being).[19] According to the respective originality

---

18. Hegel! but?

19. (Cf. lecture on truth.) {Martin Heidegger, "Vom Wesen der Wahrheit." In *Wegmarken*, GA9, 177–202. The lecture was first delivered publicly in 1930.}

and clarity in which Being is manifest, and according to the grounding of this manifestness itself in the essence, the possibility of conceptualizing and the possibility of the concept are decided.—The whole world is now speaking of a new concept of science supposedly on its way. What is meant is that it would be achieved with a so-called "new spiritual impetus" and a so-called "proximity to life." It would be just as superficial to oppose such wishes and cravings by attempting to preach in favor of the trusty old science of 1890 as the paradigm.

Assuming we understand ourselves at all as existent, as ones who "are" on our own part beings in the midst of beings as a whole, comporting ourselves to beings, then we have no choice about whether or not we want to understand and conceptualize Being. We have the choice only of whether we conceptualize it well or badly, whether the conceptualized acquires greatness for us or remains small, and whether the temper of our existence is to be determined by the clarity and severity of a *fully developed concept* or by just any accidental, confused frenzy.

§17. Transition to Parmenides: the first explicit and coherent unfolding of the question of Being

After we first acquainted ourselves, by way of an immediate apprehension, with the oldest transmitted testimony of Western philosophy (cf. above, p. 12), the task then was to consider how matters stood with our own project. That has now happened. Thereby it became clear: if, as was said at the outset, we want to seek out the beginning of Western philosophy, then that means we are to re-ask the question of Being as the ground of the possibility of our existence, i.e., ask this question *in such a way* that we thereby co-begin the initial beginning.

The task is now only this: having clarified what we want, we are to undertake a co-asking of the beginning question. That means we must now inquire into the place we first encounter an explicit and coherent unfolding of the question of Being. That occurs, according to tradition, in the so-called didactic poem (a φυσιολογία δι' ἐπῶν, according to Suidas; Diels A 2: λόγος περὶ φύσεως) of Parmenides of Elea. The chronology is a matter of controversy. We can say, with the most certainty and prudence, around the turn of the 6th to the 5th century, and that is sufficient. Diogenes Laertius reports, and a few others, including Theophrastus, also say that Parmenides would have heard Anaximander (cf. Diels A 1). This report may be correct or not; it cannot be verified. In any case, it shows that the ancients already assumed a somewhat close connection between Anaximander and

Parmenides. The extent of this connection will be shown by a comparison of the two doctrines.

We will start at once with the interpretation of Parmenides's didactic poem. What the previous endeavors at interpreting Parmenides have accomplished will be mentioned when discussing the respective issues. For the rest, however, those works will not be presented in more detail. Not because they are insignificant but because they are so unavoidable that one cannot speak about them at first. Our concern is *primarily* with securing a philosophical understanding of the beginning of Western philosophy and only *secondarily* with initiating ourselves into the procedure of appropriating an earlier philosophy, i.e., into the *method of interpretation.*

With respect to all previous interpretive attempts, even Hegel's, it should be said that they made their work philosophically too easy, in part by invoking as a highest explanatory principle the view that the beginning is precisely the primitive and therefore is crude and raw—the illusion of progress! (In this regard, nothing further to say about the previous attempts.)

The interpretation of Parmenides is closely coupled to the question of his relation to Heraclitus, who presupposed Parmenides and contests against him. The notion that in essentials they are in the sharpest opposition is thereby presupposed as valid. In the end, however, this presupposition is precisely an error. In the end, Parmenides and Heraclitus are in the utmost agreement—as are all actual philosophers—not because they renounce battling, but precisely on account of their own respective ultimate originality. For nonphilosophers, who adhere only to works, opinions, schools, names, and claims, the history of philosophy and of philosophers does of course present the appearance of a madhouse. But that can quietly remain as it is. | 32

PART THREE
The *"didactic poem" of Parmenides of Elea, 6th–5th century*[1]

"For present things are dear to humans."
Hölderlin, "The Peregrination"[2]

§18. Introduction

a) On the text and the translation

First of all, brief comments on the "externals" of the text before us. The mimeograph is so arranged that the translation can be entered beside the text. The work has not been handed down in its entirety; the greater part, however, is indeed contained in the fragments. Whence do these derive? Various disparate sources. Nowhere a comprehensive overall plan transmitted; thus to be established out of the fragmentary material, initially found scattered and loose. The ordering of the fragments depends on the understanding of their content. The order on the mimeo is that of Hermann Diels; cf. the separate printing of 1897[3] and then included in *Die Fragmente der Vorsokratiker,* several editions since 1903.[4] The number assigned to the various fragments is in each case placed above: D 1, D 2, etc. [D = Diels]. My arrangement is partially different; in each case it is to be inserted beside the Diels number.

The respective source is indicated beneath the numbering of the fragment.[5] The fragments are precisely quotations, drawn from later authors: e.g., D 7 from Plato's *Sophist* and Aristotle's *Metaphysics,* D 3 from Proclus, *Platonis Parmenides,* D 6 from Simplicius, *Aristotelis Physicorum,* etc. For the larger fragments, every fifth line is numbered in the left margin.

I will first provide a translation. Then an initial commentary on the main concepts and propositions and accordingly a first understanding of the content; predelineation of the inner structure and glance at the development of the guiding questions.

---

1. The interpretation is insufficient, even if much is grasped essentially. {Trscpt[2]}

2. {Friedrich Hölderlin, *Sämtliche Werke,* vol. 4, *Gedichte,* compiled by N. von Hellingrath, 2nd. ed. Berlin: Propyläen, 1923, 170.}

3. {*Parmenides Lehrgedicht. Griechisch und Deutsch von Hermann Diels. Mit einem Anhang über griechische Thüren und Schlösser.* Berlin: Reimer, 1897.}

4. {1903; 1906; 1912; 1922.}

5. [These references to sources are not given.—Trans.]

b) The releasement into the meaning and content

As much as possible, we must *release* ourselves into the whole, as alien as that whole might seem at first. But we have indeed somewhere preserved the remainder of a kinship and line of descent. The task is to unfold this remainder into its original fullness. (Understanding of Being.)

The meaning and content of the work as well as the spirit of Parmenides accessible only if we *conjure up* that spirit. This conjuring necessarily among our means of interpretation. Lay people, among whom I also count a certain class of "so-called scientific philologist," see therein at once only a modernization. They see the contemporary means along with what is contemporary in that which is achieved thereby and to which it leads. What thereby comes closer to us they do not see, because they do not want to see it, and that because at bottom these old issue are insignificant to them. As if the issues were there only so that a science of them can be developed, or as if books were written only so that reviewers might not be put out of business.[6]

c) Attitude toward my own interpretations

It has now become fashionable to refute my interpretation of earlier philosophers by saying, "That is Heidegger, but not Hegel," or "Heidegger, but not Kant," etc. Certainly. *But does it follow ipso facto that the interpretation is false?* That cannot at all be decided "ipso facto," especially not as long as one believes that there would be an interpretation true *in itself* and *binding on everyone at all times.*—The truth of one interpretation versus many others depends primarily on the level the interpretation occupies in its questioning and in its claim to understanding. If just any concepts and propositions are taken over from an arbitrarily adopted philosophical theory, namely, Heidegger's, and the interpretation is measured up to these, then all my interpretations are in fact false. What is decisive, however, is not this but precisely the necessity and originality of the guiding questioning under which the interpretation stands. The so-called "correct" interpretations are not attributable to x or y, but to "no one"—they are also on no one's authority.

Instead of this, the usual procedure is the reverse: with great diligence one detects "falsehoods," and at the conclusion or beginning one remarks that there is neither place nor occasion to become involved in Heidegger's own philosophy and that that would lead too far. But this amounts to shirking the essential and pursuing a purely formal quibbling under the semblance of scientific exactness. This by

---

6. Sil.! [*sic*] Here insert a "personal remark" called for in accord with the issue. Attempt at a new interpretation of Parmenides.

way of answering the question often directed to me, namely, why I do not respond to the German criticism. Up to now I have not felt myself seriously attacked, nor do I find myself actually defended by my so-called disciples. Needless to say, I do not believe my interpretations are flawless, nor am I unaware of the really weak portions of my endeavors.

All of this is trying to say, in brief: pay attention primarily not to the means and paths of our interpretation, but to what these means and paths will set before you. If that does not become especially essential to you, then the discussion of the correctness or incorrectness of the interpretation will a fortiori remain inconsequential. | 32a

§19. Interpretation of fragment 1.
Preparation for the question of Being

a) The grasp of the circumstances and images

This didactic poem has a rather long introduction and thus does not commence immediately with the simple question "what are beings?" Parmenides's introduction operates by presenting images. The aim and task of this presentation and the details of its content can be grasped only through a comprehension of the genuine didactic substance of the poem.

Presumably, this introduction will help prepare for the question of Being, and we will have to ask whether this *inceptual* posing of the question concerning Being coincides with the one we attempted to unfold in meditating on that understanding of Being which pertains to existence and which we considered the most question-worthy.

In case the two questionings do not coincide, we will have to determine why not and also whether the non-coincidence is necessary and which differences are required here by the matter at issue itself. Only in that way can we decide to what extent it is or is not right to speak here of an introduction, a proemium, or whether this does not perhaps actually belong to the matter itself, with the matter for its part belonging necessarily to an "introduction." At first we want to gain acquaintance with this introduction in a preliminary way, using a translation that will likewise only be preparatory.

D 1, 1–32

    Ἵπποι ταί με φέρουσιν, ὅσον τ᾽ ἐπὶ θυμὸς ἱκάνοι,
    πέμπον, ἐπεί μ᾽ ἐς ὁδὸν βῆσαν πολύφημον ἄγουσαι
    δαίμονος, ἣ κατὰ πάντα τη φέρει εἰδότα φῶτα·
    τῇ φερόμην· τῇ γάρ με πολύφραστοι φέρον ἵπποι
5   ἅρμα τιταίνουσαι, κοῦραι δ᾽ ὁδὸν ἡγεμόνευον.

ἄξων δ᾽ ἐν χνοίῃσιν <ἵει> σύριγγος ἀυτήν
αἰθόμενος· δοιοῖς γὰρ ἐπείγετο δινωτοῖσιν
κύκλοις ἀμφοτέρωθεν, ὅτε σπερχοίατο πέμπειν
Ἡλιάδες κοῦραι, προλιποῦσαι δώματα Νυκτός,
10   εἰς φάος, ὠσάμεναι κράτων ἄπο χερσὶ καλύπτρας.
ἔνθα πύλαι Νυκτός τε καὶ Ἤματός εἰσι κελεύθων,
καί σφας ὑπέρθυρον ἀμφὶς ἔχει καὶ λάινος οὐδός·
αὐταὶ δ᾽ αἰθέριαι πλῆνται μεγάλοισι θυρέτροις.
τῶν δὲ Δίκη πολύποινος ἔχει κληῖδας ἀμοιβούς·
15   τὴν δὴ παρφάμεναι κοῦραι μαλακοῖσι λόγοισιν
πεῖσαν ἐπιφραδέως, ὥς σφιν βαλανωτὸν ὀχῆα
ἀπτερέως ὤσειε πυλέων ἄπο· ταὶ δὲ θυρέτρων
χάσμ᾽ ἀχανὲς ποίησαν ἀναπτάμεναι πολυχάλκους
ἄξονας ἐν σύριγξιν ἀμοιβαδὸν εἰλίξασαι
20   γόμφοις καὶ περόνῃσιν ἀρηρότε· τῇ ῥα δι᾽ αὐτῶν
ἰθὺς ἔχον κοῦραι κατ᾽ ἀμαξιτὸν ἅρμα καὶ ἵππους.
καί με θεὰ πρόφρων ὑπεδέξατο, χεῖρα δὲ χειρί
δεξιτερὴν ἕλεν, ὧδε δ᾽ ἔπος φάτο καί με προσηύδα·
ὦ κοῦρ᾽ ἀθανάτοισι συνάορος ἡνιόχοισιν,
25   ἵπποις ταί σε φέρουσιν ἱκάνων ἡμέτερον δῶ
χαῖρ᾽, ἐπεὶ οὔτι σε μοῖρα κακὴ προύπεμπε νέεσθαι
τήνδ᾽ ὁδόν (ἦ γὰρ ἀπ᾽ ἀνθρώπων ἐκτὸς πάτου ἐστίν),
ἀλλὰ θέμις τε δίκη τε. χρεὼ δέ σε πάντα πυθέσθαι
ἠμὲν Ἀληθείης εὐκυκλέος ἀτρεμὲς ἦτορ
30   ἠδὲ βροτῶν δόξας, ταῖς οὐκ ἔνι πίστις ἀληθής.
ἀλλ᾽ ἔμπης καὶ ταῦτα μαθήσεαι, ὡς τὰ δοκοῦντα
χρῆν δοκιμῶσ᾽ εἶναι διὰ παντὸς πάντα περῶντα.

1) Steeds, which bring me at any time as far as my mettle desires, conducted me.

2–3) For they brought me while proceeding on the much-heralding
way of the goddess, the way that through the all (beings as a whole)
bears onward every person who is knowledgeable. (οἶδα; cf. *Hermes*
60, 185,[7] the knowledgeable one, who *knows* what is at issue—
"knowing one's way about"! From what and toward what he has
set out in advance, who correctly set out in what is *essential* and
now "*stands*" in that.)

4–5) There (on this way of the goddess) I drove along; for there many
indicating-showing steeds (others than mine!) conducted me, pull-
ing the chariot, but maidens pointed the way.

---

7. {Hermann Fränkel, "Xenophanesstudien." In *Hermes. Zeitschrift für classische
Philologie*, 60 (1925): 185.}

6–7) . . . the axle in the brackets emitted a whistling sound—and glowed—turning rapidly in two well-rounded rings on either side . . . (all this happened)

8–10) *whenever* the sun-maidens ran in escort, after they had left the house of the night, out into the light, brushing back from their heads the concealing veils.

11–13) Over there is the gate of the ways of night and day; and a lintel encloses it along with a stone threshold; the (bright) clear expanse is filled with great doors.

14) Far-pursuing Dikē holds their reciprocally (closing) opening keys. (In that they on the one hand close, do they open?)

15–16) *They* (the goddess) thus spoke to the maidens in flattering discourse and warily persuaded the maidens to push back for them the staked bolt from the gate without delay;

17–19) but this, in opening up, made of the doorway a wide-yawning gap, since the gate turned backward the bronze-sheathed doorposts in the high-squeaking brackets; these (the doorposts) were attached by tenons and spikes (pegs).

20–21) There now straight through them, on the carriage path, the maidens drove onward the chariot and horses.

22–23) And the kindly disposed goddess received me, grasped my right hand with hers, and thus taking up the word she addressed me:

24–26) "Youth—a companion of immortal charioteers, since you arrive at *our* home with the horses that convey you, be welcomed; for (cf. 1, 2) no evil fate has sent you forth to travel this way (that of the goddess). νέεσθαι—to go off (to war) on it

27) for truly *apart* from human beings, outside their trodden paths the way leads—| 33

28–29) (not an evil fate), but rather precept as well as compliance. Yet it is necessary (for you, who now enter upon this way) that you experience everything, just as much the unquaking heart of fully spherical unconcealedness (cf. s.s. 35, p. 43 top)[8] as also the views of humans, wherein there is no relying on what is unconcealed.

30–32) But in all (nevertheless) you should come to know *even this,* namely, how the semblant is constrained to draw semblant(-like) through everything, making everything, *forming* everything." Cf. D 8, 60f.

Let us try to presentify more determinately what is said here and configure it into a unitary nexus. That will not happen effortlessly. Even though Parmenides speaks unmistakably *in certain images,* yet

---

8. {Heidegger, *Einführung in die Metaphysik,* op. cit., 120.}

we must from the start beware of yielding to a mania for symbols and then interpret in an artificial way, as happened in the 2nd century AD to Sextus Empiricus, in whose writings this fragment has come down to us. This later time disposes of all others, except for the presuppositions for understanding Parmenides. Mystagogy, then and now, has nothing to do with philosophy.

The initial task is to grasp quite soberly the factual matters, including those pertaining to the images.

1) The first point is this: Parmenides travels with a team of steeds to the home of the goddess—Ἀλήθεια. He traverses this way *to* the goddess. *This* way is not discussed further. To be sure, something essential is said about the traversal of it: ὅσον τ᾽ ἐπὶ θυμὸς ἱκάνοι. This way and its reach are determined by the ἐφικάνειν of the θυμός, by Parmenides's own desire in advance. He *himself by himself* puts himself on the way; no mystical-mysterious enchantment or rapture sets him off.

This setting himself on the way happens *repeatedly,* ever again, (optative); determinative is θυμός.

What the Greeks mean by this term is rendered best in German by the old word *Muot, Mut* [mettle, spirit], as we still use in *Freimut* [frankness, freedom of spirit], *Großmut* [magnanimity, greatness of spirit], *Langmut* [forbearance, long-suffering of spirit], *Schwermut* [melancholy, heaviness of spirit], *Übermut* [arrogance, overabundance of spirit]—*wie einem zu Mute ist* [how one is mettled, how spirited].

Mettle is disposition and attunement in one; "*zumuten* [demand] something of someone"—push him toward something so that he takes it up in his *Mut* [with spirit, wholeheartedly], in a good frame of mind, with a good disposition. Mettle: *the directed, disposed, desiring reaching out in advance.* Later *Gemüt* [heart, temperament] is used for *Mut;* so it is in Kant whenever he reduces to their root all the human faculties insofar as they lie ready "in the heart." Later and for us, temperament is again narrowed to the domain of feelings in distinction to thinking and will. θυμός is urge, urge-formation, urge-direction, and disposition in one. θυμός, *animus,* heart—Parmenides is moved onto the way to the goddess not by some sort of curiosity, but by the directed, disposed, desiring pre-reaching out of *his entire humanness.*

2) This home of the goddess has a gate. There is *again a way* leading forth from this gate. It is the way *of* the goddess, not *to* the goddess; it is the way the goddess herself travels. In traveling on this way, the sun-maidens are the conductors.

Let us heed from the start with full attention: it is matter of ways—ὁδοί. "Way"—we can understand it as a traversable span between two stopping points. We can consider a "way" in the sense of driveable ground as paved thoroughfare. But "way" also in the sense of the *pano-rama* and the *outlook* the road offers, i.e., the *region* through which the road leads. Every way has its *prospect*. And that is what is at issue here. ὁδὸς πολύθημος (1, 2)—much-heralding; not, as Diels takes it, the fa-mous way, the much-heralded way. For who is supposed to herald it, since it is now first disclosed and the many do precisely not know of it? On the contrary, the way is much-herald*ing*; it offers many a pros-pect, it opens access to. . . . To what? If it is the way of ἀλήθεια, then obviously to the unconcealed as such.

This way is accordingly distinguished at 1, 27: ἢ γὰρ ἀπ᾽ ἀνθρώπων ἐκτὸς πάτου ἐστίν. πάτος, the trodden path, constantly traversed by everyone; *apart* from this. What counts is not to follow in the tracks and steps of the crowd; apart from their opinions and fancies, not to be determined by what they say and hear and believe.

It is a matter of ways: more precisely, it is a matter of *taking* them, *keeping* to the ways taken, in order to be *underway* on them, to pursue the way and its essence, to go after—μετά—μέθοδος—*method*. | 33a

b) The disclosure of method

The essence and necessity of method are disclosed. Method is not a prerogative of science; on the contrary, science can and must be me-thodical only insofar as it is rooted in philosophy.

We are standing in the middle of a basic meditation on method; to be sure, not method as formal, detachable technique. Then what? The way Parmenides is supposed to take under the guidance of Ἀλήθεια is *apart from* the common path of humans. And *yet not* something pecu-liar in the sense of the practices of a secret doctrine, the techniques of some mystery rite; on the contrary, *the way places us for the first time in the open realm*—taken in its full meaning. The prospect decisive! The goddess (Ἀλήθεια) says at 1, 28: χρεὼ δέ σε πάντα πυθέσθαι—you must experience *everything*, πάντα. How everything? 1, 29: ἠμέν—ἠδέ: both unconcealedness as well as human views, which are thus distin-guished from truth as some sort of untruth.

Yet did we not precisely hear that the way of the goddess would be far remote from the path tread by humans? Now, however, Parmenides is indeed supposed to experience these views and so must travel this path too. No; he is not supposed to frequent the path tread by humans and become acquainted with their views, δόξαι; instead, Parmenides is to experience on this path, i.e., come to understand, what this path as such is all about. He is not supposed to hear opinions and thereby half-truths and half-falsehoods but, instead, is to gain insight into the essence of the view of δόξα, thus gain the *truth* about δόξα. And correspondingly: he is not to gain sundry truths, in case there are such, but is to grasp the essence of truth and the essential truth.

The truth about δόξα, however, is obviously to be gained only on the way of truth. But the converse also holds: only if insight is gained into the truth about δόξα can the prospect offered by the way of truth be fully surveyed.

πάντα, everything, includes: 1) the essence of truth; 2) the essence of δόξα. But is this actually everything? No; ἀλήθεια and δόξα—what about the "and"? That is, why at all next to ἀλήθεια some sort of untruth? Why and how next to ἀλήθεια does δόξα come to sovereignty, so much so that it commonly draws humans onto its way? That must be clarified. Only then is insight gained into ἀλήθεια and δόξα. Therefore, the πάντα is not exhausted by the ἠμέν—ἠδέ; instead, it goes on: ἀλλ᾽ ἔμπης καὶ ταῦτα. "But in all this you must also gain insight into how the semblant in its own manner, according to its essence, comes to be all-sovereign." Only when this is experienced is the entire way of the goddess measured out.

The genuine meditation on the ways, on method, is the question of the essence of truth (this, however, is the question of Being! understanding of Being) and of the essential possibility of truth in relation to untruth. The one who would grasp this must understand untruth, must not avoid it, but instead must enter into the *most intimate confrontation* with it. The decisive insight is announced here right at the beginning of the didactic poem and is actualized in the poem's content proper.

Thereby we repeat: this way of Parmenides has nothing in common with myths and mysteries, for characteristic of the initiate into raptures and transports, who appeals to his special apparitions, is that he is carried off into his own private realm and feels sheltered there. Sheltered and protected from all untruth. But the way of Parmenides proceeds into the open realm, where it is precisely the entire opposition between truth and untruth that *first comes into the open*. It is a matter of the way that the one who is open opens up and keeps open—it is a matter of method pure and simple.

§20. Interpretation of fragments 4 and 5

a) First meditation on the ways of questioning

If we keep present before us this comprehensive outlook of the way of the goddess, then it is easily shown that the verses which now follow in Diels (1, 33ff.) and which Sextus Empiricus also had already placed there, cannot belong at this point. Moreover, Simplicius lets us see that Sextus Empiricus omitted from his citation the decisive verses 31 and 32, which refer precisely to the essential connection between ἀλήθεια and δόξα. To understand that would have demanded too much of the facile manner in which Sextus Empiricus accounts for the symbolism of this "introduction." Therefore he peremptorily left them out. The reason lines 1, 33–38 do not belong at this point is to be demonstrated on the occasion of the positive ordering. Moreover, all interpreters and editors prior to Diels have seen here in a much more accurate way. Reinhardt accepts the older ordering.[9]

It would correspond to a very natural progression of the presentation if the goddess, having given Parmenides an overall outlook on what he must experience, now pursues the meditation on the ways more searchingly. So D 4 must follow 1, 32: | 34

D 4

    εἰ δ᾽ ἄγ᾽ ἐγὼν ἐρέω, κόμισαι δὲ σὺ μῦθον ἀκούσας,
    αἵπερ ὁδοὶ μοῦναι διζήσιός εἰσι νοῆσαι·
    ἡ μὲν ὅπως ἔστιν τε καὶ ὡς οὐκ ἔστι μὴ εἶναι
    Πειθοῦς ἐστι κέλευθος (Ἀληθείῃ γὰρ ὀπηδεῖ),
5   ἡ δ᾽ ὡς οὐκ ἔστιν τε καὶ ὡς χρεών ἐστι μὴ εἶναι,
    τὴν δή τοι φράζω παναπευθέα ἔμμεν ἀταρπόν·
    οὔτε γὰρ ἂν γνοίης τό γε μὴ ἐὸν (οὐ γὰρ ἀνυστόν)
    οὔτε φράσαις.

1–2) Very well, now I will proclaim and do you take in charge (preserve) the word you hear, *which ways* you are to fix your eyes on as the *only ones* of a disclosure through questioning.[10]

3) The one: how it is[11] and how (it, the "it is") impossibly nonbeing.

4) The path of grounded trust is this, it (πειθώ) follows in the steps of unconcealedness.

5–6) The other, however, how it is not and also how necessarily nonbeing, this one therefore, so I proclaim, is a footpath of which one can never be persuaded whatever.

7–8) Neither, namely, are you able to cultivate acquaintance with nonbeing (for it is not at all to be brought forth (procured)), nor can you indicate it with words (show it in full clarity to someone) . . .

---

9. {Karl Reinhardt, *Parmenides und die Geschichte der griechischen Philosophie.* Bonn: Cohen, 1916.}

10. Cf. s.s. 35, p. 42. {Heidegger, *Einführung in die Metaphysik,* op. cit., 117ff.}

11. Cf. below, concerning 8, 3—ὡς ἐὸν . . . (p. 41, top).

D 5

... τὸ γὰρ αὐτὸ νοεῖν ἐστίν τε καὶ εἶναι.

... for the same is apprehending as well as Being.[12]

Parmenides is therefore now *underway* on the way of the goddess, a way far removed from the paths of humans; he is about to traverse its entirety. Where does it lead and which outlook does it bestow? We already heard: πάντα is supposed to be experienced. Yet not simply so as to become acquainted with some matter at issue or other; on the contrary, of concern are also the way and likewise the holding to the way. The question of the way is no less essential than the question of the matter at issue; indeed, henceforth the two will no longer be separable.[13]

Here is the first of the meditations concerning which ways the disclosive questioning in general can fix its eyes on. The way is one of a seeking out (δίζησις)—ὁδοὶ διζήσιος—seeking out and also seeking for knowledge. It is sought out in order to attain something in its manifestness (what sort of ways in general? δίζησις!), thus for the sake of knowledge; investigative-decisional seeking is *questioning*. Now to be clarified in advance and held fast: what in general can be disclosed in questioning and what not, which direction the questioning must take and which it cannot or should not. This latter must be kept in sight just as clearly and constantly as the former. Again talk of ἡ μέν-ἡ δέ (4, 3 and 4, 5): two ways at first. This division into two, however, not simply equivalent to the earlier one from the introduction 1, 29f.: ἀλήθεια—βρωτῶν δόξαι—ἡ μέν—ἡ δέ. Here the one way—Πειθοῦς κέλευθος. The path on whose course we can rely on something. The way of *grounded questioning* which rests on something firm, heralding it. The other way—παναπειθὴς ἀταρπός—the footpath onto which there can be absolutely no persuading—is utterly without prospects. Our reading, in line with Proclus, is παναπειθής, thereby exactly preserving the oppositional relation that indeed sharply divides the two ways. These ways—

---

12. Cf. D 8, 34ff.

13. Whether and how we find this interconnection. Therefore beings *as experienced*. What sort of experience is *basic experience*? / The first and highest demonstration—what must be manifest for that. / Both give each other the reciprocal authorization of having to belong together. / Being "in itself" I impossible—in what sense? substantially! not to be believed! but a task / not such that Being would stand in relation to something else, and what that other could be—but such that the essence of Being consists in this "relation" to an other—this other itself subsists only as relation to Being.

one of them must be taken, the other is completely impassible—are not distinguished simply in such terms, but at the same time we are told what can be disclosively questioned on the one way and what is entirely closed off on the other (cf. p. 34a).

On the one way, the disclosive questioning (δίζησις) concerns "how it is," ὅπως ἔστιν—how the "is" is. ὅπως ἔστιν—the sentence has no subject; better: the *predicate is itself the subject* and vice versa. How the "it *is*" is precisely what I understand when I address beings and express what has been understood? (It) "is." Thus: *how matters stand with Being.* This is to be disclosively questioned as well as, in unity it, how Being impossibly nonbeing, i.e., how Being utterly *repudiates* the "non." On the other side: how it is not, of what essence is the not-is, how matters stand with the null "is" (how matters stand with the "is"; *not Cogito!*). Nothingness—how here, with the "non," by necessity all Being remains absent. For Being forms no "non." The "non" dislodges Being and is represented only by nothingness. But there can be *no persuasion toward nothingness* and no relying on it. For nothing can at all be produced from it, ἀνυστόν—and so there is no possible acquaintance with it and no way to indicate it.

What immediately follows here is fragment 5, which provides the grounds for the sharp distinction between the two types of way and for the corresponding prospects: where there is Being there is also apprehension, and conversely: where apprehension, Being. But where nothingness, there also nothing to be apprehended and so no apprehending, no possibility of a way; and conversely: where nothing is taken up and apprehended, there also no Being. "Ap-prehend" [*Vernehmen*] is supposed to render the Greek word νοεῖν, which means to take into *sight*, specifically: a) to look at and to *take away* what is looked at; b) to *take* into sight, to look something over, take it in, consider it, *take it into consideration.*

The distinction between the two ways is grounded in the essence of Being, which is already grasped here in a decisive respect. We can express this essential characterization briefly as follows: Being offers itself only to the understanding, and every understanding is an understanding of Being. Being and the understanding of Being[14] are *the same*, they belong together in unity. Why νοεῖν, ap-prehension (a taking-up that takes away), rendered as *understanding*, with what justification—that will be shown.

---

14. Initially—presence and the present belong together. 1) how?—*more originary* time—because both not the same *and yet indeed the same*; 2) why precisely *praesens*? 3) what about the other *ecstases*? 4) essence of presence corresponding!

b) The statement that Being and apprehending
intrinsically belong together as a statement grounding
the distinction between the ways

The statement that Being and apprehending intrinsically belong together comprises *a* basic assertion about Being. For a long time it has been customary to take the statement as *the* basic assertion and to see in it the particular "standpoint" of Parmenides. The statement is thereby interpreted in an inappropriate sense (idealistically—beings posited only in thinking, and so there are no beings in themselves). This only incidentally. The significance of the statement within Parmenides's fragments takes a very different direction: an essential connection is here lit up between the access to something and this something (the matter at issue) itself. Within a meditation on the possible and impossible ways to beings as such, the statement has a *prescriptive role*. It will therefore be taken up again later, at 8, 3ff.; above all, however, it is now immediately enjoined once more and indeed with an essential supplementation. For, as was shown, the meditation on the ways is not exhausted by the earlier distinction between the one and only way rich in prospects and the other utterly without them.

34a   What guides the whole didactic poem, and is decisive, comes first. |

1) The way of grounded questioning. What is here disclosed in questioning? ὅπως ἔστιν, "how it is" = how the ἔστιν, how the "*it is*." How matters stand with the "is"; thus questioning with regard to what I mean when I address some being in virtue of itself and thus say: it, the being, "is." How does one think about the "is"? ἔστιν; a sentence—without a subject. Better: the predicate is itself the subject.

Yet not only: how do matters stand with Being? But also: καὶ ὡς οὐκ ἔστιν μὴ εἶναι—how Being impossibly nonbeing; the "non" is not seemly for Being; how *Being repudiates every "non."*

The way rich in prospects, if followed in disclosive questioning, therefore affords a prospect into how matters stand with Being and how precisely Being repudiates the "non."

2) The other way (παναπειθής ἄταρπος) leads whither? ὡς οὐκ ἔστιν: how matters stand with the not-is, with that which has utterly no "is," no Being, with *nothingness*.

καὶ ὡς χρεών . . . and how there (where the οὐκ) the necessity reigns, where the "non" reigns, Being must μή, Being must remain absent. That "non" dislodges all Being. The only representative of the "non" is nothingness.

Yet this way is indeed no way; already *in its beginning it is at its end;* it literally leads to "nothingness." On this way, therefore, nothing to produce, ἀνυστόν. Where no acquaintance, there also no assertions.

Yet *why* are the two ways so *utterly separate?* The one *rich in all prospects,* the other *completely without any prospect!* The ground of it is provided at D 5. "Where Being, there also apprehending, and vice versa." But where nothingness, there also no apprehending, and vice versa. νοεῖν, apprehending; to take into sight at all, and specifically: a) to look at, to take up what is looked at, take it away; b) take into sight, look something over, consider, take into consideration. Apprehension: a taking-up that takes away; (ap-prehension—for interrogation in court) (standing forth).

c) The absent grounding of the statement

The grounding of the differentiation of the ways goes back to εἶναι = νοεῖν; it goes back to Being, indeed in such a manner that something is said about Being. What? Being is the same as apprehending. Being itself is what it is as apprehending, and vice versa (basic assertion about Being). *Both belong together;* but heed well: it is not said that Being would have, among other relations, a relation to νοεῖν as well. On the contrary, *Being as such has warrant only in apprehension, and vice versa.* Being "as such" has no warrant; Being "as such" does not essentially occur as Being. If we grasp νοεῖν, ap-prehension, taking away, as understanding (whereby it still remains to say what understanding means here), then we can also grasp D 5: *there is Being only in the understanding of Being.* Being and understanding belong together.

Should we simply believe that? Or is there a highest demonstration and verification of it? To what extent does Parmenides provide these? Where is the way to actually test and secure them, so that we have something we can rely on? Can this belonging together be made *insightful in its necessity?*

Sufficient evidence: where Being an understanding, and vice versa. But proves only that we always come across it so; from this, however, does not follow that it is in itself so by essential necessity.

Up to now, has not happened, and the reasons for this omission legion. Main reason: the statement was taken too lightly. Neither Being nor apprehension was brought[15] to that clarification which would give insight into their belonging together.

The statement was taken too lightly, and "advancements" were made.

The statement was given a sense such that it was easily refuted; or it was given no sense at all, and the significance of the sentence within the work as a whole was not seen.

The idealist interpretation: all beings are posited by thinking; thinking as judging; beings are not "in themselves" but are only by virtue of

---

15. [Reading *man brachte* for *man braucht,* "one requires."—Trans.]

thinking; in opposition, the appeal to the fact that things "are," even when we are not thinking of them. This constatation is correct; yet Parmenides's statement is not thereby refuted. For the statement does not at all say that beings are thinking; on the contrary, it says Being belongs together with apprehending.

§21. Interpretation of fragments 6 and 7

a) Further clarification of the ways. The third way

Sufficient for now. We see: the statement grounds the separation of the ways. The statement thereby possesses a role of the *greatest bearing*. This is evident in the fact that it is immediately taken up again in the further clarification of the ways. For the clarification is by no means at an end. Quite to the contrary. Now D 6. |

35

D 6

> χρὴ τὸ λέγειν τε νοεῖν τ' ἐὸν ἔμμεναι· ἔστι γὰρ εἶναι,
> μηδὲν δ' οὐκ ἔστιν· τά γ' ἐγὼ φράζεσθαι ἄνωγα.
> πρώτης γάρ σ' ἀφ' ὁδοῦ ταύτης διζήσιος <εἴργω>,
> αὐτὰρ ἔπειτ' ἀπὸ τῆς, ἣν δὴ βροτοὶ εἰδότες οὐδέν
> 5 πλάττονται, δίκρανοι· ἀμηχανίη γὰρ ἐν αὐτῶν
> στήθεσιν ἰθύνει πλακτὸν νόον· οἱ δὲ φοροῦνται
> κωφοὶ ὁμῶς τυφλοί τε, τεθηπότες, ἄκριτα φῦλα,
> οἷς τὸ πέλειν τε καὶ οὐκ εἶναι ταὐτὸν νενόμισται
> κοὐ ταὐτόν, πάντων δὲ παλίντροπός ἐστι κέλευθος.

1–2) The setting down as well as the apprehending must persist to the effect that Being (the act of being [*das Seiend*] qua Being) is the "is." Nonbeing has no "it is"; by all means I command you to retain awareness of that.

3–4) Thus I first keep you away (exclude you) from this way of disclosive questioning (namely, the one altogether without prospects), but then also from the way humans, unknowledgeable humans, manifestly

5–7) forge for themselves—humans with two heads, for helplessness (ignorance of ways) aligns their errant apprehension; they are carried here and there, especially dull as well as blind, bewildered, the entire class of those who do not discriminate;

8–9) for their precept is: the present at hand and the not present at hand are the same and also not the same. This is so because in *all things* the path can be turned against itself.

D 7, 1–2

οὐ γὰρ μήποτε τοῦτο δαμῆ εἶναι μὴ ἐόντα·
ἀλλὰ σὺ τῆσδ᾽ ἀφ᾽ ὁδοῦ διζήσιος εἶργε νόημα.

For on no account will you compel together Being with nonbeings
(which properly should be *nothingness* and indeed *are not,* whereby the
attempt essentially forces Being on it). Instead, keep your apprehension far from this way of questioning.[16]

This treats of the ways: 1) the only one rich in prospects, leading to
something that can be relied on; 2) the one utterly without prospects,
leading altogether to nothingness; 3) which one?

Previously: 4, 3 and 4, 5. The one rich in prospects, the other without prospects. Thus to stay away from the latter. Yet the staying away
is not at an end. On the contrary, the goddess spoke explicitly αὐτὰρ
ἔπειτα! So a second way not to be trodden. Therefore, adding in the
one passable way to be trodden—*three* ways. What is this third (i.e.,
second impassable) way?

We see at once that this third way is depicted at length and with
more vividness than either of the previous two ways. And indeed the
characterization is carried out after the aforesaid basic assertion, the
axiomatic statement, is enjoined (χρή!!) once again.

We must briefly comment on the basic concept emerging here in
fragment 6. τὸ λέγειν (cf. below, p. 38) as "(of) Being" must remain. τὸ
ἐόν—participle of εἶναι. Obviously not just an arbitrary participle (but
(τό) (? not in the text) ἐόν a new and peculiar step. Thus a participle
in an essentially and wholly determinate respect.) Previously already
true—Homer, cf. especially *Iliad* I, 70. μετοχή (Dionysos Thrax)[17] *participium,* Notker's [archaic German] *teilnemunga* [taking part].[18] Namely:
1) with regard to the πτῶσις (*casus*) of the noun; 2) with regard to the
χρόνος (*tempus*) of the verb. E.g., shining, flying: 1) the flying thing,
the shining thing (the what in the how)—naming of the named of

---

16. Cf. 6, 3–4, πρώτης γάρ . . . (6, 3 = 4, 5) | αὐτὰρ ἔπειτα . . .

17. {*Dionysii Thracis Ars Grammatica; qualem exemplaria vetustissima exhibent sub-
scriptis discrepantiis et testimoniis quae in codicibus rexentioribus scholiis erotematis apud
alios scriptores interpretem aremenium repretiuntur.* Edidit G. Uhlig. Leipzig: Teubner,
1883, §11 (23, 1); §15 (60, 2).}

18. {The translation of *participium* as *téilnémunga* is mentioned in "Eine San-
galler Schularbeit." In *Denkmäler deutscher Poesie und Prosa. Aus dem VIII–XII Jahr-
hundert,* ed. K. Müllenhoff and W. Scherer, vol. 1, 3rd. ed. Berlin: Weidmann,
1892, 260.}

this noun: the shining thing, etc.; 2) the act of flying, of shining (the how in the what)—the shining in the shining thing. τὸ ἐόν (that as such)—the act of Being [das Seiend]—Being; cf. the immediate nexus. "There must be the saying . . . to be Being."[19]

This third way is the one humans forge (πλάττοναι) (plastic) for themselves and specifically the εἰδότες οὐδέν—in clear opposition to 1, 3 εἰδὸς φώς—from φάω—φημί?, i.e., in opposition to the knowledgeable person, singular, the individual, who knows what is at issue, who stands in the essential (to be there with νοῦς and λόγος!). Thus *not the way of humans pure and simple,* for even the first way (the only way rich in prospects) is a way of humans, but now the humans are named as they usually are and accordingly as they usually forge for themselves their way through the whole (6, 9), precisely thereby "humans." Important here to forge this out of itself, i.e., without special concern about whither and through what the way is supposed to lead. The third way, the common way of humans, set in relief against the first, the second now no longer mentioned; altogether without prospects (question: why then altogether? Only for the sake of completeness? Cf. below).

Despite the claims of interpreters, it is not at all a matter here of an insult on the part of Parmenides, derision, a disdainful critique of the unknowledgeable masses; on the contrary, Parmenides here presents an essential characterization of humans in a *very definite respect.* This essential characterization has its *necessary sharpness due to the basic position* from which it is spoken and is able to be formulated at all, i.e., due to the point of view bestowed only by the way of the goddess.—We will now simply try to summarize this characterization in its main points. The first characters already discussed—εἰδότες οὐδέν, πλάττονται.

Knowledge embraces many things: 1) I know the university closes at 6 o'clock in the evening—I have a determinate item of knowledge; 2) I know through what and how the electric current travels "of itself"—I possess an explanation for this state of affairs; 3) I know about the plight of an individual and individuals and am always prepared to help—"concern"; 4) I know "very well"—I am clear about what above all is at issue. These kinds of knowledge have their respective appropriateness, mode of verification, claim to validity, and, especially, truth.

---

19. {This entire paragraph from the margin of the manuscript page to be understood as a commentary on the first appearance of ἐόν in D 6, 1. The introductory sentence was taken from the notes of Helene Weiß.}

That humans are "unknowledgeable" does not mean they have absolutely no cognition; on the contrary, in the end they know too much about too many things. Unknowledgeable—they do not possess the *norm of essential and authentic knowledge.* δίκρανοι—two heads—their head is now there and now here, and indeed without being struck by or even suspecting this discordance. As humans, they possess νόος, i.e., the capacity to apprehend, to take in and take away, but *this* apprehension is not piloted correctly. Instead, ἀμηχανίη (cf. ἀπορίη)— helplessness, waylessness—has in their case taken over the ἰθύνειν, the basic alignment, the directionality. They lack the knowledge of ways that is necessarily presupposed in every correct entering upon and traversal of the way. They set out on their way without a knowledge of ways and let themselves be led by this lack of knowledge. Their taking in and taking away, their entire apprehension, is now like this, now like that, proceeding to and fro, without direction, at sixes and sevens—πλαγκτός—errantly they take in and apprehend! Led by ignorance of ways, they drift about in errancy (each runs after the others, each always follows the others, and no one actually knows why). They do not at some point first enter into errancy; on the contrary, they are constantly in it and never come out of it. In accord with this is now their fate (cf. 1, 26)—they are carried and cast to and fro, their words commandeered by the wind and waves that randomly toss things about. φοροῦνται.

b) The lack of the correct indication of the way

κωφοὶ ὁμῶς τυφλοί τε—κωφός, dull, altogether dull in sense, although here not applied to the senses in general, but restricted, since indeed blindness is expressly named as the dullness of eyesight and seeing. κωφός here to be related to hearing and speaking (cf. later, ὀνομάζειν— γλῶσσα). But what is actually meant? Of course this does not intend to say that all people are deaf and mute and blind, i.e., that the sensory organs are disturbed in their functioning. On the contrary, people see very well and hear and speak; but they see and yet do not see, hear and yet do not hear, speak and yet say nothing. Apprehension as taking in and being taken in and being taken out of—not the correct νόος— ap-prehension—Being! Understanding of Being. | 36

Moreover, this precisely *because* the correct indication of the way of apprehension is lacking to humans in advance. This apprehension, however, as we already know, is originally νοεῖν of εἶναι—understanding of Being. Their understanding of Being is errant (νόος πλαγκτός), erroneous, not simply false, but, as errant in a much more fatal way, it does not come to a standstill (cf. below, 6, 8–9), is haphazard, accidental (not grasped and a fortiori not conceptualized) and above all not as such experienced and seized, but always only alights now on this being, now on that. Humans see beings and hear about them, speak about them, but all this remains dull, without the sharpness of the penetration into the essence; the entire comportment of these humans proceeds and staggers only alongside beings, as it were, external to them.

So it is with everything that comes to these people, and everything does come into their hands, even philosophy. There they merely slurp up impressions and believe they are philosophizing when they fancy themselves stirred and meditative and talk about existence—but make themselves scarce when the work begins.

τεθηπότες—bewildered. The diverse manifold they stumble across in this more-or-less-satisfying frenzy enthralls them, surprises them, tempts them from one thing to another—but they remain with any one thing only for a fleeting moment, and then they bounce to something else, for they lack the sight of the essence and Being of things. Therefore, these humans cannot be detained by anything, they cannot sustain anything, and they cannot attain the tranquilly persistent restraint of wonder, the constancy of meditation, or the keen air of steadfast questioning. On the contrary, all that remains for them is erratic surprise and desultory bewilderment—they merely find things "interesting."

ἄκριτα φῦλα—τὸ φῦλον, phylum, class, consanguinity, all those of the same provenance as regards their way of thinking, the plural of those in the same category to whom is lacking κρίνειν, judgment, discrimination. They throw everything into the same pot, even if the only commonality among the things is the extrinsic one of bearing the same name or label and of agreeing with one another only to the most fleeting glance. Since these persons do not judge and discriminate, they can also not choose, not differentiate according to might and rank; therefore, they also lack the possibility of decision and decisiveness. Instead, they let themselves be borne here and there as the wind blows. All this lies in the words κρίνειν and ἄκριτον. The class of those who do not divide, discriminate, differentiate (choose), decide. It is not that they simply fail to do these things on occasion; quite to the contrary, here is, so to speak, the inner law of the class.

c) The lack of the understanding of Being

In our interpretation of the πλαγκτὸς νόος (6, 6), we already indicated how the dullness and the directionless to and fro of human comportment have their ground in the fact that humans lack the necessary prior knowledge of ways, *lack the required understanding of Being*. That is now explicitly stated at 6, 8–9, and we are shown which understanding of Being guides these people. It is not a consequence of their dull sense, but the reverse: the dullness is grounded in their peculiar understanding of Being. That is now finally adduced, because the understanding of Being constitutes the *essential ground* of this entire manner of being a human, or of distorting humanity, and because the entire characterization of the third way is polarized precisely around that understanding. οἷς τὸ πέλειν . . . νενόμισται—they have *in advance posited it as a law* for themselves, with the connotation that this positing is not well grounded in the matters but is merely held to be so—presumably the law—νομίζειν like δοξάζειν. Then to what do they hold fast in all their comportment to beings? How do these people understand Being? Answer:

To them the present at hand and the οὐκ—not μή—not present at hand are the same and not the same. What is that supposed to mean? The word πέλειν primarily means step forth, loom up, appear to, and signifies presence at hand, emergence (cf. Homer *Odyssey*, XIII, 60: γῆρας καὶ θάνατος τά τ᾽ ἐπ᾽ ἀνθρώποισι πέλονται[20]—are present to, do not simply appear there, but always are *among the present, essentially occur along with*). πέλειν also means become, step forth, come forth—τε καὶ οὐκ—not full nonbeing—μή, instead, not step *forth*, its opposite, step back, disappear, vanish. Stepping back—also likewise Being.

What is thus expressed in the οἷς . . . νενόμισται: this class characteristically adheres to the stepping-forth and stepping-back of things, to change and alteration. For what do the changing things show? E.g., the changing coloration of the sea or the mountains: in changing, the color is such and already also not such, and is not such and already again such.[21] The changing thing is both: *suchness and non-suchness* are the *same*. Yet in change and alteration always a becoming different, for in transformation, precisely where suchness and non-suchness are the same, we say at once and with equal justification, as a consequence of the transformation, that the current suchness is different than the previous one—they are *not* the same. Humans then waver between Being and nonbeing, to humans these are the same and not the same. Indeed, humans have some understanding of Being and nonbeing, of sameness and non-sameness, or else they could not even waver;

---

20. {*Homeri Odyssea*. Edidit G. Dindorf. Editio quinta correctior quam curavit C. Hentze. Leipzig: Teubner, 1904.}

21. (Ontologically the same) I ontically—different?—in change, Being and nonbeing, *suchness and non-suchness, are together*—(belonging to the *same*?)

but they do not have these in an understanding that conceptualizes or even clearly grasps. Humans do not know what they are wavering between—their understanding of Being is a non-understanding.

Parmenides is not trying to say that those of the ἄκριτα φῦλα would themselves be aware of this characterization and formulation of their understanding of Being; on the contrary, it is his own interpretation, one whose execution already presupposes quite determinate insights. But this interpretation of the common understanding of Being as a non-understanding of Being is consciously put forth here, because the task is precisely not simply to portray, and a fortiori not to mock, the doings of the multitude. On the contrary, the aim is to acquire and to express in advance an *essential insight* into what sort of way the multitude forged for itself here. This way, which stands under such a νόμος, leads to experiencing exclusively that which is changing, playing out, stepping forth and stepping back.

This way is finally characterized in a summary: πάντων δὲ παλίντροπός ἐστι κέλευθος—in *everything,* wherever the way leads, it turns out that things are at once not what they just were and that therefore the way must ever again turn back in the opposite direction—turning ever again (πάλιν—again; τρέπω—around, against, counter; πάντων— through and through; (the semblance of the ἕν)) and indeed the way is otherwise only repeated, renewed, and is so without direction— counter—in the opposite direction. It is the way of an essential to and fro between suchness and non-suchness, between selfsameness and non-selfsameness. The *ever-turning* way that is precisely the *appropri-* 37   *ate path* in *errancy.* |

d) The three ways in their interrelatedness

The third way has this in common with the first (the only one rich in prospects, the only one actually to be traveled), namely, that in distinction to the second (which is utterly without prospects and leads to nothingness), the third way does indeed lead to something.[22] Therefore in every case it is not without prospects; it bestows some sort of outlook, namely, the outlook upon that which changes, that which alters. The view that makes up δόξα—opinion. Yet the third way, in common with the second, is prohibited by the goddess. Indeed, because of the particular character of the third, the prohibition must become an *actual warning.* The second forbids itself by itself, since it leads to nothingness and therefore stops even as it begins. The third way, however, offers a certain prospect, precisely the one the crowd of hu-

---

22. The third has something in common with both the other two ways, but respectively different relations. Therefore especially distinguished.

mans spontaneously pursues and clings to. This prospect entices and captivates. Yet let us understand the warning in the face of the third way correctly, i.e., not merely as a restraint. The warning provides information about the *essence* of this way, and the insight into the essence of this way and into the essence of the prospect offered by this third way is supposed to be explicitly appropriated. To refrain from this way as such means precisely to have insight into the ground for its being impassable. The appropriation of this insight thus necessarily belongs to the meditation on ways with which the journey on the way of the goddess commences.

We can only now understand the goddess's words declaring that Parmenides should experience everything, cf. 1, 28. Everything—unconcealment just as much (ἠμέν) as also (ἠδέ) the βροτῶν δόξας (1, 30), which is precisely the third way, the only one, along with the first, that offers any prospects. Yet there is no reliance on the views presented by the third way, for in each case they concern something that is such and is not such, something changing and unstable. But what Parmenides is supposed to experience is precisely the third way itself, i.e., *not* the changing and inconsistent *vastness* of individual human views. The goddess of unconcealment leads him only to unconcealment, and it is precisely unconcealment as the essence of this third way that he is to experience, as was said above: not the individual changing views of human beings but, instead, the essence of a human view as such (cf. 1, 31–32). Indeed still more, but the necessity of δόξα, thus the necessity of the third way, is supposed to become clear.

The first way, which alone is properly rich in prospects and which offers the entire wealth and pure fullness of Being, would not be understood as such and would also not be the one to travel on if the essential affiliation of the third way to the first were not grasped in unity with the first. Yet something is still missing for the clarification of the ways, namely, the very way spoken of right at the beginning: the way *to* the goddess. Neither itself—nor the second, nor the third, but instead: out from the crowd. From the third to the first! Therefore, no first without the third, although that is not dealt with further. *Consequently, four ways.* Third way: δόξα, 6, 4 = 1, 30. Second way: παναπειθὴς ἀταρπός, 6, 3 = 4, 5. First way: ἀλήθεια, πειθώ, 1, 29 = 4, 3. Fourth way: 1, 1. Thus, we need to note where Parmenides is coming from as a knowledgeable man when he makes the decision to set out for the gate of the dwelling of the goddess. As this single knowledgeable man, he *steps out, detaches himself, from the crowd,* from those who do not discriminate and do not decide. He leaves the παλίντροπος κέλευθος, 6, 9, the ever-turning path and seeks the Πειθοῦς κέλευθος,

4, 4, where confidence and reliance can be grounded. Nevertheless, he remains φώς, a man, and *does not become a god.* He remains in the crowd and yet is not a slave to the crowd. He walks and resides among the crowd and participates in the affairs of the crowd, and yet, without the crowd seeing it, he travels the only way rich in prospects. But he travels this way with certainty only if he has fixed his eyes on all possible ways in their essence. He travels with certainty among the errant ones, himself errant, only if he has intuited the *essence of errancy* and by means of this intuition has mastery *in advance.* Therefore, the entire weight of the meditation rests on the insight into the essence of the third way, because this way, despite the prospects it constantly offers anew, is nevertheless not to be taken, *assuming human beings in the course they follow are precisely supposed to rely on something.*

Accordingly, D 7, 1 follows immediately upon D 6. "For on no account will you compel together Being with nonbeings." The word here is ἐόντα, not ἐόν, Being, and these ἐόντα, these beings, which pass as what "is" and yet are *properly not so,* should basically not count as ἐόν. They should count as nothingness, and *yet they are not entirely this;* hence the hopeless attempt to compel Being onto them. Basically and literally, cf. D 7, 1: δαμῇ—δαμάζω—"conquer," especially said of a man who compels a maiden to be subject to him. Being is not to be compelled onto these null beings, not to be attributed to them. They are never to be set down as what properly is and therefore nothing can be grounded on them, instead . . . keep far away . . . your νόημα.

This latter word, as in Homer, does not here yet possess the meaning of the apprehended, the content and object of an apprehension; but understanding, comprehending (νοεῖν) as it proceeds along this way does not acquire that which alone is *compelled together necessarily* with νοεῖν, namely, εἶναι, Being.

e) Conclusion of the preparatory meditation
on the possible and impossible ways

This final, deepest grounding of the impassability of the third way is connected once again to the decisive warning, which then follows at 1, 34–37. This concludes the preparatory meditation on the possible and impossible ways and on their essence. That meditation leads immediately to the traversal of the first way (cf. 7, 2 = 1, 33).

D 1, 34–37

ἀλλὰ σὺ τῆσδ᾽ ἀφ᾽ ὁδοῦ διζήσιος εἶργε νόημα
μηδέ σ᾽ ἔθος πολύπειρον ὁδὸν κατὰ τήνδε βιάσθω,
35   νωμᾶν ἄσκοπον ὄμμα καὶ ἠχήεσσαν ἀκουήν

καὶ γλῶσσαν, κρῖναι δὲ λόγῳ πολύδηριν ἔλεγχον
ἐξ ἐμέθεν ῥηθέντα. μόνος δ' ἔτι θυμὸς ὁδοῖο
λείπεται . . .

[33 = 7, 2. See above.]
34) and by no means should much-fissured custom compel you in the
   direction of this way,
35–36) so as ever to employ circumspective seeing and noise-filled
   hearing and idle talk; instead, discriminate and set down before
   yourself the demonstration of the multifarious conflict,
37) the demonstration expounded by me.[23]

Only on the basis of 6 and 7 do we know of a third way, against which
a warning must be issued, and on the basis of 4 and 5 we understand
the justification and necessity of the warning; without this (4–7), lines
1, 34–37 are not at all intelligible and (versus Sextus) can therefore
not follow 1, 30. On the contrary, what we have here is the conclusion to the preparatory meditation on ways.

Here the way of the crowd of those who do not discriminate is once
again placed before our eyes, and a new essential moment is carried
through. βιάσθω—a certain βία, not arbitrary whims but *force and compulsion* to this way of δόξα—a *peculiar sort of necessity*. ἔθος πολύπειρον—
just as humans at first are preoccupied with appearances and run after them, so this constant preoccupation is ameliorated because it will
thereby undo itself: breaking the preoccupation with custom. To take
things in the customary way, however, means above all to have eyes
and ears for what is run-of-the-mill, what is of great variety, and re-
curs in the most banal variations, such that custom can prove itself at
any time in many ways and can persuade people. | 38

Again we see how in this comportment the senses—eye, ear, tongue—
are without the proper piloting and directionality that would be sup-
plied by a correct understanding of Being. People see very well, and
indeed circumspectively; they hear, but their ears are full of noise;
every person speaks of something different, and *in the end* it is simply
the one who *speaks loudest that prevails*.[24]

Explicitly named here is the tongue, its prominence in the sense of
endless prattle (cf. κωφοί—6, 7).

---

23. [Remainder of lines 37–38, μόνος . . . λείπεται, not translated here. = D 8,
1–2 below, except the text there has μῦθος in place of θυμός. Discussed by Heidegger
in §22b.—Trans.]

24. νωμάω, νέμω, νομίζω. 6, 8—agree, acknowledge.

In deliberate and very sharp opposition to γλῶσσα stands λόγος, indeed in the closest connection with κρίνειν, precisely the comportment that distinguishes the knowledgeable individual from the unknowledgeable crowd. But it is said here that Parmenides must discriminate, distinguish, and decide with regard to the exhibited ways, something the ἄκριτα φῦλα cannot do. And this discrimination must be λόγῳ. λέγειν is gleaning, gathering, bringing together *into unity* and thus setting down before oneself and giving a fixed position. What is primarily essential for λέγειν is not the word as linguistic utterance but, instead, the *type of inner comportment* in the use of words, whether we apprehend words and by following them along, parroting them, manage to know something and test and secure this knowledge by appeal to the words, or whether we from our own resources accost the things, gather together the dispersed and accidental, set it down before ourselves, and on the basis of this comportment now first address what has been set down and by ourselves give it a *fixed stamp, give it up*.

Between these two there is now the third possibility, which Parmenides calls γλῶσσα and which will later be described more fully, namely, prattle, which in one respect listens in on idle talk but at the same time in a certain way also, again without a substantive understanding of Being, of itself introduces matters and states of affairs and their differentiations. γλῶσσα—the tongue—not as a thing-like, corporeal organ, but the *opening* (cf. ὄμμα—eye), i.e., the tongue industriously wagging.

In contrast, λόγος and λέγειν belong to the comportment of the *first* way, on which the proper understanding, νοεῖν, of Being is acquired.[25] And that is the reason we have already encountered λέγειν (D 6, 1): χρὴ τὸ λέγειν τε νοεῖν τ'ἐὸν ἔμμεναι. The apprehension of Being is an understanding of Being that *thoroughly discusses in the manner of setting down* and *so seizes* and comprehends Being on the way to *conceptualizing Being*.

The goddess now names the meditation on ways that she has presented to Parmenides: ἔλεγχον πολύδηριν—ἐλέγχειν primarily means to disgrace someone, put someone to shame, unmask someone; from there, show someone up in public, let be seen—ἀποφαίνεσθαι, uncover, exhibit. What was just now mentioned is the exhibition of the essence of the three ways: the first way is unavoidable, the second is inaccessible, the third is accessible but is to be *avoided*, wherein already lie the constantly affiliated *passability, unavoidability, and inaccessibility*.

---

25. Appendix on λόγος *and* λέγειν for Heraclitus.—Basic regarding λόγος: saying—assertion, proposition—judgment—"logic."

The exhibition is πολύδηρις—δῆρις, strife, battle, contest (Heraclitus) because controversial.

Not as if the goddess and what she says are controversial or doubtful in themselves; nor of course are they so for her. What was exhibited is multifariously conflicted only for the one who is supposed to discriminate and decide. He must make his way through the multifarious distinctions and conflicts and must do so *from his own resources.* He, and indeed no one, can be relieved of that. Only the one who here rightly decides also immediately implants in himself θυμός—that disposition (1, 1) by which he desires in advance to proceed along the only way rich in prospects; he arrives on this way only if he has previously brought himself to the gate of the ways of night and day (1, 11).

§22. Interpretation of fragment 8

a) Traveling on the first way

All this has now happened, and there commences presently the actual traveling on the first way, which means the task is to grasp and exhaust the entire prospect offered by this way, that which is visible while underway on this way.

Meditation on the ways through and from ἀλήθεια: thus not to be grasped as a precursory and empty deliberation, but itself already a following of the ways, a traveling on them (cf. later, regarding "circle"). Everywhere the step already taken: νοεῖν—Being; nothingness—?; semblance—δόξα.

In the presentation, the meditation is, as it were, turned back to a position prior to and outside of all ways, but humans, insofar as they are, are already *underway* toward Being *and* involved in semblance and constantly beyond nothingness, and they can disclose only what is *bestowed* on them.

D 8, 1–33

> μοῦνος δ᾽ ἔτι μῦθος ὁδοῖο
> λείπεται ὡς ἔστιν· ταύτῃ δ᾽ ἐπὶ σήματ᾽ ἔασι
> πολλὰ μάλ᾽, ὡς ἀγένητον ἐὸν καὶ ἀνώλεθρόν ἐστιν
> οὖλον μουνογενές τε καὶ ἀτρεμὲς ἠδ᾽ ἀτέλεστον·
> 5   οὐδέ ποτ᾽ ἦν οὐδ᾽ ἔσται, ἐπεὶ νῦν ἔστιν ὁμοῦ πᾶν,
> ἕν, συνεχές· τίνα γὰρ γένναν διζήσεαι αὐτοῦ;
> πῇ πόθεν αὐξηθέν; οὔτ᾽ ἐκ μὴ ἐόντος ἐασέω
> φάσθαι σ(ε) οὐδὲ νοεῖν· οὐ γὰρ φατὸν οὐδὲ νοητόν
> ἔστιν ὅπως οὐκ ἔστι. τί δ᾽ ἄν μιν καὶ χρέος ὦρσεν

10 ὕστερον ἦν πρόσθεν τοῦ μηδενὸς ἀρξάμενον φῦν;
    οὕτως ἢ πάμπαν πέλεναι χρεών ἐστιν ἢ οὐχί.
    οὐδέ ποτ᾽ ἐκ μὴ ὄντος ἐφήσει πίστιος ἰσχύς
    γίγνεσθαί τι παρ᾽ αὐτό· τοῦ εἵνεκεν οὔτε γενέσθαι
    οὔτ᾽ ὄλλυσθαι ἀνῆκε δίκη χαλάσασα πέδησιν,
15 ἀλλ᾽ ἔχει· ἡ δὲ κρίσις περὶ τούτων ἐν τῷδ᾽ ἔστιν·
    ἔστιν ἢ οὐκ ἔστιν· κέκριται δ᾽ οὖν, ὥσπερ ἀνάγκη,
    τὴν μὲν ἐᾶν ἀνόητον ἀνώνυμον (οὐ γὰρ ἀληθής
    ἔστιν ὁδός), τὴν δ᾽ ὥστε πέλειν καὶ ἐτήτυμον εἶναι.
    πῶς δ᾽ ἂν ἔπειτα πέλοι τὸ ἐόν; πῶς δ᾽ ἄν κε γένοιτο;
20 εἰ γὰρ ἔγεντ᾽, οὐκ ἔστ(ι), οὐδ᾽ εἴ ποτε μέλλει ἔσεσθαι.
    τὼς γένεσις μὲν ἀπέσβεσται καὶ ἄπυστος ὄλεθρος.
    οὐδὲ διαιρετόν ἐστιν, ἐπεὶ πᾶν ἐστιν ὁμοῖον·
    οὐδέ τι τῇ μᾶλλον, τό κεν εἴργοι μιν συνέχεσθαι
    οὐδέ τι χειρότερον, πᾶν δ᾽ ἔμπλεόν ἐστιν ἐόντος.
25 τῷ ξυνεχὲς πᾶν ἐστιν· ἐὸν γὰρ ἐόντι πελάζει.
    αὐτὰρ ἀκίνητον μεγάλων ἐν πείρασι δεσμῶν
    ἔστιν ἄναρχον ἄπαυστον, ἐπεὶ γένεσις καὶ ὄλεθρος
    τῆλε μάλ᾽ ἐπλάχθησαν, ἀπῶσε δὲ πίστις ἀληθής.
    ταὐτόν τ᾽ ἐν ταὐτῷ τε μένον καθ᾽ ἑαυτό τε κεῖται
30 χοὕτως ἔμπεδον αὖθι μένει· κρατερὴ γὰρ ἀνάγκη
    πείρατος ἐν δεσμοῖσιν ἔχει, τό μιν ἀμφὶς ἐέργει.
    οὕνεκεν οὐκ ἀτελεύτητον τὸ ἐὸν θέμις εἶναι·
    ἔστι γὰρ οὐκ ἐπιδευές, (μὴ) ἐὸν δ᾽ ἄν παντὸς ἐδεῖτο.

1–2) But uniquely still the contemplation (cf. above) (contemplative breakthrough) (manifestation) of the way (cf. 1, 37) remains (on which is to be seen) how matters stand with Being; on this (way) there is[26]

3–4) indeed much that shows itself: how Being without a rising and without a setting, whole, alone there, as well (in itself) not stirring as also not at all first needing to be finished (πῆ),

5) it was not formerly, and it will not be at some future time, for as present it "is" all at once

6–9) unitary—cohering—for which origin for it (for Being) could be disclosed in questioning? But how, whence, any supplement? Neither can I allow (οὔτε) (8, 12, grounding) you to say, nor to apprehend, out of nothingness; for neither sayable nor unsayable how the "is" (Being) could remain null. What concern is supposed to have impelled it

---

26. Cf. s.s. 35. {Heidegger, *Einführung in die Metaphysik,* op. cit., 117ff.}

10–11) later or earlier to emerge if commencing with this nothingness? (involve itself and so) Therefore it must either be altogether
permanent or not at all.

12–14) . . . *nor* (cf. line 7) will the power of reliance (on the essence
of Being) ever grant that out of a sort of "Being" (a being of some
sort) anything could break forth besides such (only thus "is" *in addition* something like a being at all); on account of this I has Compliance (Dikē) released neither arising nor perishing (into Being)—by
loosening (so to speak) the fetters[27]

15) instead she "*holds*" it fast[28] I . . . Simplicius!

16–21) Either Being or nothingness has sovereignty. Yet it is now decided how by necessity the *one* way is to be abandoned as unappre-
hendable and unnameable. It is not the one of unconcealment, and
the *other* is to be traveled as the way that actually persists. But how
could Being have a future? How then also a past?

20–21) For if it (previously) *was*, it *is* not,[29] (that also not) if it is first
supposed to be at some time in the future. Thus is (for Being) emergence extinguished and perishing not to be found.

22–25) Also there is no taking it apart, for it is entirely the same with
itself.

23–24) Also there is no supplement that (coming to it in addition)
would prevent its cohering (density), nor a privation (in the sense
of gaps = holes); for it is entirely full (Being only) of Being.

25) Throughout its coherence it is whole, for Being (only) comes near
to Being.[30]

26–33) While (immovably) to motion (change) it is far away in the
bounds of powerful fetters, without starting, without stopping, for
rising and setting have been driven far away; reliance on the unconcealed drove them away.[31]

29) Remaining the same in the same, it *rests* in itself.

30–31) And thus it abides steadfastly in that very spot, for powerful
compulsion *has* it in the fetters of the boundary that encloses it
round about.

39 (margin)

---

27. *Noncompliance*—to take on *contours*—I limits I—appearance—I cf., however, 8, 42—πεῖρας πύματον precisely not over and against another being which
again is "null"!

28. Compliance is a *holding.*

29. Here "is" means only the pure present.

30. Everything negative is driven far away, cf. 8, 28.

31. The genuine apprehension—νοεῖν I the imaginative projection both a casting away and a *driving away.*

32–33) On account of that is the precept that Being is not (first) in-completable. Since nothing is lacking to it; otherwise, it would be deprived of everything.[32]

D 2

Λεῦσσε δ᾽ ὅμως ἀπεόντα νόῳ παρεόντα βεβαίως·
οὐ γὰρ ἀποτμήξει τὸ ἐὸν τοῦ ἐόντος ἔχεσθαι
οὔτε σκιδνάμενον πάντῃ πάντως κατὰ κόσμον
οὔτε συνιστάμενον.

Yet just behold how what was previously absent has steadfast presence for apprehension, since (no apprehension) can cut up the coherence of Being = Being, neither to a bestrewal everywhere throughout the whole world nor to a standing side by side.[33]

D 8, 34–51

    ταὐτὸν δ᾽ ἐστὶ νοεῖν τε καὶ οὕνεκέν ἐστι νόημα.
35   οὐ γὰρ ἄνευ τοῦ ἐόντος, ἐν ᾧ πεφατισμένον ἐστίν,
    εὑρήσεις τὸ νοεῖν· οὐδὲν γὰρ <ἢ> ἔστιν ἢ ἔσται
    ἄλλο πάρεξ τοῦ ἐόντος, ἐπεὶ τό γε μοῖρ᾽ ἐπέδησεν
    οὖλον ἀκίνητόν τ᾽ ἔμεναι· τῷ πάντ᾽ ὄνομ(α) ἔσται
    ὅσσα βροτοὶ κατέθεντο πεποιθότες εἶναι ἀληθῆ,
40   γίγνεσθαί τε καὶ ὄλλυσθαι, εἶναί τε καὶ οὐχί,
    καὶ τόπον ἀλλάσσειν διά τε χρόα φανὸν ἀμείβειν.
    αὐτὰρ ἐπεὶ πεῖρας πύματον, τετελεσμένον ἐστί,
    πάντοθεν εὐκύκλου σφαίρης ἐναλίγκιον ὄγκῳ,
    μεσσόθεν ἰσοπαλὲς πάντῃ· τὸ γὰρ οὔτε τι μεῖζον
45   οὔτε τι βαιότερον πέλεναι χρεόν ἐστι τῇ ἢ τῇ.
    οὔτε γὰρ οὔτεον ἔστι, τό κεν παύοι μιν ἱκνεῖσθαι
    εἰς ὁμόν, οὔτ᾽ ἐὸν ἔστιν ὅπως εἴη κεν ἐόντος
    τῇ μᾶλλον τῇ δ᾽ ἧσσον, ἐπεὶ πᾶν ἐστιν ἄσυλον·
    οἷ γὰρ πάντοθεν ἶσον, ὁμῶς ἐν πείρασι κύρει.

50   Ἐν τῷ σοι παύω πιστὸν λόγον ἠδὲ νόημα
    ἀμφὶς ἀληθείης·

34) But apprehension and that for the sake of which there is appre-hension are the same.

35–36) For not without Being, in which (that) is pronounced, will you disclosively question apprehension; for neither was, nor is, nor will be anything outside of and next to Being.

---

32. It would altogether not be—if it harbored even the least *"not."*
33. Cf. *p. 40, section b.*

37–51) . . . —since therefore destiny has fettered it into something whole and without motion, and so there remains for it only the name. All that humans have postulated, thinking it is the uncon-
cealed. | 40
40–42) Arising as well as setting, suchness especially and non-suchness (cf. 6, 8f.), change of place, and change of surface in the light.[34]
42–45) Since here the *boundary* is the outermost, it (Being) is ter-minated, encompassed with ends, the same in all directions, the (dense) mass of a well-rounded sphere—from the middle outward everywhere equally strong; for neither in any way more powerful nor more weak can it be here or there.
46–48) For *neither* is there nothingness, which would hinder it from attaining its self-sameness, *nor* is there a being which here or there could have more or less of Being. For it is wholly without articu-lation.
49) So then the same in all directions, it rests uniformly in its bound-aries.
50–51) With this, I end my grounded speaking and apprehending of the unconcealed.

{ . . . }[35]

For the sake of the reliability and significance of the interpretation of this fragment 8, we must note that it is handed down only en bloc by Simplicius in his commentary on Aristotle's *Physics* A 3, 187a1. Cf. Diels's edition, p. 145f.[36]

Our interpolation, between 8, 33 and 34, of Diels's fragment no. 2 is not meant as an alteration of the text found in Simplicius. Frag-ment 2 is transmitted by Clemens Alexandrinus, but with regard to content, it belongs within the context of the questioning at issue in fragment 8. Indeed, it provides a decisive clarification of the leading question there. Accordingly, we take fragment 2 as Parmenides's own commentary on that part of his own text. Where it was actually situ-ated can no longer be ascertained.

Our translation already introduces paragraphs, thereby foisting onto the text an extrinsic articulation, one that must be grounded in what is presented in the text itself. That requires bringing ourselves closer to the inner structure of what is said there. The further ques-tion will be whether and to what extent the matter requires such a

---

34. To be intuited.
35. {Two illegible words}
36. {*Simplicii in Aristotelis Physicorum libros quattuor priores commentaria,* op. cit.}

structure. What matter is at issue here? To be sure, we know that already in advance, even if only very generally.

b) The manifestation undertaken by the goddess Ἀλήθεια

Lines 1–3 uniquely still remain—λείπεται—the way of truth; for we must be warned, and are warned, from the other two ways. This one *remains*—the one *to be traveled*. According to the directive sense of ὁδός, or θυμός, to travel this way means to bring into view the prospect offered by the way, to examine what is evident there. λείπεται μῦθος ὁδοῖο—there remains the manifestation of the way—does μῦθος first stand here in opposition to λόγος? μῦθος—the differently proclaimed true word, the merely accepted word. λόγος—the word freely spoken in accosting the things on one's own. Also, was not precisely the priority of λόγος just now emphasized (κρῖναι δὲ λόγῳ—λέγειν—νοεῖν and ff.)? Thus here a proclamation that needs to be interpreted. The opposite of all philosophy dubious; and so here [i.e., at 1, 37] θυμός. But μῦθος does not need to mean proclamation [*Verkündigung*], in the sense of divine revelation, something merely to be accepted, something not understood and not understandable. It can also mean manifestation [*Kündung*]. In this sense, the goddess manifests the way, makes known the prospect offered by the way.

Yet are not these the same? Divine accomplishment or divine assistance—are not both precisely not the human being relying on his own resources? These questions are justified, but only as long as we are not clear about which goddess is here doing the manifesting.[37] Ἀλήθεια, Unconcealedness, precisely the goddess who allows the unconcealed to show itself as such. A remarkable goddess. She does not force anything but, instead, leads, precisely as herself, to the place where the one who is led must set himself (κρίνειν) on his own resources in order to satisfy the goddess's lead. The goddess leads by *liberating*, by thrusting one into the *open realm*. The manifesting she undertakes is thus quite peculiar. It is that μῦθος whose understanding requires precisely λόγος and *only* λόγος.

The goddess can be relied on—not on account of some sort of inspiration or any other testimony or submissiveness, but on account of the unconcealed as such and its free appropriation.

Why then speak here of a *goddess* at all? Answer: in order to present and make clear the unusualness and sublimity of this way, that it requires a deliberate *turning away* from the common crowd and a unique *turning toward* a traveling apart. This way demands the high-

---

37. Not one of the gods or goddesses seeks—Zeus, Apollo, | Athena |.

est and most eminent piloting, full free clarity about the way, radical meditation on method.[38]

Therefore, the μῦθος ὁδοῖο does not at all lead back into the mythical—just the opposite. No occasion to alter the passage in accord with 1, 37. But also not the converse [i.e., no need to alter 1, 37 in accord with 8, 1]; θυμός also [i.e., as well as μῦθος] provides a good context. Over and against the distractedness and aimlessness of the crowd, there remains now only the closed, intrinsically aligned contemplation demanded by the way that shows how matters stand with Being. If both passages (1, 37 and 8, 1) are the same, then both transmissions of the text are justified; if they are not the same, then the transmissions are justified a fortiori.

It is now said of this way: σήματα πολλὰ μάλα—much shows itself— σήματα are determinations of the way,[39] specifically insofar as it offers prospects. It is indeed rich in prospects, the only one rich in prospects. Thus the σήματα are not pointers toward the way, nor properties of Being, but are *prospects onto this*—onto Being—respects in which Being becomes clearly seen. |

To travel the way of the goddess means to bring into view the unconcealed, that which shows itself of itself, in all the respects offered there. The task is thus to see *Being* clearly. Nothing else is meant by putting into effect the first way, the only one rich in prospects. Yet what sort of seeing is this in which Being is supposed to come into view? We know of it already—cf. D 5 and 4 inclusive. Seeing—it is already called fixing the eyes on, taking into view—νοεῖν. Only νοεῖν and λέγειν (the apprehension that sets down and thoroughly discusses) allow grasping, conceptual understanding. To transform the indeterminate and unfamiliar understanding of Being into a conceptualizing of Being—that is questioning into the concept of Being.

c) The σήματα of Being

α) the character of the enumeration

At 8, 3–6, the σήματα are enumerated, the prospects on Being, ἐόν, the respects to be pursued so that understanding will explicitly begin, i.e., a grasp of how matters stand with Being, what is to be maintained about Being. Through the ὡς ἀγένητον . . . ἐστιν—at the same time, this provides evidence for our earlier interpretation of 4, 3 and

41

---

38. Yet thereby the essential regarding ἀλήθεια and the divine is still not attained.

39. ταύτῃ ἐπί—not ἐόν!

4, 5. ἡ μέν—ὡς ἔστιν = ὡς ἐὸν ἐστιν. τὸ ἐόν, a being with respect to its Being—is. Always asked thereby: how do matters stand with Being? At first we simply encounter an enumeration: ἀ-γένετον—ἀν-ώλεθ-ρον—ἀ-τρεμές—ἀ-τέλεστον, οὐδ᾽ ἦν—οὐδ᾽ ἔσται; further: οὖλον—μουνογενής—νῦν ὁμοῦ πᾶν—ἕν—συνεχές. The enumeration not in the order of the text, but divided into two groups of respects. The first group comprises respects with ἀ- or οὐδέ—without rising, without setting, "without" or "not even"; in linguistic form, negative expressions. It could be deduced that Parmenides is here referring back to something, he is contradicting someone, carrying on a polemic, and the adversary is not far to seek: Heraclitus. Certainly, the latter would be an adversary, and battling him would be worthwhile and not a mere polemic; but the question is whether Parmenides's whole work is designed merely to be a confrontation with other philosophers or whether everything is not rather presented with a *positive* intent, such that these negative expressions then take on a quite different meaning. We need to see that they are necessary and how so.

β) The first group, the negative σήματα

Let us first examine what is denied here, how the negation itself is to be understood, and why negative expressions occur here at all; cf. p. 43. Being is without γένεσις and (ὁ) ὄλεθρος, rising and setting—cf. above, Anaximander: φθορά. There we said to think not of causal development, coming to be, and passing away, but of emergence and disappearance; so in that sense we also need to take rising and setting (cf. the sun). Being is without τρέμειν, without trembling. Homer (*Iliad*, XIII, 19) speaks, for example, of the trembling of the mountains and forests under the tread of Poseidon (earth tremor). The movement to and fro of something that nevertheless remains in its place, such as the fluttering of a robe (by transference then quivering—as quivering in . . . to be in fear)—that is what is denied here. Cf. above, 1, 29, the goddess Ἀλήθεια—ἀτρεμὲς ἦτορ—unquaking, in the sense of untrembling, entirely self-resting, unwavering, without the to and fro of errancy, strict clarity, entirely *from the inside* self-consistent (why?), for only in that way can the goddess be attended by Πειθώ, Reliance. Unconcealedness does not waver, cannot waver, precisely because that of which it is unconcealedness, namely, Being, is as such ἀ-τρεμές.[40]

Furthermore, Being is ἀ-τέλεστον. Already in antiquity this word caused interpreters difficulties, which were avoided by equating the word with ἀν-ώλεθρον, taken to mean "imperishable," thus in the sense

---

40. Precisely *"trembling"*—to and fro—Higher present— ← which *at the same time disappears* → nexus.

of the ever and ever, and correspondingly ἀ-τέλεστον is "without end," and Diels also takes it that way. But we must immediately note: in such a clearly articulated and essential enumeration of the respects in which Being is to be regarded, the same respect cannot simply be cited twice, and that is the only way the interpreters would be relieved of their difficulties. Moreover, the word ἀτέλεστον is again employed in the didactic poem, at 8, 32: ἀτελεύτητον.

What does it mean now? τελέω—τελευτάω, "to bring to an end." End, but not that at which something merely stops, desists, but end (positively—| finished—| closed)—finishing off. ἀ-—Being is *without* this. It does not mean Being is never finished, is endless but, instead, is such that something like first needing to be finished, produced, must remain altogether foreign to it. Being is indeed constantly treated below as in advance struck within fixed boundaries; therefore quite nonsensical to translate ἀτέλεστον as "endless." What is denied here is production, finishing off; not that Being would then remain unfinished, but that Being repels the entire realm of production and manufacture, because it is "finished" right from the start (not first to be manufactured—not first unfinished). The other two negations with οὐδέ—"not even"—ποτ᾽ ἦν—οὐδ᾽ἔσται. The ποτέ here in both cases has a double meaning: like our "not"; formerly and in the future (at some time to come). Being remains without the alteration of past and future, outside of these.

Let us again survey the negations: without emergence, disappearance, trembling, production, temporal change. In short: without any to and fro, from-to, without any passage from one thing to another, without transition, i.e., *without becoming.* These negations exclude from Being all becoming. Being here grasped in pure and very sharp opposition to becoming (cf. above, p. 27).

That makes clear *what* is denied. We still need to ask *how* the negation is to be understood. Negation, as an assertion, is a rejection, specifically a rejection of predicates and properties. We have deliberately and with good reason avoided taking the enumerated terms as properties or even predicates of Being. For such are not at all at issue here. Parmenides is speaking only of σήματα, of what shows itself in the prospect on Being, of respects. But what is a negative respect supposed to be? It requires a non-spectating into, a disregarding. But how? Not that we purely and simply deprive ourselves of the prospect on Being. To the contrary, regarding, seeing with respect to emergence, disappearance, etc., but in such a way that we thereby realize: in such a respect we are thrust away from Being; Being does not *permit* us to approach it in such respects. Yet thereby we are precisely given to understand how matters stand with Being.

The regarding is intrinsically a disregarding, a looking away (cf. p. 49, bottom) in the active and transitive sense. Through a determinate sort of seeing, keeping away, keeping free of emergence and all becoming. Regarding—inspecting. Why then negative respects? That still not clarified! The answer put off until we discuss the other, positive respects (cf. p. 43).

These negations using "without" are thus not trying to say that Being is missing something, suffers a lack; on the contrary, what is denied is not worthy of Being and does not measure up to it. *Its measure is different.* What is its measure? We can in a certain way grasp it from the respects that thrust themselves forward in the disregarding. It is at the same time expressed positively when we follow up the second group. |

42

γ) The second group, the affirmative σήματα

The second group, without negations; heed well that the groups are not presented successively but instead are intermingled; (not negating—negative) therefore positive. Positive respect such that following it Being itself can be grasped in the prospect. οὖλον (epic-Ionic) instead of ὅλον—"whole." That does not simply mean "complete," no piece missing, "all together"; on the contrary, it has no pieces at all, out of which it would be patched together. Therefore pieces cannot be broken off from it. Whole or not at all. *Wholeness*—this *first* philosophical respect *requires a seeing* in the direction of a preeminent *"unity."*

μουνογενής—like ἀτέλεστον, this word has up to now caused difficulties. Diels speaks of a "latent contradiction,"[41] which would hereby enter into the doctrine of Parmenides. How so? Because the poem previously said ἀ-γένητον, and so every γένεσις is denied Being, including μόνο-γένεσις. Therefore Parmenides cannot have written μουνογενής. Accordingly, the ancients already tried to alter the text.

μουνογενής—*singly* born, singly generated; yet previously said: altogether no coming to be here. γένος certainly means origin, genus, sex; in the word in question, however, the stress is obviously on the μοῦνος, unique, singly. Thus not two, not the one and the other, not two sexes. Accordingly, it is said at 12, 5 that in the domain of semblance all birth is from the ἐναντίον of man and woman. With Being, however, not this "opposition" but, instead, the "singly."[42] Being

---

41. *Parmenides Lehrgedicht*, op. cit., 74.

42. Unique—*uniqueness also alters the sense of origination*—the whence—it *itself* | Hither—from somewhere |—but it itself simply there—| its *own origination* | *uniqueness* of the "there"—| *"merely there"* | and otherwise nothing.

is hither from itself, is its own lineage; μουνογενής *does not contradict* ἀγένητον but is merely the *positive version* of what is said there negatively.

νῦν ὁμοῦ πᾶν—(in) the present at once—the all. νῦν stands primarily opposed to ποτέ. Being "now," not "at one time"; but here the "now" does not mean the now that a moment ago was not yet and when recorded is no longer now, the fleeting, variable, changeable now. Altogether not the "now" as commonly known. Instead, the now that *at once provides the "all,"* allows a grasp of the whole, and specifically such that *no succession* of piecemeal transitions is necessary or possible; instead, ὁμοῦ. Given at once with the νῦν is the πᾶν.[43]

The νῦν thus not coordinated to an individual "this here" (out of the manifold of dispersed things) and to the succession of such individuals. The now that cannot in the least be measured or compared by means of the ποτέ, i.e., the before and after. The now that thus escapes from the past and future. Yet the now should not rashly be equated with the *nunc,* which a later Christian age called the *nunc stans* (the standing now, in distinction to the *nunc fluens,* the fleeting now) and equated with eternity. "Eternity" is not at issue here—quite apart from the fact that the concept of eternity and what this concept is supposed to refer to are highly problematic. In order to indicate the *unusualness* of the word νῦν here, we translate it as "present"—initially only another word. Here follow the final respects, ἕν—συνεχές.

ἕν, the neuter form of εἷς, μία. "One"; so faint and general an expression that not much can be drawn from it, indeed obviously nothing, since it stands opposed to all multiplicity and variety. Yet the expression and its meaning are richer than may seem. For already the fact that to Being are attributed πολλὰ μάλα σήματα—very many respects—must require a new characterization of the unity of this "one." The unity contains, so to speak, everything essential that belongs to the "one" as such, everything that constitutes unity. Therefore translated with "unitary" as *the essence of the "one" that encompasses qua unity everything one-like.* To be sure, no clarification in Parmenides, but certainly more than the empty "one." Let us try to clarify it on our own.

ἕν means primarily "one" and not two, three, etc.—the *first.* What above all comes first—(unity qua firstness).

ἕν then means the one in distinction to the other, i.e., in distinction to that which in general allows and bears otherness, alterity, alteration. It means the one and thus the self-same—(unity qua sameness).

---

43. Temporality of presentification purely from presence; ὁμοῦ—apprehension *in itself* → in one.

ἕν furthermore means the simple, that which of itself excludes (ἀδιαίρετον) everything multiple, *in such a way* that variety must be foreign to it—(unity qua simplicity, unifoldness).

ἕν also means the unique, that which is not merely opposed to the other as never equated with the other, but that which excludes *all* otherness and does not allow itself to be equated whatsoever (μουνογενής)—(unity qua uniqueness).

ἕν finally means the "one" qua whole, οὖλον—(unity qua wholeness). Firstness, sameness, simplicity, uniqueness, wholeness.

How then is the ἕν the unitary? Because it encompasses all these unities: firstness, sameness, simplicity, uniqueness, wholeness. But is it then still one, if it admits into itself a manifold? Indeed, does not Parmenides contradict himself in the most blatant way by calling Being ἕν and at the same time speaking of πολλὰ μάλα σήματα? But, as the beginning of philosophy precisely shows, we must be extremely cautious concerning the usual eagerness to hunt constantly for contradictions in the field of philosophical questioning, motivated by the apparently certain opinion that contradictions are ipso facto objections.

Let us wait and see. The manifold accruing to the ἕν is merely a manifold of unities that precisely unfold out of the "one" as unity (cf. temporality!). *This* multiplicity does not destroy the unities but, instead, forms them in their full essence. Therefore it is no accident that the school of Parmenides (Melissos and Zeno) claimed precisely this respect on Being qua ἕν as the preeminent predicate of Being. And it has remained so up to Hegel—admittedly without the full essence of unity having been clarified ("identity"); it meant now this, now that (cf. German Idealism).

Plato gave the name *Parmenides* to the dialogue in which he most radically and amply develops the question of Being, and he grasps this question as the question concerning the ἕν. Aristotle wrote a great treatise about the ἕν, which has come down to us as the tenth book (I) of the compilation known as his *Metaphysics.* |

No accident, as was said, because the ἕν is the simplest concept and yet harbors a peculiar richness as its own proper domain. To be sure, it has nevertheless up the present day not been decided or even questioned why Being can and must be grasped precisely in terms of unity and how the unfolding of the proper domain of unity is to be understood and grounded.

συνεχές—here primarily is expressed the σύν versus the movement out of one another and from one another that pertains to all transition, change, and scattering; the σύν as of something coherent, holding together, insofar as in general a manifold is indeed both holding and held in it, a manifold lying in it and toward it as ἕν. The thing holds and is in itself consolidated and remains so.[44] Every attempt at separation is here from the outset without prospects. *What is gathered in itself,* therefore appropriate to Being as ἕν—that is συνεχές. But also λόγος is coordinated—*gathering.*

δ) Concluding judgment regarding the groups: comprehensive questioning

The *positive* respects do in fact easily fall under the ἕν: ἐόν is ἕν; i.e., beings understood with respect to their Being signify unitariness, the latter in the manifold sense we have indicated. Then all the more does the question already touched on present itself: over and above the positive respects, what is the point of the negative ones? Is indeed the claim that they are polemical terms and rejections of the views of others regarding Being the only intelligible explanation for the duality of the respects? If taken only negatively, then it would not be well to assume mere polemics; but we are thinking positively, since polemics do have a rightful place here.

It can hardly be contested that the negative terms involve something like repudiation and accordingly confrontation; the question concerns only the aim of the repudiation. Is it directed against fortuitous opponents and defenders of other views, or (cf. below, regarding pp. 37–41) is there still some other possibility? This much is certain: Being offers itself only to νοεῖν and λέγειν—conceptual understanding. And that is the *mode of seeing* that corresponds to the prospect of the *first* way. To keep to this way, however, means never to tread the way of human opinion. Yet the latter way is constantly tempting, since the person who follows the first way does of course remain human. To keep to the first way therefore intrinsically means not straying onto the third way, not participating in what it proffers, not accepting the prospect it presents, disregarding the respects it has in preparation. And which are these? They are determined by the understanding of Being that rules over the third way. There Being signifies precisely change, the "now this, now otherwise." Being as becoming, emergence and disappearance, the to and fro of life, the march of production, formerly this, in the future that.

The negations within the guiding respects of the first way are not directed arbitrarily and fortuitously against just any theory; on the contrary, they are essentially aimed against everyday opinions and

---

44. The "very many" are indeed easy to see; or the essential and all *other* consequences of the essence and these *adversely* according to the respective levels and strata form the domain of change and becoming.

delusions. The negations are therefore *necessary;* precisely in them is carried out the always-needed turning away from the beaten path. Only thus does the looking in accord with the prospect of the first way come to be secured. Being and the understanding of Being must *hold out against semblance and entanglement in it.* But semblance is Being as becoming; *becoming for Parmenides is the semblance of Being.* What then does Being mean?

We must admit that, even now, after the adducing of the respects, we have no fixed concept of unity but only a very unsteady notion of it, whereby we do not understand how Being is in that regard supposed to be determined in essence. (Indeed, what does "essence" mean?) Certainly we must not be gullible and, like the many, adhere to mere words, even ones that are grand and high titles for the essence of Being. Nor may we expect anything from a mere enumeration that would operate like a decree, for the latter is completely out of place where a conceptual grasp is required. And not merely a conceptual grasp of random states of affairs, but the concept of Being, a concept [*Begriff*] that embraces [*einbegreift*] everything—comprehensiveness [*Inbegriff*].

Thus, even the understanding and conceptual grasping of Being are embraced in this comprehensiveness and accordingly must come to the level of a concept. The asking of the basic question of philosophy, the asking of the question of Being is—as I have developed it in earlier lecture courses—*comprehensive questioning* (cf. the beginning of "Was ist Metaphysik?").[45] Therefore, this conceptual grasping must necessarily also grasp itself. It is a self-grasping not because the human self would be what is first or most securely given to humans; indeed, nothing is further from humans than themselves and their essence. Nor is it self-grasping, because the human being as an ethical agent and existence would thereby be what is highest and most important, the cynosure of all concern. Nor is it because every orderly process requires self-reflection. Method itself and its elaboration are indeed wrested only from Being and from the essence of Being, but the conceptual grasping is by essential necessity a self-concept—because it is, as a conceptual grasp of Being, the first and last comprehensiveness. Philosophy is comprehensive questioning, because it asks the question of Being and asks *only* that question.

The enumeration of the σήματα is primarily nothing more than an indication of the respects toward gaining the prospect on Being and

---

45. {First edition: Martin Heidegger, "Was ist Metaphysik?" Bonn: Cohen, 1929. Now in *Wegmarken,* GA9.}

therefore must necessarily *prove* itself in order to demonstrate Being in its claimed essence. We will now investigate whether and to what extent and by what means that happens.

d) Being as ἀγένητον

α) A guiding respect concerning Being

8, 6–14. We begin simply by noting what follows the enumeration. τίνα . . . αὐξηθέν; Two questions, introduced by γάρ: "For, which origin of it could be disclosed in questioning? How and whence any increase (accretion)?" These questions have to do with γένεσις, coming forth, and with αὐξάω, supervening, and thus also with the first respect on the list, ἀγένητον. Being is without origin, for whence could one be disclosed in questioning? More particularly, assuming Being had an origin, then a whence would thereby be posited (cf. below): whence— πόθεν—and how—πῆ—Being would then proceed further—in short— αὐξηθέν.

Clearly, here begins the justification of ἀγένητον as a respect guiding the prospect on Being. The justification occurs so as to prove that γένεσις is necessarily inappropriate to Being. Therefore, to be proved is that Being is not such and such. But how can one at all prove not-being and not being-such-and-such? Proving is always indeed a *showing* and some sort of exhibiting. | Yet nonbeing cannot be shown; only   44 a something is showable, a being-such-and-such. Certainly—if we understand showing as an immediate displaying. To prove, to exhibit and display the character of ἀγένητον in its justification, means to show the inappropriateness of γένεσις in relation to ἐόν. Thus we only need as it were to consider Being and determine that nothing like γένεσις occurs with regard to Being—a negative finding. *Therefore, we must already in advance know positively how Being looks, how matters stand with it.*

Do we know that? Do we hold the essence of Being, as Parmenides would have it understood, clearly before our inner gaze, so that we can just as certainly infer that γένεσις does not occur there, γένεσις does not occur in ἐόν?[46] Obviously we do not. Indeed, respects are enumerated "positively" but are not exhibited and proved. The proof commences precisely with the *negative* respects.

Yet even if the essence of Being were clearly in sight and we could establish that nothing like γένεσις occurs there,[47] the required proof would still not be carried out thereby. For what is to be shown is not

46. a) whence ἐόν.
47. b) into *occurring*—factically.

merely that we do not find γένεσις with regard to Being, that γένεσις does not factically occur there, but that γένεσις utterly cannot occur there, is altogether inappropriate to the essence of Being. Thus, the task is to show that γένεσις cannot at all pertain to Being—*impossibility of pertaining*. And the impossibility of something pertaining could never be demonstrated by referring to an absence. But with such a demonstration we must also prove Being and must be able to prove Being.

The "not" and the "un-" are never to be exhibited immediately and as lacking mediation, but only by way of the positive essence of Being, i.e., mediated by that essence. In any case, only by way of something! Therefore a showing necessary, but, in accord with the circumstances, only a *mediate*[48] *showing* possible.

How does Parmenides now proceed to justify ἀγένητον? He poses a question: "For, which origination of Being is to be sought?" This "for" means: assuming and granting that Being would have γένεσις, then which one does it have? The discussion and the proof thus concern that and how Being has γένεσις; but this is exactly the opposite of the thesis to be justified. In assuming the opposite, nothing less happens than the positive establishment of Being; i.e., we must now again attempt to demonstrate mediately what has been assumed. The task is to seek a γένεσις, i.e., to seek first a *whence*. Whence Being; assuming that it as such does come from somewhere and must do so—then whence can it come?

What are the possibilities of the whence? We see that Parmenides, right after posing the question, begins the discussion of the possibilities of a whence, an origination for Being. He says (8, 7): οὔτε, neither. . . . *The circumstances of the problematic require that a "nor" follow this "neither."* In Greek, a second οὔτε. The text as handed down does not provide such. Therefore, we need to look and see where this second οὔτε can have stood and even must have stood. Again, that could be decided only on the basis of an understanding of the entire content of the text. What is then the first possibility for a whence, an origination, of Being? Manifestly that which is not Being, thus nothingness. Accordingly, verse 7: οὔτ᾽ ἐκ μὴ ἐόντος—neither could Being derive from nothingness, nor. . . . Nor what? Which possibilities besides nothingness? Being, but that would then not be an origination, since origination always requires a whence other than that which originates from it. What is other than Being, besides nothingness, is semblance. And the peculiarity of the semblant is to look like a being, i.e., in some way—πῇ—to be and yet not to be.

---

48. [Here and throughout this discussion reading *mittelbares Zeigen* for *unmittelbares Zeigen*, "immediate showing."—Trans.]

β) The problem of "indirect proof"

In the text as it now stands, the discussion of the first οὔτε (7) con-cludes with verse 11. Then follows οὐδέ ποτ᾽ ἐκ ὄντος, thus in any case further talk of the whence. Yet nothingness as the whence is discussed beginning with 7, therefore μή cannot occur here again. Furthermore, since ἐκ τοῦ ὄντος would make no sense, it can only be ἐκ πῇ—out of beings of a sort. That is the only second possibility of the whence of Being, and it already came into question; but even this is not correct, οὔτε—neither the first nor this one. Verse 12 now begins οὐδέ, which without difficulty or violence can be rewritten as οὔτε and from all that was said must be rewritten so. *We thereby smooth out the text.*

The task is now to come closer to the content. Let us briefly review the substantive nexus. In the enumeration of the respects, the first one is this: Being is without origin. This thesis is now to be proved. As a negative assertion, it says something expressible only mediately, not immediately, through a relation to the appertaining positive ele-ment, Being. In opposition to the thesis, the assumption is made that Being has an origin. The task is to demonstrate that. Therefore seek-ing the whence. Which ones are possible? 1) nothingness 2) a sort of Being. These exhaust *all the possibilities* of the whence. If it could be shown that both are out of the question, then there would be *altogether no whence* for a γένεσις of Being, and so such a γένεσις itself would be impossible. Therefore, Being *necessarily,* by its very essence, is *without* γένεσις, is ἀ-γένητον. Such is called an "indirect proof." We say: me-diate showing. But the "indirect," "indirect proofs," are not all the same. And we have grounds for supposing that at issue here is a *quite peculiar sort of "indirect proof."* | For it is not a matter of proving just any   45 statement in the usual sense, i.e., a statement expressing something about this or that being and specifically in a negative way. On the con-trary, it is a matter here of a saying, a negative saying, of Being.

To establish the types of proof is one of the occupations of "logic." This discipline, however, deals only with the saying and "thinking" that are familiar first and for the most part, namely, the saying and thinking about beings and specifically in the already enunciated form of an assertion. "Dialectic" is in fact only a facade, apprehended through the lens of the usual logic. But this logic does not deal with the say-ing of Being as a disclosive questioning, does not deal with philoso-phizing. The latter has its own logic, of which we know the equiva-lent of nothing. It would also be a mistake to believe this logic could be acquired by combing through the *procedure* of *previous* philosophy. For there is no guarantee that we correctly grasp its procedure, rather than adhering to externals, as long as we have not grasped what philosophy is driving at and what it disclosively questions. In any case, what the logic of exact thinking says does not without further ado hold for the logic of philosophy. What the former says, superficially and schematically enough, about "indirect proof" does perhaps not apply to what we provisionally call the mediate showing of philosophizing.

That means we must not arm ourselves with a handbook of logic and put Parmenides to the test and even censure him, or, which is just as stupid, praise him for having already followed or even { . . . }[49] recognized the principles of contradiction and identity. On the contrary, we must base ourselves on his issues and participate in his questioning, his kind of demonstration and proof, in order to be directed to what his sort of proving exhibits. Then we will be automatically compelled into the correct "logic." So much about proof—what was said holds for the entire work of Parmenides as a philosophical work. According to the matter at issue, according to what is here placed in question and disclosively questioned, namely, Being, the corresponding truth, as a preeminent one, is of its own kind. Standing in accord to truth as philosophical truth—here as the truth of Being closer to the essence of truth—is the claim of proof and provability and in correspondence also the assignment of the burden of proof and the direction and structure of the course of proof. In correspondence also demonstration, exhibition, and grounding. We will not now treat this more particularly or extensively but will instead first ask with greater determinateness: what course is taken by the proof for the character of ἀγένητον, which indeed is to be demonstrated and exhibited as a σῆμα for ἐόν, a genuine gaze into the prospect on Being?

γ) The understanding of Being in δόξα, according to which Being has an origin

In order to demonstrate ἐόν as ἀγένητον, the assumption is made that Being has an origin. It is not an arbitrary and contrived assumption; on the contrary, it merely makes explicit what is already meant in the understanding of Being distinctive of common human opinion. To assume that Being originates therefore means to conform to the ordinary human view. But the conformity is not for the sake of merely grasping the view; the purpose is to place it in question, i.e., to investigate what it properly means. If Being is supposed to have an origin, then a whence is posited for Being. This whence must in any case be, and embody, something other than Being itself. The whence: that which Being first and foremost is not. What Being simply is not in

---

49. {Two undecipherable marks.}

the most obvious and clearest way, namely, nonbeing, is nothingness. Thus the question: is nothingness possibly the whence of Being? Parmenides answers: no. He grounds this answer in two steps:[50]
1) This whence is neither φατόν nor νοητόν, neither to be said nor
apprehended. Nothingness cannot at all be addressed or understood.
We can therefore neither say nor understand that nothingness is the
whence of Being. Being as originating out of nothingness is not understandable and not sayable. What is Parmenides getting at by grounding the proof in this way? Is he saying that nothingness is out of the
question as the whence because we know nothing about it? Thus a
retreat into the *asylum ignorantiae*? Is he simply taking refuge in ignorance? Such an interpretation of Parmenides's argument does not
touch the essential. Parmenides is saying more, namely, that nothingness cannot in the least be the whence because indeed Being at all
only where saying and apprehending (λέγειν-νοεῖν).

δ) Appeal to the axiomatic statement about Being

We see that the rejection of nothingness as a possible whence for Being manifestly invokes the *axiomatic statement:* where Being, there apprehension, and where no apprehension, no Being. The appeal to the
axiom requires this interpretation. Nevertheless, by conceding the legitimacy of the interpretation, we at the same time raise a difficult
substantive objection against this procedure. What does it mean to offer the axiom as a ground of proof in view of the fact that this statement about Being has itself not at all been proved and indeed cannot be proved as long as the essence of Being has not been shown in
advance?[51] And this latter task is supported by the proof of the ἐὸν
ἀγένητον. Then grounding this proof can in no way invoke that which
is first of all to be proved. That would amount to a very crude viola-
tion of the simplest rules of logic—i.e., it would be a circular argument. We cannot take this, "our" objection against Parmenides, seriously enough, but precisely for that reason we will now not press
it, since we will have to bring it up again and again in regard to the
proving that still remains. Our main concern, however, is not to refute Parmenides but, instead, before all else, to understand him and

---

50. Nothing comes from nothing—1. therefore not only out of *nothingness* come
no beings, but 2. out of *nothingness no Being.* Compellingly different questions—
the denial of the first thesis does not signify the denial of the second, and conversely the affirmation of the second does not include the affirmation of the first—
"Being comes from nothingness."

51. Un-demonstrated, un-demonstrable, as long as the essence of Being not
shown →

indeed to understand his poem as a whole. That requires us to consider not only his grounds of proof but also the aim of the proof. Accordingly, we must keep in mind that it is not because we know nothing of it that nothingness is not a possible whence; on the contrary, it is because nothingness cannot *be* such a whence. This ground of proof is supported by a second one:

2) τί δ' ἄν μιν—D 8, 9 and 10. Supposing that nothingness is the possible whence for the origination of Being, then Being must emerge— φῦν—out of nothingness, come to appearance out of nothingness. There must reside in nothingness, accordingly, a motive for the fact that Being did once arise out of it at some moment or other. Then when? That cannot be said,[52] but indeed at some moment, and the question is why then and not earlier or later. What provides the motive in nothingness for the choice of this and not that temporal point? How in the world is an earlier or later, a then and when, supposed to be claimed where there is indeed nothing and thus no time? Even if Being is supposed to begin out of nothingness "accidentally," a temporal position would still have to be occupied; where is this if the whence is nothingness? |

46   The result is that nothingness cannot at all be a whence of Being, nor could it begin the origination as such. If Being must have its origin in nothingness, then it has none. Therefore, 8, 11: either Being is not at all, or—ἀ-γένητον—it is without origin; i.e., if Being, then *altogether permanently* there. Heed well: Parmenides does not argue that Being cannot originate in nothingness and therefore is ἀγένητον; he concludes instead: therefore Being is either altogether permanent or is not at all. I.e., he says: *if there is Being, then it is altogether permanent.*

ε) Semblance as a possible whence of Being

Yet even this last statement is not fully grounded; i.e., the possibility of an origination of Being is still not completely excluded. For there is still a second possible whence. Although this is not nothingness, it nevertheless satisfies the whence inasmuch as it cannot constitute Being itself. It is πῇ ἐόν, a being of a sort, the semblant, that which looks like Being and yet is not Being.

What about this second possible whence for Being, the origination of Being out of semblance? It must likewise be rejected. How? By appealing to ἡ ἰσχὺς πίστιος, the power of reliance. There is reliance only on unconcealedness, and there is unconcealedness only of Being. Thus again, as in the first ground of proof, here an invocation of the apprehending of Being, an appeal to the axiom. Accordingly, we are again involved in a circle. In virtue of the understanding of Be-

---

52. If whence—then *hence* | *at some moment or other* |—circle.

ing (in its essence) it cannot be admitted that besides semblance, and arising from it, anything could come forth other than precisely semblance. An origination of Being from it is impossible. For semblance and all change are intrinsically permeated with the "not," and out of negativity (i.e., here then from permeation by the "not") there could only[53] come forth the "not," the null. Semblance is insufficient as the whence for an origination of Being.

Beyond these two possibilities of a whence, there is no other. If Being cannot in any respect have a whence, then it is *necessarily* without origin, ἀ-γένετον, supposing there is Being at all.

ζ) Δίκη as disposing Compliance

13–15. There now follows a summarizing reference to the proper ground of the proffered arguments against the origination of Being, thus arguments for its lack of origination. So that Being should from the start necessarily reject everything negative, Δίκη has also from the start not released arising and perishing for Being as ontological characters; that is now determined more precisely. She has never slackened the fetters in which she holds Being, so that Being, thus loosened, could so to speak slip off into nearby semblance. Heed well: the fettering of Being is not the consequence of the impossibility of an originating (arising and perishing). It is the reverse: these latter are essential consequences of the fact that Compliance holds Being fast. Compliance disposes [*Der Fug verfügt*]. And this disposing is twofold: 1) it disposes of Being by giving the law to Being, prescribing the law; 2) it has Being at its disposal, has Being in its dominion, in its possession.

The proof of ἀγένητον as an imminent respect is not merely negative but, instead, opens the prospect upon the essential determination of Being, namely, that Being stands under disposing Compliance, is held therein. Yet we know that Being as such belongs together with νοεῖν, and this latter is what it is only as the disposal. The axiom expressing the belonging together of Being and apprehension is therefore not merely invoked as ground of proof but, in and through this invocation, is itself first proved in a peculiar way, namely, in the only mode of proof appropriate to it as an axiom and a principle. More precisely: the axiomatic statement is not proved as a statement, is not deduced from another statement or shown to be underiveable. On the contrary, we are referred to that which the statement itself expresses, the disposing Compliance, the Dikē that holds Being. Nothing further is said about this holding. But it is the site of Being. We must, by way of understanding, hold out, with Being properly disposing of us, and

---

53. [Reading *nur* for *nie,* "never."—Trans.]

by originarily understanding and knowing—qua *existente*—we must apprehend and must expressly place ourselves in disposal! We—those who in the ground of their essence have taken on the disposal—must as such understand (insofar as each of us is in every case a being).

η) The impossibility of a whence is the same as the impossibility of a whither

We have overlooked something in this now completed discussion of Dikē, in reference to whom the proof of ἀγένητον concludes. Parmenides suddenly speaks here (14) of ὄλλυσθαι, not merely of γενέσθαι, which alone had been at issue. Accordingly, ἀνώλεθρον is drawn into the result of the proof of ἀγένητον. Interpreters have inferred that the previous verses must have also contained an explicit proof of ἀνώλεθρον. Yet none is to be found. The transmitted text therefore has a lacuna, or, which is even more attractive, Parmenides forgot about the proof.

Indeed antiquity already knew of the forgetfulness and unworldliness of philosophers. Plato (*Theaetetus,* 174a) relates how Thales fell into a well while gazing at the stars and was then mocked by a Thracian servant girl for wanting to observe the highest heavens and thereby being oblivious to what was right at his feet. It is nevertheless advisable not to take forgetfulness as a principle of interpretation, even if that is the easiest way out. The question is whether it is instead the superficiality of the interpreters themselves that is in play here. In other words, we must ask if an explicit proof of ἀνώλεθρον, in addition to the proof of ἀγένητον, is at all necessary.

In the end, it is precisely the fact that such a proof is missing which shows the actual content and spirit of the proof of ἀγένητον. The proof demonstrates that every sort of origin must be denied Being, not simply as an origin, but because thereby a whence is posited and along with it something which Being necessarily is not. The impossibility of an origin is grounded in the fact that it requires bringing Being into connection with something negative. But precisely that happens if it is said, as common opinion would have it, that beings pass away, 47   that Being involves perishing, passing away, or, in general, | passing into something which is then no longer Being. Thus, with the thence of perishing, something negative would necessarily be brought into relation with Being. So we see that the correctly understood rejection of the possibility of origination also already proves the impossibility of perishing. The withholding of this proof shows precisely that Parmenides knew very well what was the theme of the proof and the ground of the proof. Thus everything is in perfect order, and we are left marveling at the sureness and rigor of these allegedly "primitive" thinkers.

e) Parmenides's axiomatic statement
and his essential statement

Let us not let go of the fact that the proof of ἀγένητον (and of ἀνώλεθρον, we may now add) has recourse to Δίκη as the holding and firm possessing of Being and thus recourse to the realm expressed in the axiomatic statement. This recourse is carried out explicitly and openly, not as if Parmenides made use of it incidentally, as a last option, and even against his own aims. Indeed, ultimately the proof is carried out only in aiming at this recourse, for we know the proof of ἀγένητον is a defense against the γένεσις . . . ὄλεθρος of the common, mistaken understanding of Being. In this connection, the task is to acquire and maintain the *ontological content* of Δίκη, i.e., to carry out the correctly directed attunement of the understanding of Being. That means to acquire purely and securely a regarding, a disregarding, and simultaneously the respect. The rejection of γένεσις and ὄλεθρος derives all its power and all its right from the directedness toward Being. Therefore now

16–18. Being is sovereign or nothingness is, or else there is no sovereignty at all. One who has acquired this insight has intuited Being in its essence. Thereby, however, the basic decision takes place and so does the separation from those who do not differentiate at all; that now means: their differentiating is not guided by a view of Being in advance. Yet this basic decision, κρίσις, is not primarily a separation from but, rather, an acquisition of the ground, an acquisition of the standing and holding amid the possessions of Dikē, in her disposing. More clearly: the axiomatic statement is a self-positioning into the disposing—grounding!

The insight signifies: Being no "not." For Being, there is no complicity with the "not" and the negative, the way perhaps semblance, which indeed is not simply nothing, could very well be accepted as Being. In its full strictness and uniqueness, Being excludes everything negative. The separation of the first way from the second is thereby expressly grounded. Indeed, this also speaks of the third way, namely, that we must ever be warned against it, since it is not the way of Being.

Nevertheless, is the separation of the ways actually grounded in the essence of Being? There is certainly a relation to this essence. But is Being itself demonstrated in its essence? Has it up to now been shown anywhere that and why Being is utterly without a "not," is unnegative? Correctly observed, we always encounter only the *assertion* that matters stand thus with Being. This protestation, however, is not at all grounded through its many repetitions; on the contrary, only its arbitrariness comes to light. We will call this statement—Being utterly un-negative—Parmenides's essential statement about Being. It has up to now been no more grounded than the axiomatic statement—Being and understanding the same. The belonging together of both has neither been shown nor grounded; or is a positive and direct proof altogether inappropriate precisely here, an irrelevant and unreasonable demand? Yet note well that we propose all this not as objections against Parmenides but as naming that which we immediately fail to see. Whether justifiably or not is another question. *Only in that way,* however, can we come closer to the full strangeness of the procedure in these fragments.

Let us recall fragment 4, 3–5. It is said there: the first way about Being, the second about nothingness. Now: either Being or the "not" and in correspondence the ways. Apparently we are no farther along. Yet it must not be overlooked that with the acceptance of the proofs of the σήματα an explicit clarification of the essence of Being is acquired, even if only negatively and by already postulating in advance a positive essential determination.

f) Being is the present. Parmenides's temporal statement

The proof of the σήματα is now taken up again at 8, 19ff. Indeed, the sequence of these proofs does not correspond to the sequence of the enumeration of the σήματα. Conforming to these, what should now follow is the proof of οὖλον, μουνογενές, thus the proof of positive respects. Instead, what comes next is the proof of 8, 5—the οὐδ᾽ ἦν οὐδ᾽ ἔσται. Being was not and will not be. This is the relation between Being and time.

19–21. Parmenides will then also leap over the prior negative respects, ἀτρεμές, ἀτέλεστον. We are not told why. We see only that the discussion of Being and time immediately follows the recourse to Dikē and to the basic and essential statements about Being. The discussion is dense and crabbed, three or actually only two lines, since verse 21 already speaks again of γένεσις and ὄλεθρος; thereby a certain connection manifestly results between the question of Being and reason and the question of Being and time.

Of course, 8, 19–20, which speaks of a temporal relation of Being, must be taken together with 8, 5, which provides the σήματα, οὐδ᾽ ἦν οὐδ᾽ ἔσται, without "was," without "will be," for (ἐπεί) this σήμα views Being with respect to time. A grounding is thereby inserted within the enumeration of the σήματα; all the others are merely listed one after the other. Ultimately, that is not accidental. Here an explicit confirmation of the coupling of the negative and affirmative respects.

At first, however, we will follow up the proof in 8, 19–20. In form, the same course of proof as in the case of ἀγένητον. Then once more a question like the one above at 8, 6: "For how could Being have a future?" As above, the question presupposes assuming the opposite of the asserted σῆμα. Suppose Being should first be at some future point. How could that happen? And correspondingly: suppose Being formerly has been, how could that happen?

Supposing Being simply once was, i.e., supposing the essence of Being consisted in a having-been, then there is here no "is." Likewise, if the essence of Being is a will-be, then just as little is there an "is." Then the "is" would never arrive. Being would contain a "not" and would already not be. | 48

We say "is" where there are beings, for this "is" expresses Being. Being only where the "is." Therefore if Being once merely was, so that it first becomes Being, then the "is" utterly never is what it expresses. Then there is only nonbeing. If Being is Being, then it is necessarily pastless and futureless, without relation to past and future. If the "is" signifies Being, then Being must necessarily have a relation to the present and only to the present. Verse 8, 5 says so in a completely unequivocal way. If Being is supposed to have any relation to time, then only to the present.

To the extent that they have at all tried to shed light on these statements of Parmenides, interpreters up to now have been content to say that he here teaches the timelessness of Being. And if timelessness is completely equated with eternity, everything is then in perfect order. It conforms with the Christian teaching that the most proper being is the eternal being. And it accords with the theory of Hegel, whose philosophy presents the fulfillment of Western philosophy, i.e., one transformed by Christianity. Yet all this completely disregards the fact that it is not purely and simply clear what eternity signifies here, whether it is the same as timelessness and whether the latter is in turn the same as super-temporalness. Parmenides never claims, either in the passage now under discussion or anywhere else, that Being is timeless, without a temporal relation; a fortiori there is nothing here about eternity.

Quite to the contrary, what Parmenides says altogether unequivocally and emphatically is that Being has a relation to the present and only to this. Pastless and futureless are not at all the same as timeless. The present is even so fully time that only on its basis are the past and future usually grasped. The former is the no-longer-now, the latter the not-yet-now. In this manner, time is conceived on the basis of the νῦν up to this very day. The νῦν counts precisely as the basic phenomenon of time. And precisely in relation to the νῦν (present), Being is ὁμοῦ πᾶν; everything that constitutes Being, everything that pertains to Being, stands above all in relation to the νῦν. Being is altogether the present. To speak here of the timelessness or eternity of Being is at once purely arbitrary and superficial.

The discussion of Being with respect to time results not merely in the negative—pastless, futureless—but in something positive: Being stands in relation to the present and only to it. We will call this affirmation Parmenides's temporal statement about Being. But is it proved? Thus we ask again. Or is it merely, simply, asserted? For to say that Being can have no relation to past or future (otherwise it would not be Being) is precisely to presuppose that Being means the present. Certainly it is not merely, tacitly, presupposed; on the contrary, in the proof this presupposition is precisely to come to the fore. Parmenides has nothing to conceal.

The question is again only whether the coming to the fore of the presupposition can also already offer a proof of the legitimacy of the presupposition. That is not evident to us. So we find ourselves as regards this newly acquired temporal statement in the same situation we were in as regards the axiomatic and essential statements. Indeed, the whole question of Being becomes appreciably more complex; i.e., it becomes more problematic. Let us stipulate only a little. The axiomatic statement says Being stands in a necessary relation to apprehension. The temporal statement says Being stands in a necessary relation to the present. Do these statements mean the same or something different? If the same, is apprehension then the same as the present, and how is that to be conceived? If different, then do apprehension and the present belong together in some way? Furthermore, the essential statement says Being is utterly without any "not." The temporal statement says Being is only with the present. The question arises: is Being without the "not" because it is with the present, or is Being with the present because it is without the "not"? Or are both parts of this question not to be posed in such a way? What is then the inner connection between non-negativity and the present, indeed how in general are we to grasp, let alone ground, the axiomatic statement, the essential statement, and the temporal statement?

Line 21 of fragment 8 shows that for Parmenides the question of the temporal relation of Being in some fashion goes together with the question of the lack of origination of Being, for that line is immediately connected to the discussion of the temporal relation and says: thus emergence is extinguished and perishing not to be found. We know emergence signifies arising, appearance, and perishing signifies disappearance. To arise means to step *into the present*, to disappear means to go out of it. Both are, in their respectively different ways, the non-present.

Parmenides expresses that in the word γένεσις. The substantive priority, however, lies in time; i.e., Being is without emergence—perishing, without origin—future: only the present. The latter alone is the condition of the possibility of the "un" attaching to γένεσις and ὄλεθρος; not the reverse. The temporal statement has the priority.

We see again that the course of the proofs does not correspond to the sequence of the enumerated σήματα. Discussed up to now were ἀγένητον-ἀνώλεθρον and οὐδ' ἦν οὐδ' ἔσται, two negative respects, while leaping over the intervening positive and negative ones.

g) The impossibility of absence in Being

At 22–25, the discussion passes over to the proof of the first positive σήμα and the last one: οὖλον-συνεχές. In form, the proof is again a rejection of postulated respects, ones implying separation; for διαίρεσις is a taking apart, partitioning, dismembering. Apartness within Being would be the same as separation from another, distance from another, and so sheer negation, which is inappropriate to Being; if such partitioning were possible, then each of the parts would still be Being, although a part is not the whole and Being is only wholeness. If Being were composed of pieces, then in principle pieces could be added to it. Closed coherence would then be impossible, yet Being essentially occurs as such coherence; συνεχές would thus be excluded. Wholeness and sheer coherence do not permit any apartness—nor any "gap" where there would be no Being, such that Being would first become Being by traversing an interval. Along with the necessary exclusion of every gap, I there also drops out the possibility of any trembling in Being, as if Being could move to and fro in its parts. The proof of οὖλον-συνεχές is thus also a proof of ἀτρεμές. The necessity of disregarding any apartness (διαίρεσις) is grounded positively by regarding the fact that the whole is filled only with Being.

Since it is only sheer Being, nothing other than Being can come near to it; it fills all nearness and remoteness only as Being. The disregarding of the negative in the sense of apartness out of the respect on Being is here grounded by regarding the pure fullness of Being and the pure domination by Being of every nearness and thus of every remoteness.[54] What thereby lies in the sight of this positive regarding? Everything is purely filled, no void, no "away," i.e., no absence in Being as such, instead only presence. In its proximity nothing other than itself, no remoteness possible for it; instead, altogether there beyond all proximity and remoteness, completely in presence. And so

49

---

54. *Against* διαίρεσις—pure *fullness*—*domination;* no "away": but.

precisely sheer coherence in the present. Presence, bearing the pure fullness and the pure domination of proximity and remoteness, is the present. Again the temporal statement!

h) The recourse to the axiom

Thus we see again that the regarding of Being is basically a regarding of presence, the present. The temporal statement announces itself anew in its priority for grounding the σήματα. Not yet proved are still a negative respect, ἀτέλεστον, and two positive ones, μουνογενές and ἕν. The latter indeed already in συνεχές and οὖλον, in the sense of unity qua simplicity and wholeness, but not made explicitly thematic. Yet the following verses, 26ff., do not offer a discussion of these last named σήματα. On the contrary, the consideration turns back to what was already discussed. Let us see how.

Verses 26–28 have the same character as 15–19 in terms of method but have a different character in terms of content. They agree insofar as now again the proof is interrupted in order to take recourse in the axiom. The interruption now takes place, however, in the manner of a summary. It is now said that Being lacks all movement as named in the word κίνησις (ἀκίνητον); every sort of transition to and fro, not only emergence and disappearance, change of place and locomotion, but also the to and fro movement of trembling do not pertain to Being.

Without starting or stopping; that does not mean Being endures. On the contrary, Being is outside of duration, for that is always a from-to. Being is altogether lacking every "from" and "since when" and "until then." If Being is nevertheless precisely the present and presence, then this must signify something other than the ongoing occurrence we measure with a clock. All from-to signifies from before until later; the before a no-longer-now, the later a not-yet-now. All from-to (whether the from-to is determinate or indeterminate makes no matter here; both equally impossible with Being—in presence no "now" whatsoever can be postulated) moves in the region of the fleeting "now" that in itself—i.e., in every "now"—is necessarily different and never related to a limit but instead is precisely altogether the limitless, the mere "on and on," the "and so forth," the endless.

Being has nothing to do with this endlessness. On the contrary, Being is bounded—πέρας—limit, not that at which something stops and goes no further but as is explicitly said: the limits fetter and bind, they bestow bindingness. Being is not the endlessly ongoing "now" but rather is the binding present, intrinsically self-enclosed. What is not of the essence of this present, everything "un-" and "non-," all nonbeing, is driven away and thrust aside from reliance on the unconcealed. That means: the apprehension of Being grounds itself on itself, i.e., is in itself Δίκη, the disposing of Being.

We hear again: the essence of Being is not to be found and snatched up here and there in just any being but, instead, arises from the originary disposing that is its own law: binding, bond. The interruption of the course of the proof now a renewed retrieval of the posture of the νοεῖν of the originary disposing expressed in the axiom. This apprehensional regarding and understanding is a thrusting aside and driving away of everything "non-" and "un-"; here clearly the evidence for the earlier explanation of the apprehended respect, evidence for the disregarding! (cf. above, p. 41, sec. β.) Only after this renewed assurance of the basic posture of regarding the prospect on Being is the course of proof taken up again.

i) The unity of the simple-unique self-sameness of Being

α) Being as the oneness that excludes all otherness

29–33. And specifically in relation to the σήματα not yet discussed: ἕν, μουνογενές (29–30), ἀτέλεστον (32–33). Being remains the same in the same, and as sheltered back in itself it lies fast. Being is the oneness excluding all otherness. That does not simply mean set over and against something other but, rather, beyond everything othersome, outside all otherness. Indeed it is not merely stated that Being is ταυτόν, the same, but Being *remains the same in the same; remaining in itself,* it persists and holds itself in such sameness. In holding itself on the basis of itself and remaining present to itself, it is unifying, a unity-forming unity, and that is how it essentially occurs. We will say in the future: essentially occurs. In occurring thus, however, it remains fast sheltered back in itself, κεῖται, lie, rest: lie, e.g., as we say that such and such a city lies here or there. This lying [*Liegen*], as landed property [*Liegenschaft*], is presence. The expression "rest" (in general) can easily mislead, inasmuch as resting indeed still includes movement (κεῖται— rest!), captured, arrested movement. Being does not know any movedness (ἀκίνητον), even as arrested, nor therefore any rest. Lying fast—in the sense of that which remains altogether outside of rest and the possibility of movement.

Again we find what is meant only in terms of the presence of that which presences, and this presence excludes the possibility that that which presences could ever come forth from some whence or could disappear into some thence. And thus it perseveres steadfastly on that very site. It has always already taken up this steadfastness of a simple sheer object, this steadfastness of the present; | it has always already 50 persevered. This persevering cannot be conceived as the resistance of a now against the other nows that are always thrusting themselves forth only to swim away at once. It means instead a remaining that does not at all enter into the stream of nows. Yet this does not imply that remaining would be extra-temporal.[55] Such is so little the case that the non-now-like present as time is precisely what gives to the now and to the stream of nows dimensionality, direction, and stability. Since common human opinion, however, is familiar only with the now and the stream of nows, to such opinion this alone is time (cf. *Being and Time,* §78ff. and earlier). Everything that is not this time is therefore peremptorily considered extra-temporal and nontemporal. The present has always already taken hold, without a whence, alone there—μουνογενές—in the unity of simple-unique self-sameness.

β) The correct understanding of the incompletability of Being

Here (31) Parmenides again refers to the uniqueness of these unities; they are held in unity through powerful compulsion as the precept of οὐκ ἀτελεύτητον, a compulsion which stems from the essence of Being and which places a barrier around this essence and in that way ordains a structure. On that account, Being is οὐκ ἀτελεύτητον, not incompletable. Thereby the last σῆμα is grounded: ἀτέλεστον.

Yet how so? The earlier enumeration claimed Being is ἀτέλεστον. Now, with reference to the unitariness of Being, it is said that Being is οὐκ ἀτελεύτητον. Thus the exact opposite, namely, not incompletable. Accordingly, completable. In commenting on ἀτέλεστον, we appealed to this very passage at 8, 32. We were wrong, as it now appears. We must instead say that here completability is attributed to Being and that therefore in the enumeration of the σήματα it could not have been admitted that Being is incompletable. According to the current passage, Being is completable; what is this supposed to mean? That Being can at some point be produced in a finished state, whereas prior to that it was unfinished? From everything that preceded, it is immediately clear that neither completability nor indeed incompletability can be attributed to Being. Yet both are attributed in the text: 8, 4 and 8, 32.

All this is certainly so, and yet there is no contradiction, provided only that we understand what Parmenides is referring to. He is not speaking of some being and claiming it is at once completable and incompletable; on the contrary, he is speaking of Being and claiming (8, 1) that completion or finishedness is altogether irrelevant. Being has absolutely no possible relation thereto. Thus, Being is neither at one time unfinished, so as to become finished, nor is it ever fin-

---

55. Enduring is a possible consequence of the present, not vice versa. The latter to be announced through the former—already the {?} position *necessary.*

ished, for then it must once have been unfinished. "Incompletable" does not mean Being constantly stays unfinished; on the contrary, it means Being has absolutely no need of completion because in accord with its unity it has of itself its own proper completedness. Likewise, "completable" does not mean Being can at some point become finished, that it is possible for it to achieve completion; on the contrary, it means Being achieves completedness in advance, completedness is an essential possibility of Being, or, in other words, Being is of itself unity, without any possible "un-."[56]

I cannot comprehend how Diels, after his translation, could simply drop the matter, in case he ever did actually take it up. He lets Parmenides say: Being is "without end"[57] and "it must not be without termination."[58] That is of course a contradiction, especially if said of "beings," as Diels would have it. Yet thereby the question is utterly misplaced. The contradiction derives from the interpreters and translators, but not from Parmenides.

In verse 33, it is quite clearly expressed and grounded: for Being is without privation. Yet Being would have to possess a privation and a lack in order to be completable in the usual sense of able to become finished. If Being had any lack at all, however, there would be a "not" in it. But then the whole essence of Being would be destroyed. There can be no lack in Being, if it is at all supposed to essentially occur as itself. Completion, qua closedness, must be conceded to Being in advance as an essential possibility. Otherwise, the word γάρ would make no sense and have no grounding effect. If Being contained a lack, then it would precisely not be completable, and so the proof {?} of completability would not make sense. The word γάρ would therefore prove the opposite, if the task were to prove completability in the usual sense. But ultimately what is to be proved is the impossibility of becoming finished, i.e., the essential possibility of being finished. One might try to replace the word οὐκ in some way, so that the text would read: θέμις—ἀτελεύτητον. And thereby 8, 4 would be *unnecessary*.

Heed well: even this proof postulates the contrary possibility of privation, since privation—something still outstanding—directs the privative thing toward a "not yet," a "coming to be"—the future. But

---

56. "Incompletable" does not mean "never finished"; on the contrary, to first become finished is altogether impossible. Thus also not completable; on the contrary, to be complet*able*, to have *completedness*, is an *essential* possibility, one pertaining by essential *possibility, intrinsically,* to its essence. Being is incompletable— Being is *completable,* because it utterly knows no becoming finished, since to be finished is proper to Being as an essential possibility right from the beginning.

57. *Parmenides Lehrgedicht,* op. cit., 37, line 5.

58. Ibid., 39, line 34.

such is impossible, for Being is purely the present and precisely for that reason without relation to anything earlier that could be its whence. Not even that, but μουνογενές—ἕν. Thus Being by its every essence banishes the least shadow of a "not," opposes itself fully and purely against the "not."

This adamant opposition of the futureless essence of Being against nothingness brings to a close not only the proof of the last σῆμα but also the entire course of proof of all the individual σήματα. What now follows concerns the grounding of the ἕν in its simple-comprehensible {?} self-same wholeness.

A backward glance at the enumeration of the σήματα and at the course of proof of the individual σήματα yields two findings:

1) as the proofs proceed, the respects no longer appear to be merely juxtaposed or merely set one after the other. Instead, they dovetail unitarily into one vision, one prospect on Being. The unity of this prospect on Being proves to be the present, presence; such is seen in each of the respects. The present and presence dominate the entire prospect on Being.

2) the course of proof, which already incorporates the regarding of the unity of the prospect on Being, is constantly interrupted by the explicit recourse to what the axiom expresses. We have called it an interruption, but henceforth we must say that in terms of the matter at issue it is the *explicitly carried out consolidating and securing of the totality of perceiving in the unitary* respect directed toward Being in the prospect on the ἕν. Being is the present and presence. And there now follows upon the conclusion of the grounding of the individual σήματα a fresh appeal to the axiom, such that its content is unfolded *now precisely for the first time*. The axiom is so to speak the goal of the entire way; i.e., the goal is to acquire and carry out that which is expressed in the axiom.

j) The insertion of fragment 2

α) The theme of ἀπεόντα

We have now, however, inserted fragment 2 between 8, 33 and 8, 34, not as an alteration of the text but, so we said, as something like a gloss written by Parmenides himself, i.e., as his commentary on the preceding and following text of fragment 8. |

51

D 2

    Λεῦσσε δ᾽ ὅμως ἀπεόντα νόῳ παρεόντα βεβαίως·
    οὐ γὰρ ἀποτμήξει τὸ ἐὸν τοῦ ἐόντος ἔχεσθαι
    οὔτε σκιδνάμενον πάντῃ πάντως κατὰ κόσμον
    οὔτε συνιστάμενον.

Yet behold now how what was previously absent has steadfast presence for apprehension, since (no apprehension) can cut up the coherence of Being as Being, neither to a bestrewal everywhere throughout the whole world nor to a standing side by side. Cf. above, *p. 39.*

The very form of this fragment suggests the role we are assigning it, since the first words are λεῦσσε δε. Yet behold now—temporality. What are we to behold? What is at issue here? Clearly: 1) presence and absence; 2) νοῦς, apprehension. Thus coming into words at this point is precisely what we set out in relief as decisive in the entire previous course of proof.

Yet here something new emerges—ἀπεόντα, the *absent,* thus the *opposite* of what has presence. Indeed our interpretation has been compelled by the matters themselves to speak of the fact that the ἕν as the present, νῦν ὁμοῦ πᾶν, essentially repudiates everything not the present (future and past; cf. p. 49, top) and thus repudiates *non*-presence (absence). Everything not the present (absence) is driven far from Being, completely expelled from it. Here, however, not only is absence named, but the text explicitly says that the absent, although it remains such, nevertheless has presence for apprehension and indeed a *steadfast* presence. Presence *encompasses* absence. What is not the present, thus the negative, is *incorporated* into the present. *Being,* if indeed it essentially occurs as the present, is now *intrinsically negative.* A thesis thus most pointedly running counter to everything said previously. How are we to find our way through this?

It will not do, in view of the certainty and univocity of the transmission of the text, simply to maintain that Parmenides could not have said what is contained in fragment 2. Nor will it do simply to leave juxtaposed the utterly conflictual theses in fragments 8 and 2, at least not as long as the proof is missing that this conflict can and even must exist. The proof can be furnished, however, only if we *involve ourselves in the matter at issue.* Simply to insist that the conflict must be resolvable since it concerns Being and since according to Parmenides the ἕν is without any "non-," any "counter-," any "anti-," would mean to privilege from the outset fragment 8 over 2. As long as we consider the various possibilities only in these terms, then we are of course acting as if the conflict quite clearly resided in Parmenides's statements. What must be asked first of all, however, is whether it is not actually the case that the conflict appears only because our understanding of Parmenides, even and precisely the previous one, despite all of the interpretation, remains insufficient and thus whether there is any conflict at all in the text. Have we then sufficiently determined what the present and presence mean here, in order to decide about their compatibility or incompatibility with absence? Obviously we have not.

(Although in Parmenides himself no starting from the present = presence, yet the priority is now sufficiently clear and thus the endeavor of my interpretation.)

β) All absence lies in the sphere of presence

We would do well to investigate once for ourselves. What do we mean by presence and absence? παρεόντα—παρά, here beside [da-neben], here by [da-bei]; ἀπό, away [weg]; here and away! Where is here? Here before our eyes, here within range, at hand, lying in immediate reach. Yet how far does this reach extend? What is here has presence. Where is the boundary separating what is still here from what is already away? My hat, e.g., is not at hand here, it is away, although in my office. It is away from here, yet it is still here in the university. And thus in many cases; for instance, what is otherwise far away is "here" on the telephone or radio. Manifestly *no fixed boundary* exists between here and away; anything is both, but *relatively*—depending on the circumstances, depending on the person. That which for sensory perception is not immediately accessible, is away, is nonetheless still here for immediate presentification, e.g., the Black Forest, the North Sea, Berlin. In this regard, we do not need to recall having once seen the place; it is here at hand to sense quite free of recollection, and indeed in the present. Then is there any absence at all, if we take the sphere of presence so broadly and indeed such[59] that everything is here at hand at once? Assuming there are absent things, and there are such things relatively, then even they can be *absent only within a sphere of presence.* Something is absent only in the sphere of presence; insofar as something absent "is," it "is" only qua *present*—but it does not need to be perceived.

That is what Parmenides is trying to say! He is not trying to find a determinate boundary between individual present and absent things; on the contrary, he is striving to say something about absence and presence as such. Namely, that the former is incorporated into the latter. Moreover, that this encompassing presence is related to νοῦς; here no further "depending on circumstances"! For νοῦς, i.e., for its presentifying, everything that is nevertheless absent is already determined by presence—assuming that the absent precisely is. Yet we indeed said that Being tolerates no "not"; therefore what is absent, what is away, precisely is not. And yet it can be, without detriment to the relative absence; indeed it must be, precisely if and because it is absent. Precisely as absent it must have presence!

---

59. *Relatively* near—altogether no "away"—over and against astronomical distances.

We conclude that presence and the present must be grasped with the greatest possible breadth. How broadly, then? Parmenides answers in 2, 2–4: κατὰ κόσμον, throughout the whole world in every direction.[60] κόσμος is not nature in the narrow sense, as in "cosmology," but what we call beings as a whole. The unity of the wholeness of this "as a whole" is the *world*. That oneness of presence which first provides the *field* for everything relatively present and absent, this one presence in which every being is present, is consequently no longer a relative presence, an "according to circumstances."

Parmenides himself does not say so. On the contrary, he declares that this presence is such for νοῦς, thus in relation to something. Yet νοεῖν is the apprehension of Being. In other words: *all beings are relative to Being*. This Being cannot be cut up and partitioned, in order then to be dispersed in bestrewal or to be put back together (if it is at all configured in the first place). On the contrary, Being as the just-named presence is especially prior to all differentiated beings and non-beings. νοεῖν does not cut apart; it neither disperses nor puts together. Instead, *in an originary unity* it unifies presence as such. Presence is not at hand strewn about somewhere; rather, through νοεῖν it is as such first configured and held out, as something essentially occurring "against." νοεῖν waits against presence, waits for it, fosters and configures and keeps the "is." νοεῖν is this waiting-against [*Gegen-warten*]—in short: the present [*Gegenwart*]. *The originarily gathering gatheredness is apprehension* [Ver-nehmen]. It undertakes [*unter-nehmen*] presence as such, upholds it.

γ) The definitive understanding of the present and presence

We have up to now—intentionally—taken the present [*Gegenwart*] and presence [*Anwesenheit*] as synonyms. I In everyday speech, that does no harm. We say: "The matriculation ceremony will take place in the *Gegenwart* [presence][61] of the rector." We could also say: in his *Anwesenheit* [presence]. Both the present [*Gegenwart*] and presence [*Anwesenheit*] signify the mode of Being of a person and indeed of every being. *Now*, however, we are taking the present [*Gegen-wart*] as the encountering-configuring of presence. Presence: the character of the *Being* of beings; the present: the mode of the configuring envisioning of presence. What this means may become clearer by considering what we call presentification [*Vergegenwärtigung*]. If we now presen-

52

---

60. κατὰ κόσμον "*world*"—cf. I *Vom Wesen des Grundes* I. {First edition: Martin Heidegger, *Vom Wesen des Grundes*. *Sonderdruck aus der Festschrift für Edmund Husserl zum 70. Geburtstag*. Halle: Niemeyer, 1929. Now in *Wegmarken*, op. cit., 123–75.}

61. [*Die Gegenwart* can mean either presence or the present (time).—Trans.]

tify to ourselves Berlin, then we stretch the sphere of presence further out, whereby it is evident that this expansion is possible only because a sphere of presence always already essentially occurs around us. This refers not to the individual thing having presence but, rather, to presence itself. The sphere of presence does not expand by our "incorporating" more and more things that were previously absent; it is the reverse. We can "incorporate" these further beings only if the sphere, the *field* as such, is expanded *in advance*.

This presence, however, always already envelops us; i.e., presence as such is the prospect we look into, not qua something at hand but qua looking as such. Seeing is a configuring in advance of and against the prospect. More precisely: the possibility of the broadest expanse essentially occurs and is always already only factically restricted. Thereby, however, we must not take this possibility as the standard, but vice versa. *Our explicit activity is the restriction, the restrictedness, of the sphere of presence.* This configurative seeing that holds something over and against is the character of νοεῖν. We call it presenting or *presentifying* as prefiguring of presence. The present now designates the basic comportment of νοεῖν. This basic comportment as configurative seeing is in itself the projecting of presence. Envisioning is prefigurative seeing, just as is disregarding.

Conversely, this presence essentially occurs only as the projecting in the projection of configurative seeing. The present and presence intrinsically belong together (toward what is the unity of both turned? Temporality!). Thereby we have only determined more clearly the meaning of Parmenides's axiom: τὸ γὰρ αὐτὸ νοεῖν ἐστίν τε καὶ εἶναι— apprehending and Being belong together. For Being always signifies presence [*Anwesenheit*]; the latter essentially occurs only in the presence [*Gegenwart*] of νοεῖν. The axiom has thereby been interpreted originarily on the basis of what Parmenides says about Being in his σήματα and especially with the aid of fragment 2.

We now grasp the two main results of the course of proof of the σήματα: 1) the prospect on Being proves to be presence; 2) the securing and gathering of the respects on Being happen through recourse to νοεῖν and to the axiom. These two results now join into one, *into an originary understanding* of the axiom, which we can now formulate as follows: *Being essentially occurs as presence* [Anwesenheit] *in the presence* [Gegenwart] *of apprehension.* And only because the sphere of presence [*Anwesenheit*] essentially occurs do we understand Being and the "is." This presence [*Anwesenheit*] essentially occurs in the present [*Gegenwart*]. The latter is the time we *ourselves bring to maturity.* The axiomatic statement and the temporal statement say "the same."

The difficulties offered at first by fragment 2 (as if therein was expressed a belonging of the "not" and the "away" to Being) have dissipated. Parmenides is indeed not saying that absence would belong to the essence of Being qua presence but, on the contrary, that presence is so originarily one, uniform, simple, unique, and whole, that without it absence is impossible. To be sure, the whence of the absent, the "away," and the "not," if according to Parmenides they cannot derive from Being, is a further question, one Parmenides neither poses nor answers. Yet for this question his essential determination of Being (Parmenides's essential statement) does carry out the decisive spadework, inasmuch as Parmenides in general demonstrates for the first time that there is something like nonbeing, in the form of semblance. Admittedly, on the basis of his concept of Being he must say that semblance is not. Yet semblance is not equated with pure nothingness. Thus arises the question of what and how semblance is, namely, seeming. The prior question, however, is: what is semblance? How does it look in general? The course of the first way passes over (8, 51ff. and the remaining fragments) to this question and task.

k) The belonging together of νοεῖν and λέγειν

The first way has still not come to its end, however. As we said, the insertion of fragment 2 is important not only for the preceding text but also for the succeeding, 8, 34ff.

8, 34–37. This section, as the conclusion of the previous course of proof of the σήματα, once again reverts to the axiom, specifically such that its content is now presented with more determinateness. Not simply the belonging together of apprehending and Being. Instead, Being is now explicitly grasped as οὕνεκέν ἐστι νόημα, as the "for the sake of which" of apprehension. Apprehension is what it is *in the service and mission of Being.* Apprehension unifies so that Being is thereby configured and projected. And what is thus projected at the same time now qua that ἐν ᾧ, that "in which" apprehension is pronounced. We know νοεῖν belongs together with λέγειν. Apprehension cannot at all be found by itself, as something simply there at hand. We come across apprehension as soon as we ever encounter Being. In Being as uniformity and presence, we always find that which is conducive to the uniformity, that which unites and gathers, i.e., λέγειν, and in presence we find the necessary relation to the present. All language is sayable only *in Being.* Therefore: where Being is not understood, there also no language; and vice versa: where no language, there also no understanding of Being. Accordingly, animals—plants—although these can never exist [*existieren*].

If Being did not essentially occur as such, then νοεῖν would also remain a nothingness. πάρεξ τοῦ ἐόντος, if the prospect is outside of the sphere of presence, wherein anything can be sought, then the "it is" or even only the "it was" or "will be" is no being at all. But if the projection in νοεῖν did not happen, then *presence would be closed off,* and no beings could ever be encountered. Being and apprehending therefore do not stand in a congruent, reversible relation of reciprocal appertaining. Instead, Being pertains to apprehension otherwise than apprehension pertains to Being, with perhaps another sense of necessity in each case. Yet this difference thus also in the reciprocity of the relation pertains to the unitariness of the full essence of Being. Even this, however, is not the last word on the matter. (Cf. below, p. 56.)

Verses 37–40 also belong to this essential characterization of Being. Given this characterization, it is now said what results, on the basis of and in light of the essence of Being, for everything considered a being according to common human opinion, everything established by the human view regarding what should count as a being. All this, understood in terms of the essence of Being, is just wordplay, mere opinion, chatter (but not purely nothing!). *The common understanding of Being is suspended in idle talk about beings.* Entangled therein, the gaze does not become free to carry out the gathered and gathering respect toward oneness and to conceive presence as such in the present; mere ὀνόμαζειν, not λέγειν.

l) Changeable things as nonbeings

From 6, 6–9, we already know how the human throng understands Being. That understanding is now rehearsed in sharp opposition to the essential determination of Being. It is significant that Parmenides here refers explicitly to | τόπον ἀλλάσσειν, change of place, i.e., movement in the sense of locomotion, emergence here and disappearance there, and vice versa. Furthermore, Parmenides speaks of (ἡ) χρόα, the surface, the superficial, what first offers itself, shows itself. The superficial shows itself (φανόν) only to the eye; therefore what in a preeminent sense *appears and seems,* what shines, is precisely color, a changing surface in the light. There is good reason for explicitly mentioning such change here, because precisely the change of light and darkness, or day and night—as we saw earlier with regard to Anaximander—is the primal phenomenon for emergence and disappearance, γένεσις and φθορά, *here* and *away.* But that which in this manner can be here and away like day and night, that which is visible by day and hidden at night, that which is now here and now away, now has presence and now absence, is not a being. It does not satisfy Being, presence, but on the contrary itself requires presence in general as the domain of coming to be and passing away. In the day, however, already the dispersal into a diversity; at night, everything determinable becomes indeterminate and ungraspable.

At this juncture, the consideration swings from the outlook on the field of semblance back to a *final conclusive presentation* of the essence of Being in the image of an intrinsically unitary, simple, unique, completely uniform, well-balanced sphere, one struck within a hard, clear, outer boundary. The sphere. Image of the self-gathered gathering of unitariness.

No further comments now on verses 42–49. What is required is merely to view synthetically everything that preceded, i.e., to put into effect a *new* unitary respect forming over and against us in the one prospect on Being: *presence as such pure and simple*—Being.

We gain from all this the basic insight that Being could never become and that we will nowhere hunt it down, come across it, discover it, snatch it. It offers itself only if we configure it, carry out the projection of presence in general, i.e., at the same time hold ourselves out in its expanse as thus opened up. This self-opening of presence as such in the projection out of the present [*Gegen-wart*] is, however, at once nothing other than the happening of *manifestness* or, said in the Greek manner, unconcealedness—*truth*.

Here truth not because of correctness, but the reverse: here correctability and reliance because of truth, i.e., because *presence* essentially occurs as self-opening in the truth. Undue "modernization" (inappropriate and false way)—on the whole, it is not a matter of correctness and falsity but of the happening of manifestness and the happening of semblance—beyond correctness and incorrectness.

The way on which Being as such is projected and explicitly understood is thus the way of truth. Insofar as truth itself is won, i.e., insofar as Being is conceived qua *presence in the present,* the way attains its goal (50–51) *"in the truth."*

Whatever is said and discussed from this point on belongs to the prospect of the way of δόξα, the way of human views.

m) The way of δόξα

α) Coming to understand δόξα

D 8, 51–61

δόξας δ᾽ ἀπὸ τοῦδε βροτείας
μάνθανε κόσμον ἐμῶν ἐπέων ἀπατηλὸν ἀκούων.
μορφὰς γὰρ κατέθεντο δύο γνώμας ὀνομάζειν,
τῶν μίαν οὐ χρεών ἐστιν (ἐν ᾧ πεπλανημένοι εἰσίν).
55   ἀντία δ᾽ ἐκρίναντο δέμας καὶ σήματ᾽ ἔθεντο

χωρὶς ἀπ᾽ ἀλλήλων, τῇ μὲν φλογὸς αἰθέριον πῦρ,
ἤπιον ὄν, μέγ᾽ (ἀραιὸν) ἐλαφρόν, ἑωυτῷ πάντοσε τωὐτόν,
τῷ δ᾽ ἑτέρῳ μὴ τωὐτόν· ἀτὰρ κἀκεῖνο κατ᾽ αὐτό
τἀντία νύκτ᾽ ἀδαῆ, πυκινὸν δέμας ἐμβριθές τε.
60   τόν σοι ἐγὼ διάκοσμον ἐοικότα πάντα φατίζω,
ὡς οὐ μή ποτέ τίς σε βροτῶν γνώμη παρελάσσῃ.

51–54) From this (with which I stopped), come to understand the views of humans, whereby you must apprehend my discourse as full everywhere of delusion (a saying of deception and semblance). Of forms they establish two for all discussing of what is meant, such that of these it should not (be said) only the one "is." In all this (establishing) humans are the errant.

55–59) A lying over and against they have demanded according to configuration, and the respects (for the views) they strictly separated from each other (each for itself). Here, the bright glow of flame, bestowing (appearances), lightened (thin), nimbly quickened, in all directions the same, but not the same relative to the other (cf. D 10). Likewise, the other one for itself, that which lies opposite, the night, withholding (appearances), unlightened (dense), and weighing heavily.

60–61) I want to say completely how semblance is configured in the separate appearances. Thus (if you understand this) never will human opinion surpass you.

The way of δόξα is now to be traversed, and specifically based on the first way and not as humans generally proceed, namely, by taking this third way while completely caught up in it, without knowledge and understanding of the other ways. To take the third way based on the first way means to question the prospect and the respects of the third way while keeping in sight the clarified outlook of the first. The task is accordingly to find the σήματα and to present the outlook founded on them. But this does not mean to learn the countless individual views and opinions of mankind, neither so as to go along with them nor to disprove them; instead, the task is to see them on the basis of the first way, i.e., to question them in accord with unconcealedness, so as to determine how matters stand with δόξα as such and in general.

Let us briefly take up the meaning of the word δόξα and the *matter at issue* therein for the Greeks (cf. w.s. [winter semester] 31–32).[62] δόξα is view: 1) the aspect anyone presents, the view of oneself offered with

---

62. {Martin Heidegger, *Vom Wesen der Wahrheit: Zu Platons Höhlengleichnis und Theätet.* GA34, 246ff.}

some binding force, to stand in view; in general, the aspect something offers, the view of a landscape, of a city, (picture postcard) [*Ansichts-karte,* lit. view-card]; 2) view, I am of the view that such and such, I am of the opinion, some sort of determination, intrusion of appearances! in opinion. Thus on the one hand: δόξα as a character of *appearances themselves,* their aspect, self-offering (cf. 8, 53 μορφή; 55 δέμας, form—cf. thus later εἶδος, ἰδέα). On the other hand: δόξα as a character of the *comportment* toward appearances, having an opinion about them, holding them to be such and such, soliloquizing, ὀνομάζειν (8, 53; 9, 1; 14, 3; already 8, 38 inter alia), δοξάζειν (later—tragedy.) These two meanings of δόξα are not accidental. They belong together, and *indeed entirely in the decisive sense,* just as do εἶναι and νοεῖν or λέγειν on the first way; only this not a single word; ἀλήθεια certainly; cf. especially later ἀληθεύειν τῆς ψυχῆς, Aristotle. | 54

β) Errancy and semblance

Now just brief references to the most important content of the remainder of fragment 8. The respects and aspects are introduced (53) quite abruptly as two, called light and darkness (day and night). They offer the outlook on appearances now in this way and now in that, according to circumstances, i.e., now determinately and now blurred, according to the brightness or dimness, which is constantly changing, thus a prospect on seeming, ostensible, i.e., precisely *semblant beings.* Thereby it is important that there are *two* respects, i.e., that the σήματα are χωρὶς ἀπ᾽ ἀλλήλων (55–56). These ordinary opinions always set themselves apart for themselves; thus precisely the "according to circumstances" is possible. On the other hand, the σήματα of Being all converge on *one* outlook and are all basically the same. Every discussion is carried out in terms of these respects and their "according to circumstances," whereby further views come to be formed and at once dominate.

Those who commit themselves to these established respects are the *errant ones;* they move in the *to and fro,* the now this and now that, *of errancy* (8, 54). Indeed, the light of day seems to offer aspects of *beings themselves,* namely, their clear lines and contours and the articulation of surface and color, foreground and background, whereas in the dark even what is close by becomes unfixed, wavering, and blurry and disappears or else fools us like something uncertain changing here and there. But to privilege one of these two respects οὐ χρεών ἐστιν, goes against necessity, for the rising of the day is posed in between night, i.e., out of the night and back into it; day as such is *related to something else* and so is *in itself nullifying.* Does day have priority? The day rises, begins, according to ancient Greek doctrine, with the night. Day proceeds from night into night. Day is light in transition. Lacking the rigorous clarity of (stable) essentially occurring Being.

Verses 56-57 characterize the two respects, light and darkness, in sharp opposition. Bestowing appearances, withholding appearances; thin in density, compact in density; light, heavy. That a *grandiose* gaze into the phenomena is here at work does not need extensive confirmation. This oppositionality, however, is the preparation for what is to be said in the following, of which only a little survives for us in the disjointed fragments 9, 10, 11, 12, 13, 14. Yet the essential can indeed be seen: both aspects, light and darkness, are the *primary appearances* (cf. above, Anaximander). Appearance here as looming up, and this latter as setting oneself out in relief and prevailing—*appearance as predominance, coming to the fore. And even semblance never has the weak and pallid sense of an indistinct, gloomy haze.* Light and darkness configure and guide all stepping forth and receding and thus all ephemeral appearance as such and such, according to circumstances.

These appearing things, however, pass themselves off as beings; semblance is alleged Being. This configuring separately into the changing individuals, διάκοσμον (60) is to be described. Numbered among these are the household things, the nearest, the common. But what appears through is that *the entire manifold of appearing things is of this origination out of light and darkness;* that remains *unsurpassable* (61). He is, as in a race, constantly and necessarily in advance of everything that conceals views and that is established on them, even if ever so rightly. He is in advance thereby secured against these appearances being taken, despite all their fullness and obtrusiveness, as beings themselves, although the latter precisely seem to be these appearing things. All semblance gleams, shines, enthralls, and captivates precisely when the semblance unfolds into the enchanting manifold of the to and fro, on and off, open and closed—this free play of the "according to circumstances" is prevalent everywhere. As thus constant and unified it is something like *Being* (ἕν). The semblance of the ἕν appears as the prevalent, the similar, the constantly in play "according to circumstances."

§23. The δόξα-fragments 9, 12, 13, 10, 11, 14, 16, 19
(in the order of their interpretation)

a) The equality of light and darkness

The guiding sense and the aim of the following fragments must thereby have become clear. In their details, they offer insuperable difficulties to an interpretation, especially because later cosmological theories commandeered Parmenides's notion of δόξα, deflected it, and totally deprived it of its meaning. The doxographers then exacerbated the confusion by basing their interpretation of Parmenides on this earlier misunderstanding. The immediately *most important fragment* is number 9.

D 9

> αὐτὰρ ἐπειδὴ πάντα φάος καὶ νὺξ ὀνόμασται
> καὶ τὰ κατὰ σφετέρας δυνάμεις ἐπὶ τοῖσί τε καὶ τοῖς,
> πᾶν πλέον ἐστὶν ὁμοῦ φάεος καὶ νυκτὸς ἀφάντου
> ἴσων ἀμφοτέρων, ἐπεὶ οὐδετέρῳ μέτα μηδέν.

Yet ever since everything was spoken of with respect to light and night, and this done according to the powers proper respectively to the one as well as the other, so the All is at once filled with light and nonluminous night, each equal to the other, for concomitant to neither (is) nothingness.[63]

Briefly: everything that appears not only shows itself in the light, in illumination and darkness and gloom, and conceals itself there, but appearing is at the same time the "Being" of light and darkness. Things consist of light and darkness; on that, also 8, 59: where darkness and gloom, there murkiness, the impairment of brightness. But the murky is in a certain sense the denser, the more burdensome, the heavy—matter. All matter is in its own respective way elapsed, darkened light and for that reason is unthinned and untransparent. Yet in the luster of metal there is still the intrinsically steady reflection of pure brightness and clarity.

Again the essential is said about the two basic respects, light and darkness; *each is equal to the other* (cf. above, 8, 54), neither has priority, for they are both not entirely nothingness. Yet they are also not Being but are, rather, precisely between, that which partakes of both, that which looks like Being and precisely *as* so doing is *not* Being: therefore *seeming*.

b) Birth as the basic occurrence of becoming

D 12

> αἱ γὰρ στεινότεραι πλῆντο πυρὸς ἀκρήτοιο,
> αἱ δ᾽ ἐπὶ ταῖς νυκτός, μετὰ δὲ φλογὸς ἵεται αἶσα·
> ἐν δὲ μέσῳ τούτων δαίμων ἣ πάντα κυβερνᾷ·

---

63. The basic respects—pre-semblances—of all appearing.

πάντα γὰρ <ἦ> στυγεροῖο τόκου καὶ μίξιος ἄρχει
πέμπουσ᾿ ἄρσενι θῆλυ μιγῆν τό τ᾿ ἐναντίον αὖτις
ἄρσεν θηλυτέρῳ.

For of (both) the narrower regions of the sphere (day and night), the one is filled with unmixed light but the other with night (complete darkness). Between these two, however, (everything) is shot through with partial light, and in the middle of these (regions) resides the goddess, who steers all things. For in every direction she is the incentive to and the sovereign over all dreadful (because death-bearing) birth and mating. Sending the woman to the man for breeding and conversely again the man to the woman.

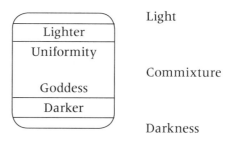

55   Diagram of the outlook on the whole of appearance. | Here beside the total outlook on appearance the *throne* of the goddess, in the middle, where, *equally distributed,* light and darkness are governable *together and uniformly in all directions* (cf. 1, 11). In her dwelling are the gates of day and night, now beyond light and darkness since it is a matter of appearance as origination and disappearance, the basic occurrences of all becoming: birth, but this στυγερός, dreadful; στύξ, underworld, Hades, death. *Every birth begets death.* In arising to presence, there enters at the same time utter absence; both at once—presence-absence, dread and bliss, impotence and power, δεινόν, *away and here, in frenzy*—Dionysus! Nietzsche's doom was that he—with all his clarity—misunderstood no other Greek philosopher as completely as he did Parmenides. Consequently, Nietzsche did not later measure up to the proper task!

D 13

πρώτιστον μὲν Ἔρωτα θεῶν μητίσατο πάντον.

But Eros was devised as the first of all the gods.[64]

---

64. (the configuring urge)—*underway*—

Thus in 9 the basic respects of all appearance, in 12 the diagram of the outlook on the whole of appearance in both those respects, only in 13 and at the end of 2 the character of the occurrence of all appearing and configuring.

c) The history of the appearance of the world

Fragment 10 ushers in the presentation of the history of the appearance of the world.

D 10

> εἴσῃ δ᾽ αἰθερίαν τε φύσιν τά τ᾽ ἐν αἰθέρι πάντα
> σήματα καὶ καθαρᾶς εὐαγέος ἠελίοιο
> λαμπάδος ἔργ᾽ ἀίδηλα καὶ ὁππόθεν ἐξεγένοντο
> ἔργα τε κύκλωπος πεύσῃ περίφοιτα σελήνης
> 5 καὶ φύσιν, εἰδήσεις τε καὶ οὐρανὸν ἀμφὶς ἔχοντα
> ἔνθεν ἔφυ τε καὶ ὥς μιν ἄγουσ(α) ἐπέδησεν ἀνάγκη
> πείρατ᾽ ἔχειν ἄστρων.

But come, you shall hear of the generation of the pure light and hear of everything that shows itself in the light (cf. 8, 58; the same and not the same) and of everything that blazes up while radiating (flaring up) in the bright sun and also disappears from it, and of whence that happens (the sinking in brilliance) and also of the origination and intrigues of the round-eyed moon, and you shall get to know whence arose the surrounding heaven and how constraint directed it and bound it to hold fast the limits of the stars.

D 11

> πῶς γαῖα καὶ ἥλιος ἠδὲ σελήνη
> αἰθήρ τε ξυνὸς γάλα τ᾽ οὐράνιον καὶ ὄλυμπος
> ἔσχατος ἠδ᾽ ἄστρων θερμὸν μένος ὡρμήθησαν
> γίγνεσθαι.

How earth, sun, and moon
pure atmospheres to us along with the milk in the sky, and outermost Olympus,
and the glowing force of the stars broke forth
into appearance.

D 14

> νυκτιφαὲς περὶ γαῖαν ἀλώμενον ἀλλότριον φῶς

Nightly[65] shining, wandering around the earth, borrowed light.

---

65. [Reading *Nächtig* for *Mächtig*, "powerfully."—Trans.]

Throughout this entire history of appearance according to the guiding respects of light and darkness, all the things that gleam and also become extinguished, faint, and dark in their nexus of appearance, a nexus that presents itself at once as movement, whether that is clearly established, coordinated with others and with other appearances, or errant, as the movement of the moon or in general the appearance of *semblance*—all these things, without their own light and *without the correct appurtenance, wander about in the contourless dark of the nights.*

We saw above: δόξα has a double meaning. In accord with the matter, that indicates a δοξάζειν or an ὀνομάζειν (δόξα 2) corresponds to the φαινόμενα. The basic meaning of this has already become familiar to us though the first introduction of the separation and characterization of the ways. Cf. fragment 6, especially 6, 5: πλαγκτὸς νόος, erroneous-errant apprehension that is not gathered into itself and thus is not secured in advance so as to apprehend and understand solely the one in its unitariness but, instead, from the beginning is attached only to whatever things just show themselves *according to circumstances* and lets itself be drawn to and fro by these, constantly tugged by the "according to circumstances." Insofar as νοῦς must express itself about the things it has apprehended, it does not address them in terms of the unity and uniqueness of the essence but, instead, names and discusses them according to circumstances, in each case according to a respect that indeed offers the appearance. This naming entrenches itself, ossifies, and forms its own world of word-knowledge that then guides all cognition and controls all proofs and proof-claims.

This giving of names to the appearances and thus the adherence to appearances do not ever stem from a grasp of Being; on the contrary, they are always established in the respect toward a view in which the beings offer themselves and which is more or less appropriate, as the case may be. Therefore, the *meaning and weight* of a word must always be confirmed and redeemed through knowledge of the essence, a knowledge that at the same time makes understandable the relative justification—indeed, the necessity—of semblance. The sole fragment teaching us something about δοξάζειν, specifically in its *necessary relation to semblance*, is 16.

d) Apprehension and corporeality

D 16

ὡς γὰρ ἑκάστοτ᾽ ἔχει κρᾶσιν μελέων πολυπλάγκτων,
τὼς νόος ἀνθρώποισι παρίσταται· τὸ γὰρ αὐτό
ἔστιν ὅπερ φρονέει μελέων φύσις ἀνθρώποισιν
καὶ πᾶσιν καὶ παντί· τὸ γὰρ πλέον ἐστὶ νόημα.

For just as apprehension at any time abides in a mixture of the much-errant body, so is it at the disposal of humans, for this (common) apprehension is the same as that which the figure of the human body thinks (opines) in all and in each. For excess (excess of weight) always constitutes apprehension. | 56

Here it is said with immediate clarity: *apprehension occurs in corporeality.* The latter is (12, 4f.) *self-mixing* and is *itself mixed* and by some sort of necessity appears sensuously in birth and death and procreation and indeed in all activity. What is meant here is not simply the sense-organs, but *sensuality,* as that bears and rules the entire disposedness of humans, precisely that which is always proper to them. And now Parmenides says here: just as that which is intended in opining, the appearing thing, is always constituted out of light and darkness, the lightweight and the heavy, so is also opining, as the case may be, either itself illuminated and light and lightweight or dull and unilluminated, heavy and ponderous; for all and for each individual ever differently. *And the respective excess of light or darkness in corporeality itself determines the apprehension and the possible sphere of apprehensibility.*

We know from 1, 34–37, how common opinion resorts to hazy seeing and noise-filled hearing and idle talk, according to the predominance of the dark and heavy, i.e., the unlit.

Therefore, it remains to note that apprehension is corporeal and that, accordingly, even the pure apprehension on the course of the first way is never free-floating in itself but on the contrary is what it is only in confrontation with the errancy and discordance of the to and fro of the body. The body, however, is not, as in the Christian understanding, evil; instead, it is the most necessary powerfulness in the sense of δεινόν—at once uncanny and much capable.

e) Being itself apprehends

If we wish to survey *the whole,* there is still one consideration to be made. Not only does apprehension always pertain to corporeality, i.e., to that which appears, but, conversely, everything that appears is thoroughly and as such always in its own way something that apprehends. Indeed no direct testimony of Parmenides about this has come down to us, unless the axiom and what corresponds to it in the appearance of the world must be grasped in such a way that not only does apprehension apprehend Being but also *Being itself apprehends.* On other grounds as well, I lean toward taking the axiom primarily and ultimately in that sense. Yet, as I said, there is no adequate documentation of it.

On the other hand, there is the testimony of Theophrastus, Aristotle's student, whose Φυσικῶν δόξαι also transmitted the two statements of Anaximander.

Fragment 16 comes down to us in Aristotle's *Metaphysics* Γ 5, 1009b21, part of a very remarkable text. Theophrastus cites precisely this passage in his treatise *De sensu* (cf. Diels I, 3rd. ed., 146)[66] and provides an intepretation important also in another respect (μνήμη—λήθη). Here we will take up only his report that Parmenides teaches:

> τὸν νεκρὸν φωτὸς μὲν καὶ θερμοῦ καὶ φωνῆς οὐκ αἰσθάνεσθαι διὰ τὴν ἔκλειψιν τοῦ πυρός, ψυχροῦ δὲ καὶ σιωπῆς καὶ τῶν ἐναντίων αἰσθάνεσθαι.

Where light and that which is light occur, there also that which is light and illuminated can be apprehended and likewise also warmth and brightness, sound and voice. Where light and that which is light are absent, as in a dead body, there *not nothing* but, instead, the *dark* and *dense,* the *closed,* the *mute.* Accordingly—the dead apprehend cold, the dead hear silence.[67] Even the dead, those who are no longer alive, apprehend. From this, but a small step to say that precisely everything dense and fixed and dark, all matter, has apprehension of some sort; an apprehension happens there. Theophrastus also reports this, by saying in connection with the cited statement: καὶ ὅλως δὲ πᾶν τὸ ὂν ἔχειν τινὰ γνῶσιν, Parmenides even teaches that all beings whatsoever in some way have something like apprehension.

Transmitted to us, still from the δόξα-doctrine, is the concluding fragment 19, with which the entire compilation of the fragments also concludes.

D 19

> οὕτω τοι κατὰ δόξαν ἔφυ τάδε καί νυν ἔασι
> καὶ μετέπειτ᾽ ἀπὸ τοῦδε τελευτήσουσι τραφέντα·
> τοῖς δ᾽ ὄνομ᾽ ἄνθρωποι κατέθεντ᾽ ἐπίσημον ἑκάστῳ.

Therefore, in the manner of appearance, this (what was presented in the appearance of the world) originated, and now still remains, and afterwards, henceforth nourished, will come to its end. Humans have thereby established the names (discussion), in this way granting to each thing that by which it shows itself.

---

66. {*Die Fragmente der Vorsokratiker. Griechisch und Deutsch von Hermann Diels.* Vol. 1, 3rd. ed. Berlin: Weidmann, 1912.}

67. [Heidegger's rendering of the passage ends here.—Trans.]

Again, ὀνομάζειν in necessary connection to appearance, characteristically words and speech. ἐπίσημον, not σήματα, not what of Being
or of appearance immediately and originally shows itself, but conversely what, on the basis of an individual respect—according to
circumstances—ἐπί, is posited in addition and as it were is fitted with
a *mask*, behind which it is concealed and through which it nevertheless at the same time can be distinguished and recognized.

Conclusion

§24. The inceptual question of Being; the law of philosophy

We have proceeded a small distance in *co-asking* the inceptual question of Being. From the interposed considerations, we know that it is not an alien and discardable question.

We need to recall from the interposed considerations, in regard to the understanding of Being—what the "is" *signifies*.

What has thereby resulted? Not much. Nothing. Perhaps this one circumstance: we have learned that that is what we should not ask if we truly want to grasp.

We have co-asked, re-asked, the question of Being. Being is starting to become *question-worthy*. We understand something of the well-worn, much-used "is"—or at least we understand that there is here something to be grasped. This grasping has its own proper law and its unique measure.

The law of philosophy—philosophy has its own law. How we situate ourselves in relation to its rests *with us* alone. We can expose ourselves to this law and thereby sustain it. *We can also keep away from it.* But as usual—

What remains: the shocking greatness of this (so slight at the beginning) labor. It is a labor that has been standing for two millennia—and it will stand *in the future*. It will stand especially against all the volumes full of the idle talk and pen pushing of *everyone* today.

APPENDIX
Drafts and plans
for the lecture course

ON ANAXIMANDER

1. {Concerning the structure of the interpretation of Anaximander}

Introduction. From the *sphere of the beginning* the oldest transmitted pronouncement.

    A. The interpretation in two phases
    B. The appropriation of the interpretation
    C. Meditation on the procedure
(Thales)—Anaximander () two statements.

The first: text; customary translation / tradition; commentary—according to the individual sections of the statements. I–III.

I.

    1) About what—τὰ ὄντα—the things; *literally* and *better:* the beings.

(Word) grammar: neuter—plural: *beings:* not simply a *"multiplicity"* —*the many individuals in their unity*—the neuter plural governs as a singular.

(Issue) *that which is*? How to be understood?

(*In general*) *beings:* e.g., the sea; the land—the sky—what is therein and thereon—plants—animals—humans—their works and destinies.

Beings: not these individual ones, but rather all, everything? Quantitatively—sum total.

No! *Not everything!* Why not? Precisely because we *never* could and *never* did grasp *everything?* Not only therefore—*no—but for a more essential reason.* To grasp "everything"—indeed, even only a quantity of several—we must seize individuals and gather them together. Yet—we never find merely *individuals*—the seizing is always a wrenching *away from;* to begin with individuals—beforehand—nothing? That certainly not.

Thus: we always already have more than individuals and more than a *quantity*—no matter how great—*more than everything and yet never the sum total—the full quantity.*

More than *everything?* "Everything": includes each thing; leaves nothing out.

Plants—everything laid out—nothing omitted—everything? Yet something still missing.

Everything—not the *whole*—"*organism"*—*the whole*—not subsequent (result)—instead, prior—even where no individual parts and pieces— bud—seed.

Wholeness and totality as *unities;* not every whole that of an organism.

That which is = the whole of beings.

Sum total—ungraspable and innumerable.

Wholeness—encompass or unfold out of itself? Either: completely outside—how? or: itself the whole?

That which is—neither individuals and particulars nor quantity and totality nor the whole.

What then? Let us hold fast and try to name it—unmistakable—the "as a whole."

Hereby: unessential: 1) the number of things known; the scope of the *cognition;* 2) a fortiori not the kind of cognition—such as scientific cognition.

N.B. how to the *farmer* that which is is more than it is to the city-dweller. The farmer's experience is into the whole and out of the whole. The city-dweller: attached to the newspaper and radio—*untold variety*—*for him* the farmer: narrow world—he: but not broad—nor narrow—but only *"scattered."*

That which is = beings as whole (≠ all beings; ≠ the whole of beings)—admittedly not grasped with full sureness! But indeed a sure feeling for it.

Cf. Text, *p. 2 bottom*! Ungraspable: because the closest and most familiar—therefore: skipped over—misinterpreted. In order to see: *not* artifices and contortions—but only need to loosen the shackling to the currently obtrusive and incidental.

The "as a whole": *in a rough way* and yet quite determinate. What is around us and before us—under us and above us, and *ourselves* included; with the most constricted narrowness and the most expansive breadth nevertheless always some sort of closure; a self-coordinated manifold; *familiar and proven*—in an *unproven affiliation* with the *new and alien*—not *"added" from the outside*—instead: *out of this.*

About what: τὰ ὄντα—beings as whole.

2) *What* is said about this?—first section of the statement.

a) γένεσις καὶ φθορά pertain to beings.

α) "Coming to be—passing away"—*un-Greek*—the understanding of the entire pronouncement is jeopardized from the outset.

γένεσις stepping forth—receding.

Difference—causal—doxal! γένεσις also not "genesis"; Aristotle κίνησις—ποίησις.

Appear—≠ Kant. Appearance—thing in itself. I Appearance—as the happening of beings as such.

Example—disappearance as a mode.

β) ἡ γένεσις—ἡ φθορά—*the* stepping-forth—*the* receding; not "a" random occurrence; *mark of distinction* I the *essential indicated.*

I *Sameness* I γ) ἐξ ὧν—εἰς ταῦτα—the *whence-whither*—our characterization of stepping forth and receding—sameness of the whence-whither I thither the result as returning there—proves to be φθορά.

Meager information—immediately ask: *what is* this whence-whither?

The usual wrong-headed interpretation of γένεσις—φθορά—because the coming to be of the world—world—nature.

Whence nature arises—matter—basic matter, prime matter—supposed advancement on the part of Anaximander—because not a determinate particular matter!

Mistake! Entirely off the mark.

At issue here cannot be a basic matter.

1) altogether not a coming to be out of and through one another—passing over into one another—not a whence as matter;

2) altogether not nature—according to which a formation develops. Beings as a whole not any particular domain, even a preeminent one.

The whence-whither—I *each and every being*! I I Plural! I

Difference—from beings—; what is then differentiated and separated: nonbeings.

Nothingness—limit! *Do not shrink back*!

Therefore initially and for a long time—saying nothing. Therefore can do nothing with the whence-whither; let stand—sameness.

d) κατὰ τὸ χρεών

What is said about beings—not this *also* inter alia—it is *the* necessity.

Not arbitrary—not choice—not mere fact—also not just some sort of invariability—instead, beings are forced to it by compulsion—with and in every appearance *the compulsion shows itself*—*the* necessity shows itself in beings.

What is enumerated about beings—what the situation is *with them*—with them—with them *as beings—the way beings are—Being.*

More precisely: stepping forth and receding (appearance)—sameness (what therefore? belonging together) of the whence and whither—the compulsion shows itself. How compelled through sameness.

About what: about beings as a whole.

Of what: of the Being of beings—first appearance of beings in their Being—with the intention—interpreted—poetized.

But not narrated—or only *established*—instead, *said.*

Why beings are as they are—said of Being—(wherein it essentially occurs)—what this essential occurrence itself is—why what is said pertains to the Being of beings—*why beings are as they are.* Why the what. The I γάρ I.

II. *why* whence-whither necessarily the same—to enter more closely into Being.

γένεσις and φθορά *related to each other*—*interrelation*—give way to each other—*basic experience.*

Evidence (cf. text): out of the most broad and free glance of humans into beings *not to lose* and we will experience it. *Making secure*—unitary glance at beings (I).

Appearance oscillates in such reciprocal giving way (back and forth).

And what *lies therein*—(διδόναι) a bestowal—| in what sense; *how determined*—in *consideration of what does it happen?* ἀδίκια—wickedness. δίκη and τίσις—ἀδικία—*what is the meaning?* Juridical-moral evaluation and concepts.

Is this a free and immediate experience of beings? Or not rather a most restricted, shackled, and new evaluation of beings—*transference*—of determinate human relations into the whole—*projection*—of subjective lived experiences into objective events?

Precisely that—which one is used to finding in primitive times and among primitive peoples—one is readily inclined—to take the statement in such a way; especially if the already mentioned bias still holds: he was actually aiming at a doctrine of the basic matter. This intention and these means *in the sense of a philosophy of nature.*

In the background of this intention—the means insufficient— admittedly—*pardon* the lack of cognitions; much poetical coloring— in fact: Theophrastus.

Anthropomorphism: 1. as lack and impasse; 2. as *advantage* and power. Not either, because anthropomorphism precisely quite impossible.

But if the postulation of a philosophy of nature falls away? Then at least *no misproportion*—physical—moral, but precisely still the whole— juridical-moral!

But whence the right—to interpret the words in such a way—late antiquity—Christianity—Enlightenment—all that must keep its distance!

Fundamental for these and other *basic words:* "indeterminate"—*yes*— not already determined in the sense of later determinateness—and *yet not vague and vacillating*—*not* the indeterminateness—of the superficial and empty, the fullness of the not unfolded and yet sure.

How then to be understood positively?

Here at the start only references: ἄδικος ἵππος—unjust—guilty— sinful—horse! *Not broken in.*

Non-compliance; compliance (belonging together); correspondence —measuring off of the correspondence.

Origin of these words and concepts—not based on anticipation; instead, the *reverse.*

Translation—interpretation—example—cogent verification—on the basis of a completed interpretation of the whole.

Thesis and grounding! Wherefore? Being . . . in consideration of the noncompliance—*that* | *beings as a whole*—noncompliance?

The second phase

Now—beyond commenting on the individual elements, to grasp the unitary content on the basis of its central core.

Gather together what preceded: beings—*Being*—appearance—bestowal—noncompliance—*time*.

Clear structure and *yet alien*—if pressed . . . but *genuinely shocking: the noncompliance.*

Precisely this passage is *even* the *core*—the whole *comes down to this—need to clarify it.*

How does the noncompliance persist—*what does it consist in*? If a character of Being, then a *further clarification* of Being, and this way precisely *for that reason* necessary—if noncompliance is *not* an arbitrary accidental—defective property of beings!

Being and appearance; appearances! Day—night and suchlike the first *reference*—illustration! Individual examples? Particular cases? Wrong!

Day and night—the *originary appearance—basic experience.* How? As framework—or most frequent?

Permits all appearances to arise: sea and land, forest and mountain, human being and animal, house and homestead.

Sovereignty of the night.

In the luster of the light, beings appear!

The light—the sun—*time*—what *installs* beings into Being. Day—brightness—fixed circumscription.

What is thereby further disclosed about Being?

Every being appears—*sets itself out in relief—raises itself up over—against.*

As stepping forth—entering into a contour—standing out in its contours—the being *"is."*

Appearance: emergence and, *as this,* entrance into contours—*emergent entrance into a contour primal experience*!

Now appearance—how Being as such consists in noncompliance.

Anaximander: beings correspond to compliance, in compliance they revert back to their whence—disappear.

How in beings, insofar as they are, noncompliance predominates—and what that signifies for the essence of Being.

The appearing thing as such out of compliance, out of order. Meaning? On the basis of the further interpretation!

Construction—what the meaning *can* be.

Appearance: *entrance into; whence* steps *forth* that which enters into *contours.*

Noncompliance: persistence in contours.

Disappearance: darkness—stepping back out of—*giving way to:* to a persistence in; taking into consideration—receding acquiesces; testifies—contourlessness.

Cf. *text.*

2. Anaximander and the first empowering of the essence

Cf. Überlegung II, *124ff.*[1]

3. Anaximander—and in general fragments—

What kind of "object" such a fragment is and accordingly what *kind of treatment,* kind of dealing with it for it!

Something cast off—which manifests *precisely* the swing and the casting—the direction into the open realm—*becoming absent*—the *reigning plight* which holds back while *co-forming* and *releases the project*—this latter as it were *kept up and kept open.* To be sure, also just as certain the "danger" of the most obtuse *belittlement.*

Supposing we enter completely into what is pro-*jected* and weighty and provide it the self-recoiling swing of the foothold. The now fixed oscillation of a trembling—which still harbors something of the dimension of the oscillation.

What would be—if no fragments—but rather *finished?* Then a fortiori—*"inceptual"*—provisional—*surpassed*—left behind—our *superiority* still more unrestrained—and the step to the beginning even less prepared and measured.

4. Anaximander

τὸ ἄπειρον—the limitless—what does not come to presence—thus also never *disappears*—the absent—over and against that—which emerges to presence and *reverts* from it.

While emerging and *withdrawing* and *circling around presence—in one way or another* over and against *absence.*

Even this and precisely it as *essentially occurring*—in the present?? *Dominant outcome.*

N.B. the limitless ≠ the *"and so forth"*—the *inexhaustible?*

---

1. {In *Überlegungen II–VI,* GA94.}

The *not unfolded greatness of this beginning.*
The fact that this presence *noncompliance* and such by necessity—
receding as *compliance—non*compliance qua: *toward* presence—compliance as *away from* presence.

5. Anaximander

Is he thinking of withdrawing (receding) in regard to the pandemo-
nium of the fall of Nineveh. Sardis—with regard to the tremors of the
cities of Magna Graecia?—Ro. Roll. [*sic*] {?}
Perhaps also.—

6. Anaximander

φύσιν
  Sophocles, 523 {*Antigone*}
  οὔτοι συνέχθειν, ἀλλὰ συμφιλεῖν ἔφυν.[2]
  Not to co-hate, but to co-love am I there.
  (I am open and manifest—as (proto)-type.)
  Cf. 562
  τὴν δ'αφ'οῦ τὰ πρῶτ'ἔφυ.
  From when she first appeared—not at all—*came to be*!

7. Anaximander

δίκη
  Compliance—*and specifically in the sense of disposal.*
  Make right—reign—reach through and take hold ≠ *equilibrium*—
elimination of the strife—*coming into*!?
  Cf. Solon—θάλαττα! {?}
  Instead—mutual self-postulation—measure—/ correspond—"giving
way" to the stronger—
  ἀδικία—noncompliance—without disposing power—*fail*—compliance—*ordains,* "separates and organizes."
  The disposal first creates compliance *and* noncompliance—posits
rank and "order."

---

2. {In *Überlegungen II–VI,* GA94.}

8. Anaximander

concerning διδόναι.

Give—give in—concede—to-(rights!)—let the compliance persist —*acquiesce.*

Thus not to pay something and to counter-pay—to *render* for . . . — instead—to let the compliance hold good.

Cf. Aeschylus, *Prometheus* 9, 30.[3] To create disposal—let hold sway the (battle) between compliance and noncompliance—all things engagements and causalities of the (battle).

The battle—struck within no limits—instead, itself *separating and organizing.*

9. Anaximander

Cf. Winke II, 109, beginning.[4]

How therein a *casting loose of oneself.*

How and where the human being finds himself.—

Away—here—he forms for himself a place.

Set out into Being.

*Compliance—noncompliance—*structure—*remote disposal.*

Itself worked forth *out of itself.*

Here first δίκη—τίσις / not *"in itself."*

What first appears in Being not for "humans" and thence asked about!

10. ψευδωνύμως, cf. w.s. 31-2[5]

ψευδωνύμως σε δαίμονες Προμηθέα καλοῦσιν . . . Continuation! Aeschylus, *Prometheus,* 85.

Yet you *have* no Forethought in you—you *are* not—as you are addressed and named.

The *name* is a perverting designation—it adverts to something— which is not at all present at hand.

---

3. {*Aeschyli Tragoediae,* op. cit.}

4. {In *Winke I, II,* GA 101.}

5. {Martin Heidegger, *Vom Wesen der Wahrheit: Zu Platons Höhlengleichnis und Theätet,* op. cit., 258ff.}

11. δίκη

Aeschylus, *Prometheus,* 9
  τοιᾶσδέ τοι
  ἁμαρτίας σφε δεῖ θεοῖς δοῦναι δίκην.
  Such a mistake—(error) / to give—concede compliance; / emphasis
on δοῦναι.
  Ibid., 30, βροτοῖσι τιμὰς ὤπασας πέρα δίκης.
  Beyond the limit of *compliance.*

12. *{Concerning the structure of the interpretation of Anaximander}*

A. The interpretation in two phases

Introduction: *two dicta transmitted.*
              Text.
              Translation—I customary—according to Diels and
              Nietzsche.
              Transmission—in Simplicius from the φυσικῶν δόξαι of
              Theophrastus.
              Procedure of the interpretation: start with the longer dic-
                              tum. Treat it in the first
                              phase.
                              In the second phase incor-
                              porate the shorter one.

The first phase of the interpretation

Break down the *longer* dictum into three sections, I, II, III.
    Commentary on the sections.
    In re I. The first opening of beings in their Being.
1) *about what* does the pronouncement speak? τὰ ὄντα
    a) the word—α) participle—as noun (τὸ ὄν)—*the beings*—but as *that
        which is.*
                β) neuter plural—governs the singular—that which
                    is—the many individuals in their unity.
    b) the issue—*that which is*—α) not this or that individual—arbi-
                    trary one.
                    β) also *not* all individuals in their sum-
                        mation—not only unattainable—
                        instead—we always possess more

γ) but the whole a fortiori not—and yet!—

δ) beings *as a whole*—essential for that is neither the number of things known nor the scope of the cognitions nor the *mode* of knowledge (such as the scientific)—e.g., the "as a whole" for the farmer—the constant scattering for the city-dweller.

The beings before—around—under—over—and in us, and ourselves included.

The most constricted narrowness and the most expansive breadth of the "as a whole" are maintained in an untouched but ever so close affiliation.

About what: about beings as a whole.

2) *What is spoken of—whereas beings as a whole are spoken about.*

a) to beings there pertain and result γένεσις and φθορά

α) the jeopardizing of the understanding of the entire pronouncement through the misinterpretation of γένεσις and φθορά in the sense of *"coming to be" and "passing away"*—("genesis").

Here the basic notion is that of a directed from-to—transition and progression or regression—succession—cause-consequence-development. *Precisely this un-Greek*—even still for Aristotle, where first γένεσις qua κίνησις, then also for ποίησις, production, εἶδος.

β) γένεσις—stepping forth—advent ("born"—arrived); φθορά—disappear—recede—go missing.

Both in one: *appearance*—l a book appears l the appearing guests—nevertheless ≠ Kant; because not the distinction between appearance and thing in itself.

b) γένεσις and φθορά not arbitrary—just any one and occasionally—instead, ἡ γένεσις and ἡ φθορά preeminent appertaining character of beings as such.

c) ἐξ ὧν—εἰς ταῦτα καί—the *sameness* of the whence and whither.

α) *according to* the basic character of γένεσις and φθορά.

From where—thereto.

Thus not: whence of a self-forming—origination and transformation—in one another

Proceed—exclude—precipitate—like *prime matter*—*thus no* "advancement" by Anaximander—because no determinate individual matter.

β) We can refrain from (α) prime matter *altogether not* at issue, because τὰ ὄντα—beings as a whole no individual domain.

d) this sameness in the *plural*—in itself a fullness? Darkness. (Superiority of the essential enabling, cf. below.)

e) Thus of what is spoken? Of something different from beings as such, something that is not a being—nothingness? But on the other hand

f) κατὰ τὸ χρεών

what the situation is with beings—the belonging together of the whence and whither in stepping forth and receding—this according to compulsion. Not arbitrary—not choice—not mere fact—instead, the compulsion shows itself in appearance *and* disappearance. Beings are compelled into the sameness of the whence-whither of their appearance | disposition {?} of the essence |.

The enumerated, that *of which* is spoken in the pronouncement about beings, concerns Being.

I. About what: about beings as a whole—of what: of their Being. Transition from I. to II.—

About beings not constatations simply with respect to their Being—instead—*why beings are as they are.* On what that depends. That means: to enter into the essence of Being.

In re II. *The essence of Being*—the more precise characterization did conceal anew the gaze at beings that *provides the basic experience.*

1) τὰ ὄντα . . . διδόναι ἀλλήλοις—altogether mutual bestowal—back and forth—off and on.

Appearance oscillates in a reciprocal—giving way back and forth.
Evidence: glance at the whole: day and night / winter and summer / tempest and calm / sleep and waking / birth and death / youth and age / fame and disgrace / shine and pallor / curse and blessing / in all this appearing and disappearing—in each case beings as such first show themselves.

This the "as a whole"—out of this the dictum speaks—but not a determinative assertion in the barrenness and thinness of a contrived natural science.

2) What do beings bestow on one another—what happens in their Being?
δίκην καὶ τίσιν . . . τῆς ἀδικίας

Justice retribution injustice—(recompense—atonement—sin—guilt—wickedness).

a) Transference of human relations into things—poetic coloring—|
    Theophrastus.

| *Anthropomorphism* (humanizing of beings as a whole):
     α) as lack and impasse—where still properly nature
     β) as advantage and power of depth.

1) This conception itself anthropomorphic—and presupposes
     α) detached—egoic self-experience
     β) disenchanted presence at hand—mere pushing and min-
        gling of matter.

2) *But neither one there*—neither the whence—nor the whither for an
   anthropomorphizing transference—*no possibility at all* of an anthropomorphizing—still not the dwarfism [*das Gezwerge*] and Christian
   pontification over one's own soul.

3) Impulse to this understanding from late antiquity—Christianity—
   Enlightenment.

b) *Adequately positive understanding of such basic words.*
     α) *Fundamental:* Undetermined—but not vague and vacil-
        lating—not the indeterminateness of the superficial and
        empty—instead, the not unfolded and broad, yet sure—
        the whole.
     β) *Individuals*—Only references—e.g., ἄδικος ἵππος—a horse
        not broken in—not a "guilty horse"—"sinful ox."
        ἄδικος—does not run in harness—does not fit in—not
        pliant—
        ἀδικία—noncompliance
        δίκη—compliance
        τίσις—τίω—appreciate—whether it corresponds—take
        the measure of something in relation to—*correspondence.*
        Compliance—*belonging together*—"juncture"—structure.
        Correspondence—proportional interrelation.

Genuine verification of these comments on the basis of the whole.

In II. essential characterization of Being as grounding for beings in
their "what" and their "how."

Here grounding! Darkness! yet especially III:

In re III. the essential ground of the essence—(cf. 6 and 7).

Time as presence of appearance and disappearance—the essential
occurrence of Being.

Summary: in all sections the translation clarifies—and yet we will
not dare to say we understand.

On the contrary—versus the initial translation (interpretation)
everything less accessible and darker.

Therefore: *Second phase.*

Translation: But whence beings take their stepping forth, thence also their receding ensues according to necessitation; for they (the beings) give compliance and correspondence to one another in consideration of the noncompliance according to the allocation of time.

κατὰ τὴν τοῦ χρόνου τάξιν—I as if related back to the whole I.

The mutual bestowal in consideration of the noncompliance happens according to . . .

The grounding is now *again led back:* χρόνος—τάξις—time—order.

These words clear—; ordinary—no danger of misinterpretation!

"Time"—"*in* time"—the processes lapse; in a respective "temporal point"; each.

a) temporal position—in succession; time—*sequence of these positions*—framework in which we calculate.

b) *testimony* of philosophy for it: Kant—the wherein of the order of the manifold with respect to the succession of the manifold—succession—consequence—cause—result—*nature—history*

c) in addition—γένεσις—φθορά—"coming to be"—"*passing away*"—time the "*transient*"—transience—eternity—"the *temporal.*"

But: in re c) we know—γένεσις—φθορά—*appearance* in the Greek sense; not succession—cause-effect—not *transience* of time!

In re b) *Kant's concept of time*—tailored for nature—theoretical-scientific calculation of the elapsing of motion—of a material thing. Quite determinate concept of time—not at all self-evident.

In re c) what to us is self-evident and customary—is indeed only the indeterminateness of something entirely *ungraspable*—almost only a word. I The *superficiality of everything customary.*

Therefore even here *basic words*—not arbitrary!

How thus for χρόνος? Kant *does not* inquire—but if already in philosophy, then in *the Greeks*! Aristotle—*Physics*—precisely an interpretation of later ones, contemporaries—customary—Plato—little—reference—οὐρανός—at first appears not to say much; genuine experience.

Testimony *outside of* philosophy; *poetry* always the *first—great* interpretation of {beings} out of *basic human experiences.*

Undetermined—individual—on purpose *precisely that:* Sophocles, *Ajax,* 646–47: here: χρόνος φύει τ᾽ ἄδηλα καὶ φανέτα κρύπτεται.

κρύπτεσθαι—*conceal* (let disappear) and specifically φανέτα—the appearing that stands in appearance.

φύει—φύσις *growth*—nature—1) domain—such as that delimited against history or art; 2) nature of something—nature of a work of art—essence—whatness; 3) living and thriving of a being—Being.

φύει ἄδηλα—lets grow—lets come to be—something not manifest. This would indeed mean: expose what is concealed—; let disappear.

But *indeed precisely the converse:* bring *forth* what is not manifest, τέ—
καί, so—as also! Namely, in *manifestness.*
φύει—*lets arise—appear*—show itself.
Double, important result: 1) time—*its basic character*—to let appear!—
puts *forth* and *takes back* not the emptied
and incidental order of position.
2) φύσις—arising—*appearing*
γένεσις and φθορά—confirmed in their basic meaning.
Time: not as order of position for succession and framework for
temporal points, instead—that which lets appear—ǀ cf. Heraclitus.
ἀναρίθμητος—incalculable—against which all calculation fails—more
important than this ≠ not . . . {illegible word}.
τάξις—τάσσω—allocation of place—*hither* for something stepping
forth—*allocation* of the present and absent in their *essence* (time as the
essential occurrence of Being) (cf. p. 5, sec. a).
Entire translation.

The second phase
The intrinsic unity and the content of the pronouncement (I)
and the incorporation of the other dictum (II)

I)
Start—in the genuine theme—*Being* of beings and here again with
that which is *most alien*—insofar as it is not drawn into insignificance
through misinterpretation as a mere metaphor.
The most penetrating revelation of the essence of Being—ἀδικία—
to Being as such pertains noncompliance. How—does it persist? In
what does it consist? First task.
1) *Renewed characterization of Being.*
Appearance—thus more precise and fuller version of the essence
of appearance (disappearance).
a) cf. above, Homer: *day and night,* etc.—not special cases—*basic ap-*
pearance: insofar as light—brightness lets everything appear and disappear—*bring something to the light of day*—let step forth and let stand
in the light;
b) i.e., *however, entrance into contours*—limits—not indifferent framework—instead, ordaining—gathering and holding power and weight
of things.
Presence
        Night—*limits become indistinct*—things merge together—
Absence Disappearing (receding—gorge—) gaping void—χάος—
        not reciprocity—instead, the void—nullity.
2) *Now it becomes clear—how in the essence of Being noncompliance, and*
in what does noncompliance consist?
Being qua appearance: but to appearance pertains disappearance—
first and properly a *reciprocity* and this latter is to bestow compliance in

consideration of the noncompliance—the noncompliance is the *emerging entrance into contours* and therein self-*understanding and not knowing*—*to consist in that.* To give compliance—*is stepping back from that.*

Being—therefore *the acquiescence to compliance, an acquiescence that is disposed (corresponds) to noncompliance.* Thus neither compliance— nor noncompliance constitutes the essence—instead, their correspondence—*absenting presence.*

Grounding of this essential grasp of Being?

II. The other dictum—

the sovereign source of beings as such, i.e., Being, is the limitless.

ἄ-πειρον   a) ≠ the endless, the "and so forth"

b) ἀ-privative—here not absence in the sense of something lacking or missing, but the "without" and "away" —of disappearance and the "from itself"—of the essence out of *superabundance* and *overfullness*. What has to do with contours—neither assuming them nor abandoning them—established neither in presence— nor absence.

Rather—these in their essence first empowered—in advance— essentially occurring as their unifying and empowering ground: | Time—| absence: disappearance and not still appearing (priority— apparently of the present—seen on its basis).

The empowering essential power, out of which and back into which all Being essentially occurs and in accord with which beings are— Anaximander envisions as time / cf. κατὰ τὸ χρεών.

N.B. From here, easy to realize the absurdity of the wrangling, how and in what guise the basic matter would be determined.

The entire confusion and derangement: people wrangle over the interpretation of the later doxographical facts and explain the singly transmitted pronouncement—as *poetic* decoration—| since Theophrastus and Aristotle and Gr. {?}.

"Result"—Being is not a being—completely different—it essentially occurs as time.

Poetry—to be sure!

And yet—the comprehending interpretation extremely daring and to all suspicion against itself? Transition to *B. Meditation on the procedure.*

13. Anaximander (Fall, 1932)

Introduction: from the *sphere* of the beginning of Western philosophy. The oldest transmitted pronouncement.

Articulation: A. The interpretation in two phases.

B. The appropriation of the interpretation.

C. Meditation on the procedure.*

Conclusion: Unity of the dictum—word and Being at the beginning and end.

*Take up the "method" in the middle and thus obtain its inclusion in the issue and thereby intensify the issue.

14. B. The appropriation of the interpretation

1. The differentiation (beings and Being)
2. The bifurcation (originarily united dawning of the modalities)
3. The mood (aloneness—ordaining [*Fu.*]—maelstrom {?})
4. The procedure (poetry).

15. C. Meditation on the procedure (Fall, 1932)

Transition: Through B, A is not confirmed but only made fully suspect; for how should Anaximander have thought of all that. | The interpretation extremely daring in every respect—admittedly. τολμητέον!

Hence necessary: meditation on the procedure. The meditation becomes justification of the interpretation as grounding of the "standpoint" in the task of beginning. And the task out of a necessitation becomes a cessation with "philosophy."

Meditation: I. Objections to the procedure
 II. Dispersal of the objections
 III. The grounding of the procedure in the task.

I. *Objections.*

1) The procedure is *unilateral;* for excluded is the whole "doxographical" tradition, one that is important precisely here where only a single pronouncement has been preserved.

2) The unilateral procedure thus becomes completely *unrestrained;* for it is exposed without restraint to the danger of utter arbitrariness. The restriction to the one statement leaves the interpretation without any possibility of testing and verification by means of comparison with other passages.

3) This unilateral and odd procedure is furthermore fully and intrinsically *impossible.* For no interpretations could illuminate a pronouncement {?} or an individual dictum simply on the basis of itself. It is indeed a commonplace that any interpretation works with definite presuppositions.

II. *Dispersal of the objections.*
(In inverted sequence, to show their origination and the claim.)

In re 3) True, every interpretation moves within presuppositions. The only question is whether these lie on the same plane as the treated "matter" and accordingly are just as accessible and evident. Or whether indeed *this open* presence of such presuppositions would already be their justification, i.e., would make a justification superfluous.

Admittedly, to judge in this way means to wallow in coarse prejudices regarding the essence of the presuppositions of an interpretation.

If the usual presuppositions for the interpretation of Anaximander were ignored, namely, a) that he belongs among the Greek philosophers of nature who treat of the basic matter and b) that this philosophizing is based on pure observation and inquisitiveness (ἱστορία), then this still does not mean banishing Anaximander's teaching to groundlessness right from the start. On the contrary.

In re 2) True, the possibility of comparison with related passages can testify that an interpretation is more comprehensive, provided the interpretation has already been attained. But it is still an error and a delusion to believe that the richer the direct transmission, the better and surer the interpretation.

How much more do we "have" of Parmenides and Heraclitus? Does that in the least make our interpretation of them better founded and less questionable?

And even for Plato and Aristotle? What do we grasp of their genuine questioning? The broad abundance of the texts merely creates an opportunity for turning off into side issues, for quick and superficial entwining of artificially invented systems and structures—from which all questioning has flown.

Thus only the danger of shirking the genuine exertions of questioning, the danger of flight into the placidity of splashing about in shoreless muddy waters.

In re 1) True, in what has been handed down a mode of appropriation always reveals itself, and, from that, something can be gathered regarding the appropriated issue—provided the issue has already been grasped in its essence and the handed down, transmitting reports and positions have been clarified in their proper intentions and aspects.

Otherwise, all that rises up is a flighty to-do with opinions—which becomes all the more vacuous the clearer it is seen that the semblance of diversity in what is handed down goes together with a reduction in the possibilities for actual understanding. And such is indeed the case with the entire doxography regarding pre-Platonic philosophy.

III. *The grounding of the procedure in the task*

16. Anaximander—hermeneutic meditation

"Prime matter"?
   Indeterminate world-pulp—mishmash?—*and similar nonsensicalities.*
   Neither causal—nor material and not in consideration of the doc-
trinal opinions—instead, in the *sense* of the basic question—ὄv—and
in the *direction* of the basic answer—οὐσία—and connection with ἀ-
λήθεια—with φαίνεσθαι.

17. The beginning.
The monumentality of the beginning

and, raising itself up therein, the remote disposal of the unasked—
unbegun.
   Monumentality—the resting in itself greatness of the produced work.
Greatness—bursts into the breadth and depth of being great, i.e., *ac-
ceptance of the concealed mission.*
   Here: the work of the happening of the outbreaking *question.*
   What we—tottering right in the middle | thrown off the path |—
succeed in taking out of the beginning determines for us the height
of the goal: as task | leaps to the front and only then is to be drawn in.
   The one great memory now and still borne on.
   The greatness a *fragment*—what *tears open* of the dark—of its greatness—that which fails—no accident!
   Thus ever again compelled away—without the comfort of a shining
possession—one that makes dispensable the appropriation and retention.
   Thus at once: out of what is early—inceptual the genuine correspondence to the remote mission—the latter obscure in its mode—
only one or another of a deep intimation broken out—out of necessity *to be sure* a virtue! In plight the necessity and to correspond with
the latter through the turn into the clarity of a mission.

18. Anaximander

Anthropomorphism of *"legal"* thinking.
   δίκη—compliance!
   Neither ανθρω-morphism nor θεο-morphism—instead, here precisely the essentially philosophical burgeoning into the "between" of
man and God—as poetizing transformation to Da-sein—Being.

19. Hermeneutic basic presupposition
for seeking out the beginning

1. The beginning is the greatest—and therefore not great enough to lay hold of.
2. We are—indeed advanced—but that means always left less equal to the beginning.
3. The beginning was previously to no avail—(N.s.) [sic].

20. Anaximander

Which plight and affliction undergone—which mission undertaken—i.e., in and out of which questioning *answered*.

21. Anaximander: ἄπειρον and ἕν and bifurcation

Here only quite in the twilight—the modalities and not as such and yet precisely their | unity | ἕν.

Compliance *and* noncompliance | *fro—into appearance.*
Disappearance—*to—back into concealedness.*
To *and* fro—| universal cadre |.
Structure of the bifurcation.

22. Anaximander: τὸ ἄπειρον and Being

Not to represent—something intuitively at hand—but self-presentation to the happening of Being—to the questioning of what it means that there are beings at all and not nothing. | Being—not beings.

If there is still something to say about τὸ ἄπειρον and its interpretation in the first statement, then this: τὸ ἄπειρον speaks out of the basic experience of the δεινόν qua the basic character of Being.

Being—the overpowerful—which empowers all things—to their greatness, i.e., to their limits. The overpowerful that in its bestowing empowering is at the same time the frightful—insofar as it compels giving way and disappearing—i.e., *receding and giving way in and under the retention of greatness*—and specifically the bestowal of noncompliance in the fetching back into compliance—(Being is *cadre*).

N.B. Here at the beginning—not slipping down into πέρας and climbing up to εἶδος. Instead, the glance into Being sees more.

Being is not exhausted in apparentness and in impressed form.

23. The second phase

Versus the dissecting and the word-analysis, the unity and toward an understanding of the issue.

The *most pressing alienation* of the *essence of Being—to Being pertains:* ἀδικία—*out of that* and at once in glancing *at* compliance.

In what the alienation persists—I can persist!

To give compliance—in the "against" of the essential occurrence {?}— and *at the same time* | *noncompliance*.

Disposing of the noncompliance while acquiescing to the compliance—to acquiesce to the compliance—dispose into noncompliance.

Thus to acquiesce as disposed.

τὸ χρεών and τάξις χρόνου.

Instead, going down out of time—instead!! *Not endlessness*—instead, *time* is the ἀρχή! Time does not have the limits of presence and absence.

Power {?} of the essence | source |.

24. Concerning the text of the dicta

Nowhere wanting to find some sort of terminology—as if Anaximander claims something as a *terminus*.

Precisely therefore also impossible to argue: e.g., he still cannot have used ἀρχή, γένεσις, or φθορά "as a *terminus*."

Thus—these *sections not genuine*.

Cf. e.g., Burnet—Jordan.[6]

25. Textual question

Where does the actual quotation begin, what is transcribed in a later conceptual language?*

In the context of what questioning did the pronouncement stand? Is the pronouncement as central and unique as the solitary preservation would suggest?

*ἐξ οὗ—εἰς τοῦτο | ἀρχή |

| *unjustifiably cast into doubt* |

---

6. {John Burnet, *Early Greek Philosophy*. London: Black, 1892. Bruno Jordan, "Beiträge zu einer Geschichte der philosophischen Terminologie," *Archiv für Geschichte der Philosophie* 24 (1911): 449–81.}

26. "ἀρχή"

ἄρχων

(ἀρχή) and ἡγεμών equivalent for Philolaos—*old Pythagorean tradition.*

Source—sovereignty—by holding back and *thus by taking back.*

27. Concerning p. 11

1.) sovereign source, overpowering egress and ingress (of beings (as such)): the limitless. / (Essential power of Being)

2.) But whence beings take their stepping-forth, thence also their receding ensues (happens) according to necessitation (compulsion); for they (the beings) give compliance—maintaining correspondence with one another, *acquiescing* to a correspondence with one another—(in consideration of) in return for the noncompliance according to the allocation of time.

Now in reverse sequence and according to a more precise version.

28. Concerning p. 11

Beings ≠ noncompliance—instead, *more acquiescent—compliance bound* and *thus correspondence*—not contour = noncompliance—instead—to merge into, or, *returning from.*

Being—*absenting presence.*

The essence—| what this ↑ empowers.

What has to do with contours—neither by assuming nor by abandoning.

Not established on presence or absence (priority of the present).

Being *and* bifurcation.

29. Concerning p. 12

An isolated treatment of Anaximander, once the interpretation is carried out (A), should bring forth a discussion of the open and yet concealed difference between Being and beings and the modalities (bifurcation) (B); the latter in unity with (A) should discharge itself in a meditation on the whole mode of questioning and interpreting and on their truth (C): *question of the beginning*!

30. Concerning p. 16ff.

We maintain that the beginning of Western philosophy is in our closest proximity. Needs to be exhibited. To that end:
the *mark* of the beginning
the pronouncement—1. *grounding* saying of Being over beings
—*why*
2. answer—intrinsically related *to questioning.*
The *pronouncement* as such altogether not the beginning; instead, possibly *the end and indeed of a questioning.*
Questioning—a creatively grounding questioning—*disclosive questioning of Being.*
Question of Being!
Where suchlike is encountered—or something bound to it—there the beginning is near.
Question of Being? Question.
The act of beginning as question of Being
The question and questioning in general.
a. Forms of questioning
b. Essence of questioning
c. Mode of Being of questioning—
d. Scope of questioning
e. Possibility of questioning in general
f. Appurtenance of questioning.
"Order" of the question of Being
a) What-question—why-question
b) What-question—as essence-question—*a single one*
c) A preeminent—abyssal one
d) *The* essence-question pure and simple—
e) *The* most originary question whatever.
But thereby—with such a characterization—the question is not asked.
Also not through repetition or imitation; instead, *posing the question*—working out the question.
The unproblematic and the problematic
    ↑   ↑
    beings   —   Being?
But Being the *most unproblematic.*
Cf. the characterization of the understanding of Being.
Question of Being superfluous—impossible—or—*to make the unproblematic problematic in the first place.*
To gaze at Being anew—whether Being is question-worthy and what about it is question-worthy.
More penetrating questioning—*what we understand by it*!

To show we understand something quite *definite* by it.
The four *oppositions* | unitary meaning of "Being."

31. Concerning p. 23

The "ought"—how related to "Being"?
1. qua the obliging of the one who ought—I ought—I am obliged—
2. qua the oughtness of what ought to be.
I ought to bring about what ought to be.
a   b
both ought.

32. Anaximander

In the Schopenhauerian manner—to fulfill Dasein (human being) through death.
The human being really ought not exist.
But—stepping forth as well as disappearing ought to be grounded.
Not only *the latter.* (Perhaps "punishment of the one who has become"—beings (appearance) place of execution of the damned?)
What is the unity of both—*manifestness*—presence and absence. πέρας—
But precisely {?} this sovereignty of the formation and of the *abundance of the visions.*
The clarity of the limit.
Melancholy of Being!
"Becoming is the punishable emancipation from Being"?[7] To *expiate with going down*! Does "the existence of multiplicity" here become "a moral phenomenon"?[8] Nietzsche.
No!!! But beings are not *Being!* And yet the latter allots the former to us.—
What *is* (πέρας)—how ought it *not* be. Precisely because it "*is*," it must pass away—as a *being,* it must account to *Being.*
But *Being is not a being!*
Why then not already long ago *nothingness?* Already long ago—*Being is nothingness*—but not *sheer nullity!*
And *how* out of Being indeed beings?

---

7. {Friedrich Nietzsche, *Die Philosophie im tragischen Zeitalter der Griechen,* op. cit., 27.}
    8. {Ibid., 30.}

Not: Being versus becoming—that which is versus that which be-
comes.
   Instead, beings *are as appearance and disappearance.*
   And beings essentially occur in *Being* (ἄπειρον).
   Even *appearing* is *acquiescing*—to give compliance.
   Being—as acquiescent noncompliance.
   Essential power—the *limitless.*

33. {Presence and absence}

It is not that what disappears pays for what remains, but *also the reverse*—instead, *both reciprocally*—insofar as they *are* at all—*beings,* i.e.,
in appearing disappearing—present absent.

34. Out of Anaximander

To acquire only *one* glimpse into the not unfolded inner diversity of
the dictum—all pre-Platonics together.
   Which glimpse?
   And which glimpse the intrinsically unitary diversity?

35. Being and ἕν

"Everything is one."
   This statement, expressed in some way or other, is already an answer to the *question* of *Being.*
   This questioning—this opening is the first—the questioning answer or the answering question: beings are! *Beings!* Hear and see! Being—! The greatest, the *insurmountable,* the *unique,* ἕν.

36. Anaximander

The sameness of the whence-whither ought to be grounded.
   The fact that the one (uniquely unitary) "ground" of presence and
absence precisely out of the essence itself.
   Presence—absence
   | Bifurcation |
   Cf. p. 9, sec. b.

Essential *power* (ἀρχή)—whence—whither—fetched back—because here that which is sovereign.

Plural—time itself. | Bifurcation!

Beings ≠ what stands in contours—instead, that which *as such* grows back out of them. In and behind *presence stands absence!*

Question: to what extent this conceptually clear for Anaximander . . . *thought apart*—not so important—on the contrary—now first *taken back* even into what is not devised—and then a fortiori to perceive the poetic power (not to admire aesthetically).

ON PARMENIDES

I. "METHOD"

1. Parmenides. ἕν—the first projection of Being

Against the uncanny, multiple, uncertain, dreadful—the excessive, the wilderness, *Being a Being*—what at once leads to a downgoing.

On the ἕν of Parmenides, cf. *s.s. 31* lecture course—w.s. and s.s. 30–31 seminars, Plato, Parmenides.[9]

2. "Beginning." To interpret Parmenides

Already since Plato—or since the ensuing interpretation of Plato, etc. Aimed at the soul or some sort of "subject" and thus everything corrupted. If this guiding notion were transplanted back into the beginning—then the beginning would appear naive, "objective," and impossible.

But above all—one never manages to ask whether in this beginning there might not lie something—which is intended precisely necessarily *prior* to the subject or also *prior* to the object and which makes the beginning something other—*properly* philosophical—yet seized again deformed as a whole.

Therefore also not to invent contrary mistakes: in order to interpret simply "objectively," indeterminately, or unilaterally in the sense of the *author*—instead, to work out the necessary hermeneutical preparation in Da-sein—| origin |.

3. φύσις

φύσιν βούλονται λέγειν γένεσιν τὴν περὶ τὰ πρῶτα. Plato, *Leges* X, 892c2–3[10]

But οὐκ ὀρθῶς!

Of each ψυχή—πρεσβυτέρα

  it properly διαφερόντως φύσει, c5.

---

9. {Martin Heidegger, *Aristoteles, Metaphysik* Θ *1–3. Vom Wesen und Wirklichkeit der Kraft*, GA33. Also, "Übung für Fortgeschrittene: Platons Parmenides," in GA83.}

10. {*Platonis Opera*. Recognovit brevique adnotatione critica instruxit I. Burnet. Vol. 5. Oxford: Clarendon, 1902. "With 'nature' they wanted to say what were the first things to originate."—Editor's translation.}

4. {Negative-positive}

Emergence—disappearance   negative
Life—
Production—
Formerly still
in the future—first   temporal *change*
Whole   positive
Alone there
The present all together
Uniformity
Cohesion.

5. Eleatics

Cf. Nietzsche, *Götzendämmerung*, VIII, 80i.[11]

6. Parmenides

the philosopher—in the midst of (beings). These not *de-poetized* and somehow only observed—instead, precisely a *poem—world-poem.*
    This *re-poetizing* in another mode of poetry.

7. δόξα. *Not to strive for the basic forgottenness*

The fact that humans, in order to attain truth—i.e., to be in it—above all—must understand i*n advance.* The moment this possibility sinks away—they come to that which *fools* them—the incidental and accidental. Not what is *turned* toward necessity.
    Standstill—entrenchment in something that—thereby becomes law.

---

11. {Friedrich Nietzsche, *Götzen-Dämmerung.* In *Nietzsche's Werke,* vol. 9. Leipzig: Naumann, 1899, 80. "In fact, nothing has yet had a more naive persuasive power than the error regarding Being, as that error was formulated by, e.g., the Eleatics: the error indeed has for itself every word and sentence we speak!"}

II. LIGHT AND DARKNESS
Ἀλήθεια:δόξα[12]

8. Parmenides

Departing from φάος—νύξ and *thence to* truth and Being.
But how? | *Various ways.*
Such ones themselves are open, and the way is something to be traversed.
Moon: νυκτιφάες.

9. Parmenides. Light and darkness, frg. 9

How related originarily to Being and truth—nonbeing and concealedness.
More exactly: how *out of* them—as what is most proximate and most permanent (powers) to Being and truth.
Semblance and appearance in them as coming-going self-showing, yet self-showing and precisely showing the things. *The latter* grown together with the former—persisting in them.

10. Light and darkness

"Here" and away.
Darkness veils—cuts us off from the things—isolates—anxiety—aloneness—*lets disappear and pass away*—receding and nothingness—μὴ ὄν.
            "away"
Clamping in "appearances"—self-showing—open/truth and absence presence—Being—becoming; coming to be—passing away.

11. The ὁδὸς ἀληθής

[The] True way [*Wahre Weg*]—
1. correct way—
2. more originarily—the way that can have no truth
3. because there no νοεῖν—φάναι possible.

---

12. {See editor's afterword.}

12. Ἀλήθεια:δόξα

and its encounter in φάος—νύξ. This encounter as "appearance."
But appearance as *encompassing*—penetrating occurrence—not *object—image.*

13. Parmenides. ἀλήθεια—δόξα

"Appearance."
δόξα, because set "over and against" truth, is immediately held to be "illusion"—i.e., falsity, which perhaps is taken for truth.

But δόξα is not necessarily δόξα ψευδής—instead, that which can be the one and the other—oscillates and precisely because it has an indeterminate proper essence—*view*—appearance.
And indeed it pertains to ἀλήθεια.
The latter—even here not simply the opposite of falsity—instead, the *more originary* essence of uncoveredness—*unconcealedness;* yet also not at all the "absolute" and infinite.
Why does *appearance* pertain to ἀλήθεια? Because *concealment* and Being and {beings}.
Beings—in each case these or those—the way we take them and have them—are *self-showing*—and cut away from self-showing as such —emerging—*appearing!*—possessing a look.
ἀλήθεια *not* at all the thing in itself—ontic "beyond"!

14. ὀνόματα and σήματα. Language

Outbreak and language—how language grasps individual present things—and yet how language may originarily at the same time preserve absence.

15. Ἀλήθεια:δόξα and language

Language—beyond ὀνόματα—σήματα!
Ἀλήθεια:δόξα and λόγος.

16. Ἀλήθεια:δόξα and light—darkness

Light—brightness—*transparency—permeability—outbreak*—space.
Ἀλήθεια:δόξα————————————————————openness
Manifestness

δόξα *light—semblance and appearance.*
Being and "seeing"—*the present*
Sight and light.

17. *Light—darkness*

Light *extends*

          limit

darkness *contracts.*

18. Ἀλήθεια:δόξα—*appearance—dispersal and* λόγος

This *dispersal (distractedness)* as the essential character of appearance—emergence here and there and individually remaining standing. | πολλά!

Dispersal and fracturedness require already gathering—because they arise out of gatheredness, better: out of un-fracturedness.

λόγος: not gathering *ontically*—instead, the gathering of beings *in Being!*

λόγος and εἶναι—"gathering"—*self-containment*—storing up.

Gathering and shelter—preserve and *retain*—from one's own resources—seize—*concept.*

19. *{Five spheres}*

Stobaeus: ↓ Aether
            ↓ fiery heaven
            ↓ axis of the earth
Parmenides's "five spheres"
one dark
one mixed, with terrestrial matter predominant
one *uniformly* mixed
one mixed, with fire predominant
one light—pure—(contains revolutions and extrusions—Milky Way—*milk in heaven—white* {?} *from lights*).

20. *{Being and apprehension}*

Being—light ↓ *sight—apprehension*
εἶναι   δόξα   νοεῖν

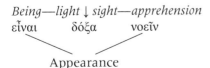

      Appearance

Sight— "seeing"
    look at   apprehend
    consider   take *in*
    observe
    view as
    ponder   take in advance
              inquire
              project.

21. Being and "space"—light—darkness

Let be—
    let through— | "through" "errancy"
    what lets through "δία"
    what can be seen through
    common field for light and darkness | *Choephori* |
    the murky and murkiness
    the first decrease in transparency
    first filling of space
    first step to non-transparency—*murkiness*
    flimsiest matter
    Decrease of light and darkness at the same time.
    Light from dark to light: red—yellow—white.
    Darkness form light to dark: green—blue—black.

22. Errancy—light and Being

Light—beheld non-sensuously
    color—sensuous presentation of light
    light and darkness
    the non-sensuous | *"Being"*
    the *light*
    the light and errancy.
    White the brightest we know—we *compare* with light—not = light.
    Black the darkest we know—we compare with *darkness*—not = darkness.

23. Darkness and Being

What lets rest | it grows dark—*to become dark*—which allows *no undertakings*—permits no *circumspection*—*contains* surprises—*threatens*—allows *disappearance* and *nothingness*—which absorbs beings.
    But is darkness—not also precisely "present"?

24. Chiaro-scuro

"makes physical bodies appear as physical bodies since light and shade instruct us about density."

Goethe, theory of colors, 852[13]

25. νύξ

On the Cimmerians—

Odyssey 11, 19[14]

ἀλλ᾽ ἐπὶ νὺξ ὀλοὴ τέταται δειλοῖσι βροτοῖσιν.

But ruinous night is spread over these accursed people.

It lets nothing come up into appearance (into being).

26. ἐπίσταμαι

Odyssey 13, 207

At the arrival of Odysseus in Ithaca.

Now *I do not know* whither to go with the χρήματα.

I am at a loss—I do not oversee.

27. ἔμμεναι

τήν (Ἰθάκην) περ τηλοῦ φασὶν Ἀχαιΐδος ἔμμεναι αἴης—Odyssey 13, 249

And this—they say—*lies far* from the Achaian land.

"Lie"—"be"—*present at hand* (remaining there for itself).

Odyssey 13, 294

οὐδ᾽ ἐν σῇ περ ἐὼν γαίῃ

Even where you *"are"* in your homeland—now you cease (arrived and in the "here").

τῷ σε καὶ οὐ δύναμαι προλιπεῖν δύστηνον ἐόντα—Odyssey 13, 331

Where you *unhappily* are—*you must persevere*—

28. νοῦς

νοήμονες

οὐκ ἄρα πάντα νοήμονες οὐδὲ δίκαιοι—Odyssey 13, 209

---

13. {Johann Wolfgang von Goethe, *Naturwissenschaftliche Schriften. 1. Bd., Zur Farbenlehre. Didaktischer Theil.* In *Goethes Werke. II. Abtheilung, Bd. 1.* Weimar: Böhlau, 1890, 337.}

14. {*Homeri Odyssea*, op. cit.}

Achilles—in regard to the wounded Machaon.

τὸν δὲ ἰδὼν ἐνόησε ποδάρκης δῖος Ἀχιλλεύς—*Iliad* 11, 599[15]

To grasp with the eyes—apprehend—have in the *eyes*—end in view
—contemplation | meditation |.

ὄμμα τῆς ψυχῆς.

{III. WAYS
THE UNDERSTANDING OF BEING
THE THREE STATEMENTS}

*29. The mistaken use of the "circle" in advance—
concerns also: Being and ὁδός*

Assignment of Being and understanding—we demand from isolated
Being the insight into the necessary appurtenance of understanding
to it and vice versa—but the decisive is precisely to make the non-
assignability evident—

From which standpoint—can that happen (temporality)? *Does Parmenides accomplish it?*

Or do we not simply find a constant dogmatic appeal to the *axiom*
Yet the inter alia appeal to "presence" ἕν *insufficient!* essentially! and
yet necessary!

30. Points in question for the entire interpretation of frg. VIII

The circle objection—p. 45, bottom, 47, top—*appeal to the axiom:* 8, 8f.;
12 ὄντος ἐφήσει πίστιος ἰσχύς—*forms* of this appeal:

The designation of the third way

Time not older than Being | Accidental |

If Being, then thoroughly permanent—without origin—(Parmenides—does he speak of "if"? Cf. 8, 11—or is that inter alia mis-
said ἤ—ἤ (*indirect proof—from negatio!* →) and why?) Parmenides does
not "conclude"—therefore[16] there is Being; instead—therefore either
Being altogether—or not at all—but now there is Being—therefore—
thoroughly permanent.—

Appeal to what? ἔστιν γὰρ εἶναι—there is Being! Basic *projection*—
empowering—ἀλήθεια—(*existo*)—δίκη—disposal of compliance—disposal = for compliance to happen—the use is resolved—at the same
time, *falling back.*

---

15. {*Homeri Ilias*, op. cit.}
16. [Reading *also* for *als* ("as").—Trans.]

If Being essentially occurs, then in the essentiality of constant presence; constant repudiation of every to and fro *and every "not"* (47, middle). Grounding?

How beings as a whole? (Totality)

"Grounding" of the axiomatic statement—8, 13–15 / *16–18*

"Grounding" of the essential statement

"Grounding" of the temporal statement

Being without a "not," because only the present; or Being only the present, because without a "not"—or?

The question of Being *increasingly more problematic*—(cf. p. 48)—(where indeed only constant sameness is maintained—seemingly only *a* thought and a very empty one with the evening starting to appear).

31. {Essence of Being}

Everything fro ← and to → γένεσις—ὄλεθρος;

everything to and fro—τρέμειν;

everything fro- qua brought forth—first;

everything—still and first I against:

everything away and in that regard I "transition";

everything is null and so *against* the *essence* and this—the *barrier*—trammel—*compulsion*—

everything—to disavow the non-essence;

for the *first pure* (and thus alone powerful) empowering and preservation of the essence of Being.

32. Not a blind appeal to and of the χρεών

instead, free empowering and thereby I *demonstration.*

Demonstration as *empowerment.*

Seeing—as *envisioning* and correspondingly exhibition and demonstration.

33. The proper way

as *breaking forth* and *breaking through*—*not* a joyous, tranquil, ever elated, lost-in-itself turn for the better.

Outbreak—which beholds.

ἀ-λήθεια

Ex-stasis.

34. Semblance of the ἕν

is the πάντα in a determinate *condition*.

35. {Three ways}

If way II, the way completely without prospects, is at all mentioned—because even decisive—precisely for the understanding of III—the *warding off of the "not"*—or what is signified by *not warding off.*
He *is* away—as *not* there!
Pertains to the knowledge of way I.

36. Mediate showing

= necessary detour over the *third way.*
Confrontation with this *not less intuitive—on the contrary.*
Ordinary concept of *indirect proof*—also *not merely* negative—but not a *contradiction.*

37. Inappropriateness of the respect through γένεσις, etc.

γένεσις *understood in the Greek sense* and *therefore also* no indirect proof in the usual sense of modern formal logic *pouncing on contradiction—instead, pouncing only* on ἐόν itself.
It would not be *itself*—whereby precisely only direct demonstration—reversal of appearances to the opposite!
Cf. with regard to ἦν = ἔσται

38. What is to be proved—

What is to be proved—I how Being is shown to be *without emergence and disappearance:* it cannot have such—*for otherwise* it would not be itself. So *what is it?*
Hence the "for otherwise" demonstrates that it is itself—must be—more precisely—what it is here projected to be.
But is this projection thereby *itself grounded?* Can it *be grounded? How?*
Proof—indeed here not as deduction from the *"general"*—only *nothingness.*

Indirect proof—that nothing else remains—if contradiction is to be avoided. But—contradiction "follows" first and out of *Being*.

Assumption of the opposite—consequence of this assumption? *Impossible*—What criterion of impossibility? *Contradiction. For which reason the contradictory*—*not being* nonbeing. What then does Being mean? ἕν. ἀγένητον *a whence*—there is not—factually or essentially.

In virtue of what does *the repudiation* of the common understanding of Being *follow*? Where the *hold*? (*Restraint!*) Is the repudiation grounded on something immediately demonstrable, and *does this demonstration happen* at once along with or even through the repudiation?

Can something be repudiated *without end*, or not?

If not, *where the limit* | *whence* the delimitation given? Evident in advance.

Is the "impossibility"—better: *inappropriateness*—of γένεσις and φθορά grounded on the inappropriateness of the *negative*?

And why this inappropriateness? *Presupposed*—*perhaps on the basis of contradiction?*—*cf. separation of the ways*—this *separation*—*consequence* of the essential determination of Being. This the barrier?

Contradiction λόγος as incidence-dictum versus the "not" and semblance.

But *wherefore this determination itself*? Because νοεῖν = εἶναι. *Why this latter?*

Everything on the immediate positive grounding of the basic statement as axiomatic statement—as ground-statement—*ground-setting* and its "logic" (N.B. are not precisely these ground-settings [principles] only indirectly proved—cf. Aristotle *Metaphysics* Γ).[17]

39. Proofs

Already here to be mentioned—that these *"proofs"* of a *peculiar* sort—hence at the same time such that we in going through them—*apprehend precisely the respects*, enter into them, and try to carry out the "seeing."

νοεῖν, λέγειν—*disclosive questioning*—projection—judging—and *yet* at the same time basically a seizing of the *beginning*. Pressed forward {?} into temporality—*taken possession* of it—*grounded* and *yet* only qua g{rounding}.

"Proof"—what it means and what it is to accomplish.

Exhibit, substantiate; | establish; | expose the ground—| *burden of proof;* distribution of the burden.

---

17. {*Aristotelis Metaphysica,* op. cit.}

40. The entire methodology of variations on a theme

always oscillating in and out from ever the same center.

Proof as an exhibiting demonstration "only" the intrinsically *established* showing forth into—the site of Being (46).

Compliance and hold—ἀνάγκη—*trammel and barrier*—limit—end—closedness.

41. Conclusion

Co-asked: the inceptual question of Being—what there disclosively questioned—placed into question.

To re-transfer into our interposed considerations.

Understanding of Being—meaning—the *"is"*—Being and understanding—*Being and becoming.*

Whether understanding does not arrive on the way to the *first comprehension*—to a comprehension—as a questioning one—the question of *Being and time.*

And *time*—|

42. {The hunger for Being}

Not for us of today, in order to become *satisfied at some time*—instead, for the future ones, so that their hunger for Being might increase.

Not for us—a fortiori not for *humanity in general.*

43. Conclusion

The proof of the respects—carrying them out *understandingly* means—*to enter into* this respecting—carrying away.

To grasp the ground and the soil therein!

Soliloquizing—comprehend—concept of Being; only as such *to be understood!,* those who in the ground of their essence have taken on the disposal (δίκη, etc.). To bear and take on!

Ex-sistite! I.e., *empowering of Being! Decree!!* cf. *earlier.*

Not unconditioned!

Only—*if existence*—freedom—*but even then!* the question—Being = *presence in the present?*

44. ἕν

the simple-unique-selfsame unifying unity.
The present—presence.

45. Concerning D 7 and p. 37

μὴ ἐόντα—plural—
    so called, what to mankind are generally beings—properly *are* not; not an ἐόν—they *cannot* and *must not* be claimed as such. μή.
    And yet they are *not simply nothing;* precisely therefore the *constant attempt* to take them as *that which is*—to compel Being onto them.
    But that is never possible—for, Being—rejects everything negative—and forgoes all that is in any way *negative*.
    Precisely therefore, however, it becomes unavoidably necessary to meditate on *how matters now stand* with the fact that *neither* can *Being* be compelled onto so-called beings nor can these be identified with nothingness.
    δόξα—semblance—*how do matters stand with semblance?*
    If that clear—then at the same time the warning *grounded* and *intelligible* and *effective*.
    ἀλλὰ . . . νόημα.
    This question stands immediately at the beginning of *philosophy.* No Being without semblance, and vice versa. But the way to understand this, and a fortiori to ground it, is long.

46. Axiomatic statement—

not in its content something we recognize like just another factual state—not that and then to be applied in the manner of feeling and mildness to existence qua personality—instead, to experience the *danger*—to be placed under the *power* of the axiom—not *poetic* coloring—δίκη, etc.

47. {Apprehension of Being}

    How presence—establishes the inspection of the ἕν—the various unities in their unity.
    How the present—lets this unity essentially occur—*empowerment of the essence.*

What secures this great conclusion posits as the *last jolt*—the apprehension of Being, an apprehension having returned into itself and disposing *out of itself.*

Why this apprehension empowered to its essence and in its essence.

48. *{Beings and Being}*

Presence—even permanence ≠ continuous duration.
From-to—that presupposes presence.
Out of it only—what *enters* into presence.
| *Semblant beings* | but not Being |
What is is only Being (paradox).
Beings into Being—all beings remain behind Being—behind its essence.

49. *{Three statements}*

Axiomatic statement: Being—apprehension.
Essential statement: Being utterly without any "not."
Temporal statement: Being a necessary relation to the present.

50. *Language*—

about beings—semblant beings.
Not in order to say *Being* in the proper sense.
Language *and a fortiori* grammar.

51. *The essence of Being*

How does Being essentially occur?
Which is the appertaining understanding (projection)?
Which is the mood of the projection of Being (empowerment)?
How does mood come to the origin?
How is all the preceding *one* in Da-sein (temporality)?
How is the essentially not inceptual beginning?

52. *"Being"*

not some sort of *thing*—which we then could and should gape at—not some sort of *process*—which we follow so as to produce something—instead—to join the poetizing, *configuring image.*

Being *is* understanding—and yet is not—understanding is Being—and yet is not—instead, Being-understanding—in each case—therefore what?

"Being" *always more than* Being—if this as conceptual content or the like a set aside—intended aside "what."

Presentifying as presentifying of presence.

Thus at first in the start and introduction of the beginning.

Letting *appear* (and thereby along with seeming).

Apprehend = pre-hending qua: letting appear—i.e., to make *appearance* as such possible—qua that which *stands* in *advance* of everything and around everything.

53. {The "theoretical"}

Truth—knowledge—science—the "theoretical."

εἶναι—ἀλήθεια—νοεῖν.

Knowledge—a *"deficient mode"*—namely, within the everyday comportment toward beings.

This comportment to *"beings,"* however, already has the mission of gaining a feel for familiar things; i.e., such comportment is *existent.*

The "deficiency"—as such—of itself makes use of the "theoretical" in the sense of indicatively silent philosophy.

The decision about the full essence of science can come only from *philosophy*—not through the direct assumption of a quasi present at hand "theoretical" element—something generally accepted—which would be carried out only by the disinterested observer {?} of *indifferent* matters!—nor can the decision come from a revision of myth! How not ἐόν and Ἀλήθεια:δόξα.

That, to be sure, only if philosophy is first brought back to *its own* problems—i.e., only if the problem of *truth* is grasped.

Science—can never *itself* pose itself on itself, or else it is deluded.

Yet that does not mean—to waive its rigor and proper significance —on the contrary—it means: still not having grasped its rigor thereby —the so-called "primacy of the theoretical."

For, what does "the theoretical" mean?

54. Parmenides—Plato

To gain *Being* by struggling against semblance—thereby necessarily to alter Being!

In which *direction*? κίνησις? What does that mean?

Dead end—dialectics—necessary?

Aristotle δύναμις—ἐνέργεια?

55. Concerning Parmenides (Being and time)

1) Presence cannot be derived from any absence (past—future). /
There completely certain. | Cf. fragment 2! On the contrary—even
what is *absent* comes to *presence* in Being and as Being.
2) but—is Being only presence—*whence* this *dictum*? Grounding?
Motive? Absence—necessary. *Essential error*—not a failing—instead,
an error, one that remains with errancy? And *yet* not to remain
there.

56. ἀλήθεια—divinity—cf. p. 40, sec. b

Origin—unconcealedness *and* concealedness and bestowal | but also
semblance.
   This as releasing liberation.
νοεῖν—λέγειν not the position-taking and comportment of the individual qua *case*—instead, qua *selfhood*. The latter qua *assumption* of the
gathering of the projection—ἕν. Unification and individuation of the
individual, qua the exclusive one, replaced into the whole. Empowerment of the essence.
   κρίσις λόγῳ.
   The constant appeal to νοεῖν and *to the axiom* (what the latter properly
says!). Not an appeal to a standpoint, not to a crude idealism | instead,
to the essence *of Being* itself. Yet precisely apprehension the first authority for the demonstration of truth. Understanding of Being.
   How matters have to stand with Being.
   Empowerment of the essence.
   Surely *grounds* the ground and abyss of the empowerment.
   Empowerment as disclosing originary exhibition and intrinsically
necessary repudiation—qua assumption of the κρίσις and the confrontation.

57. Being as the most question-worthy

Supposing *existence*—i.e., *Being*!
   If the most question-worthy—then to *disclosively question* existence
—thus make it problematic—*develop the highest questionableness.*
   That the *basic act of disclosive questioning—not* results!
   Therefore *renunciation?* No, the reverse—highest claim of existence
held fast—not abandoned!

58. "Being"

not only site and field—but an *answer* and question especially—questioning as disclosive questioning—opening up of wonder—concealedness *and* unconcealedness—but also in this way not found—what I seek—what *grants place* and at the same time *configures*.

59. Disclosive questioning

To seek—*what is sought first configured,* not pre-given, nor is what corresponds familiar, and yet not absolutely new!

Instead—the search a *leaving behind* of what is "earlier"—earlier what? *Shelteredness*—and now *non-shelteredness*—*what thereby?*

60. Being only in the understanding of Being

i.e., Being as such essentially occurs.

The *essence* and its essentiality—the latter, however, as presence.

The essence qua temporality.

61. First way

The regardful looking away toward *presence*—pure *presentification* of pure presence.

Everything *negative*—inappropriate away.

The basic experience of the "there" as such—and *only this experience* in its predominance over everything entrenched.

"οὐσία" "presence"

The "it is" and only what lies therein—νοεῖν—λέγειν—address—*call forth!*

62. {Mood}

The *restrained astonishment* in the face of Being.

The *shock* in the face of the *negative* | "dispersal."

Shock—*back in the face of—deny* (oneself).

Astonishment—carried away to?—restrained—saying—gathering.

The unity of this mood and ἀ-λήθεια.

Disclosive questioning.

Predominance of the ἕν—what *the shock* (of the predominance) *in the face of the "not."*

63. Axiom

Primal concept → primal possession.
    Empowerment of the essence.
    Being essentially occurs = empowerment happens.
    Humans exist in the proper sense.

64. Fragment 8—what is Being?

What alone accordingly "being"?

What in that way presents itself to us—consequently *semblance—not nothingness.*

Distinguish: 1.) Being—nothingness—*nonbeing and Being*—how with the "not" no effects.

Sphere and its "limit" | *the present* |

The present—presence as such set down and as measure *apprehended.*

Projection of presence as such—and *from presence* as normative at once the removal of everything *negative.*

Only *deduced theory?* Or the "not" spoken out of the basic position—precisely first and at the same time co-apprehended and considered too "lightly"?

65. The first way

A unique "thought," to be sure, but
    1. in this purity to grasp in general
    2. to maintain and to secure from all sides
    3. and only this one.

That precisely decisive—in accord with the matter at issue, there can be only this one truth.

But this one truth is also the proper one—the *essence* of truth—and what is here called a "thought"—!

Incursion—or—occurrence *of the beginning—self-containment—disclosive questioning.*

66. νοεῖν

Take in—look upon.
  Take on—look at.
  Understanding—as *projection*—the seeking-poetizing-configuring projection.
  And originarily— a) let *give itself*
                    b) draw itself *forth—bring forth*—"configure."
  The errant one—πλαγτὸς νόος—how and whither errant here—*make a mistake—go wrong*—
    a) *doubled* δόξα
    b) according to the double essence.

67. Origin and empowerment

8, 28, the originary power of νοεῖν, letting arise and also holding off.

68. {Cadre and truth}

Precept θέμις
    compliance δίκη
    compulsion ἀνάγκη
    and νοεῖν—ἀλήθεύειν.

69. The present and the "not"

Pure presentifying without privation or the "not."
    The present and the "against."
    The "not" as not *yet* and not *still*—temporal *"not."*
    This present altogether other than "eternity."

70. {Being and semblance}

According to the particulars of the fragments about *semblance*—the question of Being as a questioning of *Being and semblance*. Likewise for the question of *Ἀλήθεια:δόξα*—as a whole—*grounding of the ground.*

Is the threefoldness of the ways shown and on what grounds?
    The whole a "circle," cf. p. 44.

Outbreak—beginning—clearing the path.

> *Being and time*
>
> └─→
>
> Being and . . . | today?
> The "is."
> *Where we stand?*
> First *contemplation and intention*—
> i.e., *questioning.*

At first, ways and on them
Being—semblance—
nothingness and from
them—*only* those three
ways. Necessarily—but
why and what is that—
cf. *Being and Time* [18]

71. The first way

Which projection must be carried out—adhered to.

What the projection in purity has to anticipate and hold before itself.

How pure presence in the deepest presentification must become originarily manifest and beyond everything behind and everything in front must in passing snatch away.

Only *where Being there semblance*—but necessarily?

And what then does Being mean?

How both temporal!

---

18. {Martin Heidegger, *Sein und Zeit*, op. cit.}

Editor's Afterword

This is the edited text of a lecture course Martin Heidegger offered in the summer semester of 1932 at the University of Freiburg. The course was announced as "The beginning of Western philosophy, Tue-Fri, 5–6 p.m." [*Der Anfang der abendländischen Philosophie, Di Fr 17–18*]. The first session took place on April 26, the last on July 26.

The manuscript—as is usual for the lecture courses—consists of folio-size [ca. 8½-by-13-inch] sheets in landscape orientation. The left half of the page contains the running text, and the right is reserved for interpolations, emendations, amplifications, and supplementary remarks. The pagination, with some subordinate numbers, extends to 56; the total number of pages is 64.[1] The literary remains also include a sizeable quantity of unnumbered slips "On Anaximandros" and "On Parmenides," intended to prepare for or to accompany this lecture course. In addition, there exists a complete transcript produced by Fritz Heidegger, whose brother then inserted occasional remarks in the margins of the Parmenides portion. There are two copies of this transcript, and earlier and latter comments can be distinguished accordingly. Marginalia that seemed important to me I placed in footnotes, marked as "Trscpt[1]" or "Trscpt[2]." Finally, two sets of attendees' notes survive. One set, in the form of a typescript, stems from Eugen Fink (41 pages). It covers only the Anaximander portion. The other, in handwriting, covers the entire course and is owing to Helene Weiß (165 pages). Her notebook also contains the "mimeo" of the fragments of Parmenides mentioned by Heidegger at the start of the respective portion of the lectures.

In addition to preparing the text, the editorial task consisted primarily in establishing the tripartite structure (with many subdivisions) of the lecture course and thereby articulating a table of contents. Footnotes enclosed entirely within braces are mine. The other footnotes reproduce annotations (always on the right side of the manuscript page) that could not easily be incorporated into the flow of thoughts of the text. The current edition is the first to provide Heidegger's own pagination of his manuscript. The appendix consists of a selection from the slips; the selected passages display a common orientation to the respective issue. Mere lists of keywords and very un-

---

1. [Total: 56, plus 7 pages with subordinate numbers (12a, etc.), plus a last unnumbered page containing the conclusion, §24.—Trans.]

clear remarks were omitted. In general, the guiding aim was to furnish a text that reads smoothly. With that in mind, I silently expanded Heidegger's punctuation in various passages.

I must here mention a peculiarity of the materials obviously used to prepare the lectures. In various notes, the acronym "Aλδo" or "Aldo" occurs. A marginal remark in one of the copies of Fritz Heidegger's transcript allowed this to be deciphered as "Ἀλήθεια:δόξα." By drawing the two parts so closely together, Heidegger is manifestly stressing their unity—presumably also the unity of the usually separated sections of Parmenides's didactic poem. The capitalization of Ἀλήθεια suggests some priority.

* * *

The lecture course on the "beginning of Western philosophy" is a pivotal one. It stands out from the previous courses (on Plato and Aristotle) and prepares for the succeeding ones. It illuminates above all a lecture course such as the "Introduction to Metaphysics" from the summer semester of 1935. Heidegger himself indicated that "since the spring of 1932," "the basic features" were settled of the plan which acquired "its first configuration in the projection 'Of the event.'"[2] This "projection" is essentially related to the distinction between a "first beginning" and an "other beginning." And that distinction quite unmistakably forms the ground of the interpretations of Anaximander and Parmenides.

Each of the three parts of the lecture course has a distinctive character. Whereas Heidegger already occupied himself with Parmenides in the lecture course from the summer semester of 1922,[3] he here interprets the dictum of Anaximander for the first time. Heidegger subsequently indicated that with respect to the interpretation of certain words of the dictum "a misunderstanding made itself felt."[4] Otherwise, the later treatise as well as the still later essay on the "Dictum of Anaximander"[5] bear no relation to this lecture course. The "interposed considerations," as Heidegger called them, stand out in relief from the interpretations of the Greek fragments in a special way. These considerations construct a framework of philosophical meaning, and in that framework the interpretations first receive their sense. The interpretation of Parmenides, introduced by a verse from Hölderlin, moves very closely within the available text as handed down, and thus it pursues a claim to completeness. The interpretation includes

2. Martin Heidegger, *Besinnung,* GA66, 424.

3. Martin Heidegger, *Phänomenologische Interpretationen ausgewählter Abhandlungen des Aristoteles zur Ontologie und Logik,* GA62, 209–31.

4. Martin Heidegger, *Der Spruch des Anaximander,* GA78, 158.

5. Martin Heidegger, "Der Spruch des Anaximander." In *Holzwege,* GA5, 321–73.

fragments, in particular those about δόξα, which Heidegger omitted in later treatments.[6] A marginal remark at the beginning of the interpretation of Parmenides is self-critical: "The interpretation is insufficient, even if much is grasped essentially."

Heidegger himself alluded to the direct effect of his thinking on an interpretation of Parmenides. The notes to his "Lecture courses and seminars since the appearance of *Being and Time*"[7] refer to the 1934 study on Parmenides by Kurt Riezler. At the very outset, Riezler acknowledges he is "gratefully beholden to Martin Heidegger's breakthrough into the question of Being."[8] It is improbable that Riezler knew the full particulars of Heidegger's interpretations of Anaximander and Parmenides.

*   *   *

Prof. Heinrich Hüni was initially assigned to edit this lecture course. His preparatory work included a handwritten transcription of the manuscript up to page 24 (in the pagination of the manuscript itself), a handwritten transcription of the first three pages of the interpretation of Parmenides, as well as research into the historical data concerning the course. I thank him for placing this material at my disposal. I thank Dr. Hermann Heidegger for his untiring work (carried out with his wife, Jutta) in cross-checking and proofreading, and I am also grateful to him for entrusting me with the editing of this volume. To Prof. Friedrich-Wilhelm v. Herrmann I am obliged for assistance with all sorts of editorial issues and for deciphering difficult passages. As regards the further labor of copyholding and proofreading, I thank my friend Martin Berke as well as the following students: Christian Biehl, Philip Flock, Martin Seidensticker, and Barbara Kowalewski. Finally, I express appreciation to Dr. Alfred Dunshirn for communicating with me in regard to classical philology.

Peter Trawny
Düsseldorf, 2011

---

6. Martin Heidegger, *Parmenides,* GA54. Also, Martin Heidegger, "Moira (Parmenides, Fragment VIII, 34–41)," in *Vorträge und Aufsätze,* GA7, 235–62. Also, Martin Heidegger, "Ἀληθείης εὐκυκλέος ἀτρεμὲς ἦτορ," in *Seminare,* GA15, 403–407.

7. Martin Heidegger, *Seminare Hegel—Schelling,* GA 86, 890.

8. Kurt Riezler, *Parmenides.* Frankfurt: Klostermann, 1934 (*Frankfurter Studien zur Religion und Kultur der Antike,* vol. 5), 7.

German-English Glossary

das Abendland	West
der Abbruch	cessation
der Abgrund	abyss
abwesend	absent
das Abziehen	withdrawal
der Anblick	aspect
der Anfang	beginning
das Anfangen	act of beginning
anfangen mit	do something with
anfänglich	inceptual
das Anfragen	inquiry
das Ankommen	arrival
die Ansicht	view
anweisen	allocate
die Anwesenheit	presence
der Aufgang	emergence
auftauchen	loom up
der Auftrag	mission
der Ausblick	outlook
der Ausbruch	outbreak
das Ausfragen	interpellating
der Ausgang	source
die Auslegung	interpretation
die Aussage	assertion
die Aussicht	prospect
aussichtslos	without prospects
aussichtsreich	rich in prospects
der Ausspruch	pronouncement
das Beben	trembling
das Befragte	the interrogated
die Befreiung	liberation
die Befremdung	alienation
die Befugnis	warrant
begründen	expose the ground
begründend	grounding
bekannt	familiar
die Berechnung	calculation
die Besinnung	meditation
der Beweis	proof
bilden	configure
bloßes darüber Reden	chatter
die Buße	retribution

das Daherreden	prattle
das Dasein	Dasein
das Daß-sein	thatness
das Eingehen	entrance
einheitlich	unitary
sich einlassen	involve oneself
die Entdecktheit	uncoveredness
das Entstehen	coming to be
der Entspruch	correspondence
die Entwürdigung	dis-esteeming
das Erfragen	disclosive questioning
die Ermächtigung	empowerment
die Erscheinung	appearance
die Erschienenheit	apparentness
die Existenz	existence
die Existenzialien	existentials
existieren	exist
fertig	finished
die Fortdauer	duration
fraglich	problematic
fraglos	unproblematic
die Fragwürdigkeit	question-worthiness
der Fug	compliance
die Füge	juncture
fügen	ordain
sich fügen	acquiesce
sich fügend	compliant
die Fügung	disposition; cadre
das ganze Seiende	the whole of beings
das Gebiet	region
geborgen	sheltered
das Gebrauchsding	use-object
das Ge-fragte	the asked after
die Gefüge	structure
die Gegenwart	present (time)
das Gerede	idle talk
das Geschehnis	happening
die Geschichte	history
das Geschick	destiny
das Geschreibe	pen-pushing
die Gesinnug	contemplation
die Gewährung	bestowal
die Grenzenlosigkeit	limitlessness
die Grundfrage	basic question
der Grundstoff	basic matter
die Halt	hold
die Haltung	stance

hell-dunkel	chiaro-scuro
die Herkunft	origin
die Herrschaft	sovereignty
die Hinsicht	respect
das Hinstellen	setting down
die Historie	historiology
die Insistenz	insistence
die Irre	errancy
irrend; irrig	errant
in Rücksicht	in consideration
die Kündung	manifestation
das Lehrgedicht	didactic poem
die Leiblichkeit	corporeality
die Lockerung	slackening
der Machtspruch	decree
die Meinung	opinion
die Monumentalität	monumentality
der Mut	mettle
die Nähe	proximity
negativ	negative
das Nichts	nothingness
das Nichtsein	nonbeing
das Nichtige	nullity
die Not	plight
die Nötigung	necessitation
die Notwendigkeit	necessity
das Offene	open realm
die Quelle	spring
das Recht	justice
die Reflexion	reflection
die Ruchlosigkeit	wickedness
der Satz	statement
die Satzung	precept
schätzen	appreciate
der Schein	semblance
schlaglos	unquaking
die Schranke	barrier
der Schrecken	shock
das Schwinden	departure
schwingen	oscillate
der Schwund	receding
seiend	extant
das Seiend	act of being
das Seiende	beings; that which is
das Seiende im Ganzen	beings as a whole
die Seienden	the beings
das Sein	Being

die Seinsfrage	question of Being
die Selbst-täuschung	self-delusion
das Seyn	Beyng
das Sich-loslassen	releasement
das Sich-sagen	soliloquizing
die Sippe; die Sippschaft	class
die Situation	situation
das So-sein	suchness
der Spruch	dictum
die Stimmung	attunement
der Stoff	matter
die Strafe	penalty
die Streuung	bestrewal
die Temporalität	temporality
die Transzendenz	transcendence
die Trübe	murkiness
übermächtig	overpowerful
der Umriß	contour
die Umrißlosigkeit	contourlessness
umsichtig	circumspective
unbekannt	unfamiliar
der Un-fug	noncompliance
der Untergang	downgoing
der Unterschied	difference
die Unverborgenheit	unconcealedness
das Un-verhältnis	negative relation
unvollendbar	incompletable
der Ursatz	axiom; axiomatic statement
ursprünglich	originary
unwissend	unknowledgeable
verborgen	concealed
die Verfügung	disposal
die Vergegenwärtigung	presentification
das Vergehen	passing away
die Verhaltenheit	restraint
die Verhaltung	comportment
der Verlaß	reliance
das Vernehmen	apprehension
die Verneinung	negation
das Verschwinden	disappearance
die Verstreuung	bestrewal
vollendbar	completable
das Vorhaben	project
vorhanden	present at hand
die Vorstellung	representation
das Vortreten	stepping forth
die Wahrheit	truth

das Wahr-sein	trueness
das Was-sein	whatness
weg	away
der Weg	way
das Weg	the "away"
weichen	give way
wesen	essentially occur
das Wesen	essence
der Wesenssatz	essential statement
das Woher	the whence
das Wohin	the whither
die Würde	dignity
das Würdigen	esteeming
der Zeitsatz	temporal statement
die Zerfahrenheit	distractedness
das Zerflattern	scattering
die Zerklüftung	bifurcation
die Zerstreuung	dispersal
zugehörig	appertaining
zugrunde gehen	perish
der Zwang	compulsion
die Zwischenbetrachtung	interposed considerations

English-German Glossary

absent	abwesend
abyss	der Abgrund
acquiesce	sich fügen
act of beginning	das Anfangen
act of being	das Seiend
alienation	die Befremdung
allocate	anweisen
apparentness	die Erschienenheit
appearance	die Erscheinung
appertaining	zugehörig
appreciate	schätzen
apprehension	das Vernehmen
arrival	das Ankommen
the asked after	das Ge-fragte
aspect	der Anblick
assertion	die Aussage
attunement	die Stimmung
away	weg
the "away"	das Weg
axiom; axiomatic statement	der Ursatz
barrier	die Schranke
basic matter	der Grundstoff
basic question	die Grundfrage
beginning	der Anfang
Being	das Sein
beings	das Seiende
the beings	die Seienden
beings as a whole	das Seiende im Ganzen
bestowal	die Gewährung
bestrewal	die Streuung; die Verstreuung
Beyng	das Seyn
bifurcation	die Zerklüftung
cadre	die Fügung
calculation	die Berechnung
cessation	der Abbruch
chatter	bloßes darüber Reden
chiaro-scuro	hell-dunkel
circumspective	umsichtig
class	die Sippe; die Sippschaft
coming to be	das Entstehen
completable	vollendbar
compliance	der Fug

compliant	sich fügend
comportment	die Verhaltung
compulsion	der Zwang
concealed	verborgen
configure	bilden
in consideration	in Rücksicht
contemplation	die Gesinnug
contour	der Umriß
contourlessness	die Umrißlosigkeit
corporeality	die Leiblichkeit
correspondence	der Entspruch
Dasein	das Dasein
decree	der Machtspruch
departure	das Schwinden
destiny	das Geschick
dictum	der Spruch
didactic poem	das Lehrgedicht
difference	der Unterschied
dignity	die Würde
disappearance	das Verschwinden
disclosive questioning	das Erfragen
dis-esteeming	die Entwürdigung
dispersal	die Zerstreuung
disposal	die Verfügung
disposition	die Fügung
distractedness	die Zerfahrenheit
do something with	anfangen mit
downgoing	der Untergang
duration	die Fortdauer
emergence	der Aufgang
empowerment	die Ermächtigung
entrance	das Eingehen
errancy	die Irre
errant	irrend; irrig
essence	das Wesen
essentially occur	wesen
essential statement	der Wesenssatz
esteeming	das Würdigen
exist	existieren
existence	die Existenz
existentials	die Existenzialien
expose the ground	begründen
extant	seiend
familiar	bekannt
finished	fertig
give way	weichen

grounding	begründend
happening	das Geschehnis
historiology	die Historie
history	die Geschichte
hold	die Halt
inceptual	anfänglich
idle talk	das Gerede
incompletable	unvollendbar
inquiry	das Anfragen
insistence	die Insistenz
interpellating	das Ausfragen
interposed considerations	die Zwischenbetrachtung
interpretation	die Auslegung
the interrogated	das Befragte
involve oneself	sich einlassen
juncture	die Füge
justice	das Recht
liberation	die Befreiung
limitlessness	die Grenzenlosigkeit
loom up	auftauchen
manifestation	die Kündung
matter	der Stoff
meditation	die Besinnung
mettle	der Mut
mission	der Auftrag
monumentality	die Monumentalität
murkiness	die Trübe
necessitation	die Nötigung
necessity	die Notwendigkeit
negation	die Verneinung
negative	negativ
negative relation	das Un-verhältnis
nonbeing	das Nichtsein
noncompliance	der Un-fug
nothingness	das Nichts
nullity	das Nichtige
open realm	das Offene
opinion	die Meinung
ordain	fügen
origin	die Herkunft
originary	ursprünglich
oscillate	schwingen
outbreak	der Ausbruch
outlook	der Ausblick
overpowerful	übermächtig
passing away	das Vergehen

penalty	die Strafe
pen-pushing	das Geschreibe
perish	zugrunde gehen
plight	die Not
prattle	das Daherreden
precept	die Satzung
presence	die Anwesenheit
present (time)	die Gegenwart
present at hand	vorhanden
presentification	die Vergegenwärtigung
problematic	fraglich
project	das Vorhaben
pronouncement	der Ausspruch
proof	der Beweis
prospect	die Aussicht
proximity	die Nähe
question of Being	die Seinsfrage
question-worthiness	die Fragwürdigkeit
receding	der Schwund
reflection	die Reflexion
region	das Gebiet
releasement	das Sich-loslassen
reliance	der Verlaß
representation	die Vorstellung
respect	die Hinsicht
restraint	die Verhaltenheit
retribution	die Buße
rich in prospects	aussichtsreich
scattering	das Zerflattern
self-delusion	die Selbst-täuschung
semblance	der Schein
setting down	das Hinstellen
sheltered	geborgen
shock	der Schrecken
situation	die Situation
slackening	die Lockerung
soliloquizing	das Sich-sagen
source	der Ausgang
sovereignty	die Herrschaft
spring	die Quelle
stance	die Haltung
statement	der Satz
stepping forth	das Vortreten
structure	die Gefüge
suchness	das So-sein
temporality	die Temporalität
temporal statement	der Zeitsatz

thatness	das Daß-sein
that which is	das Seiende
transcendence	die Transzendenz
trembling	das Beben
trueness	das Wahr-sein
truth	die Wahrheit
unconcealedness	die Unverborgenheit
uncoveredness	die Entdecktheit
unfamiliar	unbekannt
unitary	einheitlich
unknowledgeable	unwissend
unproblematic	fraglos
unquaking	schlaglos
use-object	das Gebrauchsding
view	die Ansicht
warrant	die Befugnis
way	der Weg
West	das Abendland
whatness	das Was-sein
the whence	das Woher
the whither	das Wohin
the whole of beings	das ganze Seiende
wickedness	die Ruchlosigkeit
withdrawal	das Abziehen
without prospects	aussichtslos